The *Sams Teach Yourself in 24 Hour*

Sams Teach Yourself in 24 Hours books provide quick and easy a
proven step-by-step approach that works for you. In just 24 sess
hour or less, you will tackle every task you need to get the resul
Let our experienced authors present the most accurate information to get you
reliable answers—fast!

The entire spectrum of Microsoft development
technologies, from Visual Basic to Microsoft's
Web server, uses ActiveX Data Objects (ADO) as
the method of accessing data sources. When you
regularly construct database applications, you
will be programming ADO regularly.

This object model diagram and the sample recordset code will be an essential reference for quickly
creating the basic code you need for a project.

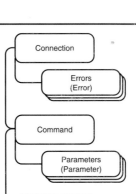

You can create a new connection and recordset by using the ADO objects with
the following code:

```
 1:    Dim myRS As New ADODB.Recordset
 2:
 3:    ' Set up connection string
 4:    Const ConnectStr = "PROVIDER=Microsoft.Jet.OLEDB.3.51;" & _
 5:    Data Source=C:\Program Files\Microsoft Visual Studio\VB98\Nwind.mdb;"
 6:
 7:    ' Create new recordset
 8:    Set myRS = New ADODB.Recordset
 9:
10:    ' Set property to automatically create a connection
11:    myRS.ActiveConnection = ConnectStr
12:
13:    ' Open recordset with query for all customer records
14:    myRS.Open "Select * from customers"
15:    ' Check if recordset is empty
16:    If myRS.BOF And myRS.EOF Then
17:        MsgBox "Recordset is empty!", 16, "Empty recordset"
18:    Else
19:        ' Make sure that you're on the first record
20:        myRS.MoveFirst
21:        ' Loop through 5 records to display company name
22:        For i = 1 To 5
23:            MsgBox myRS.Fields(1), _
24:                vbInformation, "Field # 1:" & i
25:            ' Move to next record
26:            myRS.MoveNext
27:        Next
28:        ' Close recordset
29:        myRS.Close
30:    End If
31:    ' Set to nothing to eliminate object
32:    Set myRS = Nothing
33: End Sub
```

Teach Yourself Database Programming with Visual Basic 6 in 24 Hours

COMMON DATABASE METHODS

METHOD	DESCRIPTION
AddNew([fieldList], [values])	Recordset **object—Adds a new record to the current recordset. Automatically sets the cursor to point to this new record.**
AppendChunk(data)	Field **object—Used to write binary data (such as a picture) or an object into the field of a database.**
BeginTrans() as Long	Connection **object—Begins a transaction. Use the** Rollback **method to nullify current transaction.**
CancelUpdate ([affectRecords])	Recordset **object—Cancels any changes made to any of the field values of the existing selected record. By default, the** affectRecord **property is set to cancel any changes to the current cursor record.**
CommitTrans()	Connection **object—Accepts all operations within the transaction started by BeginTrans and writes the changes into the database(s).**
Delete([affectRecords])	Recordset **object—Deletes the currently selected record(s). By default, the** affectRecords **parameter is set to delete only the record that the cursor currently indicates.**
Execute(commandText, [recordsAffected], [options])	Command **object—Executes to current** Command **against the related** Connection **object or** Recordset **object. Commands may include providing access to a table's records, executing a SQL query, or calling a stored procedure.**
GetChunk(length)	Field **object—Retrieves binary data (such as a picture) or an object from a field of a database. The length in bytes to retrieve must be specified.**
MoveFirst(), MoveLast()	Recordset **object—Moves the cursor in the recordset to the beginning (MoveFirst) or end (MoveLast) of the data set.**
MoveNext(), MovePrevious()	Recordset **object—Moves the cursor in the record-set one record forward (MoveNext) or one record back (MovePrevious).**
Open([connectStr], [userID], [password], [options])	Connection **object—Opens a connection to the specified data source. If no** connectStr **parameter is included, uses the string stored in the** ConnectionString **property of the object.**
Open([Source], [ActiveConnection], [CursorType As CursorTypeEnum = adOpenUnspecified], [LockType As LockTypeEnum = adLockUnspecified], [Options As Long = -1])	Recordset **object—Opens a connection and instantiates the recordset. If this method is executed on** Recordset **object without a specified** Connection **object, a** Connection **object is dynamically created.**
Requery(options)	Recordset **object—Re-executes the query of the recordset and updates the records to reflect the current state of the data source.**
Resync([affectRecords])	Recordset **object—Accepts a constant parameter to specify which records in the recordset will be affected (default is all records).**
RollbackTrans()	Connection **object—Cancels the transaction started by the** BeginTrans **method and revokes previous operations.**
Update([Fields], [Values])	Recordset **object—Writes any changes made to the values stored in the fields of the current record to the table. The** Update **command allows fields and values for changes to be passed as parameters.**

Dan Rahmel

SAMS
Teach Yourself
Database
Programming with
Visual Basic® 6
in 24 Hours

SAMS

A Division of Macmillan Computer Publishing
201 West 103rd St., Indianapolis, Indiana, 46290 USA

Sams Teach Yourself Database Programming with Visual Basic 6 in 24 Hours

Copyright © 1999 by Sams Publishing

International Standard Book Number: 0-672-31409-6

Library of Congress Catalog Card Number: 98-86256

00 99 98   4   3   2   1

Printed in the United States of America

FIRST PRINTING—December 1998

Trademarks

Warning and Disclaimer

EXECUTIVE EDITOR
Chris Denny

ACQUISITIONS EDITOR
Chris Denny

DEVELOPMENT EDITOR
Anthony Amico

MANAGING EDITOR
Jodi Jensen

SENIOR EDITOR
Susan Ross Moore

COPY EDITOR
Linda Morris

INDEXER
Mary Gammons

PROOFREADER
Mona Brown

TECHNICAL EDITOR
Vincent Mayfield

SOFTWARE DEVELOPMENT SPECIALIST
Michael Hunter

TEAM COORDINATOR
Carol Ackerman

INTERIOR DESIGN
Gary Adair

COVER DESIGN
Aren Howell

LAYOUT TECHNICIANS
Ayanna Lacey
Heather Hiatt Miller

Overview

Appendixes

Contents

About the Author

DAN RAHMEL is a Visual Basic programmer with over 13 years of experience designing and implementing information systems and deploying mid-sized client/server systems using Visual Basic and Visual FoxPro. He has authored several books including the *Visual Basic Programmer's Reference*, *Developing Client-Server Applications with Visual Basic*, and *Server Scripts with Visual JavaScript*. He is a regular contributor to *DBMS*, *Internet Advisor*, and *American Programmer* magazines.

Dedication

I would like to dedicate this book to the unsung heroes at Microsoft who, though much maligned, have produced an Insanely Great family of programming products.

Acknowledgments

Writing this book has been extremely enjoyable due to the contents of the book itself and the people I had the pleasure and opportunity to work with.

Combining the creation of the book itself with the superior Sams staff often made the difficult seem easy. I'd particularly like to thank Chris Denny and Tony Amico who pointed the direction for the book and worked with me to produce it on an insane schedule. Also thanks to Vince Mayfield, who provided a superior technical review that ensured that any mistakes that are found in this book are strictly my own.

I'd like to thank my parents (Ron and Marie), siblings (David and Darlene), and friends (David Rahmel, Greg Mickey, Ted Ehr, Don Murphy, Ed Gildred, Juan Leonffu, Weld O'Connor, Bernard Arroyo, Thomas Rommell) for their tireless support.

To David Rahmel, who provided ADO expertise and made fantastic suggestions on how to improve the book, my many thanks.

Most of all, I'd like to thank the reader. By buying this book, you make it possible for all of us in the book industry to labor to produce good work. When pulling the long hours to complete a book, knowing that every little improvement will help your audience is what really makes the difference. Thanks.

I hope you find this book as useful as the people at Coherent Data (www.coherentdata.com/cscentral) and Hobby Planet (www.hobbyplanet.com) already have. I also hope you'll provide feedback with any suggestions you have or mistakes you find. We have a page on our Web site dedicated to taking your suggestions. Please stop by.

Tell Us What You Think!

As the reader of this book, *you* are our most important critic and commentator. We value your opinion and want to know what we're doing right, what we could do better, what areas you'd like to see us publish in, and any other words of wisdom you're willing to pass our way.

As the Executive Editor for the Visual Basic Programming team at Macmillan Computer Publishing, I welcome your comments. You can fax, email, or write me directly to let me know what you did or didn't like about this book—as well as what we can do to make our books stronger.

Please note that I cannot help you with technical problems related to the topic of this book, and that due to the high volume of mail I receive, I might not be able to reply to every message.

When you write, please be sure to include this book's title and author as well as your name and phone or fax number. I will carefully review your comments and share them with the author and editors who worked on the book.

Fax: 317-817-7070
Email: vb@mcp.com
Mail: Chris Denny
         Executive Editor
         Visual Basic Programming Team
         Macmillan Computer Publishing
         201 West 103rd Street
         Indianapolis, IN 46290 USA

Introduction

You may need to create a database already for some already defined purpose. Maybe you need a database application for home, work, or a social organization. Perhaps you just have an interest in learning about one of the most fascinating and lucrative fields in computers.

People that use computers to manage information are vital to almost every aspect of our world. This book can be your gateway to understanding databases and the applications that access them, as well as help you solve your day-to-day information problems.

Who Should Read This Book

If you need to create a database, from the simple to the complex, begin with this book. You will quickly gain confidence as you progress from one hour to the next, building increasingly powerful Visual Basic database implementations.

The book assumes a working knowledge of the Visual Basic language and programming environment. If you have never used Visual Basic, *Sams Teach Yourself Visual Basic in 24 Hours* is an excellent introduction. With a working knowledge of Visual Basic and this book, you can get started.

This book only peripherally addresses database servers and larger database projects. If that is your ultimate target, but you don't have a firm grasp of basic database project concepts, this book is for you. The firm foundation provided in this book will aid you substantially when moving to more complex database systems.

What This Book Will Do for You

The *24 Hour* organization of the book will guide you to create database applications to fit your needs. When you complete the 24 hours, you will have several sample projects that demonstrate a majority of the key technologies that you will use on any future database project.

You will have a complete grounding in database design and development. Your knowledge for small to medium systems will be well rounded when you complete this book. You will also have established a great stepping stone of understanding if you want to enter the world of large-scale database design.

Can This Book Really Teach Data Construction in 24 Hours?

Yes, because this book leads you through the construction of real working examples. As you sit down and master each hour, you will be building a substantial foundation of knowledge and working projects. Many of your own database applications can be constructed simply by modifying the projects that you have already created.

Additionally, there are numerous tips, notes, and cautions to speed your grasp of some of the different aspects of the technology. Following along, creating the examples should make every page interactive and exciting.

What You Need

This book assumes that you have a Windows 95/98/NT machine that you are familiar with already. All of the construction of the projects also requires that you have Visual Basic 6.0 installed in either the Professional or the Enterprise Edition. Since the database tools are necessary, the free Control Creation Edition cannot be used for most of the implementation.

If you have Microsoft Access installed, this can also be a help. Although not required for any of the portions of this book, editing data or adding security is easier from Microsoft Access.

Conventions Used in This Book

Each lesson highlights new terms as they appear, and a question-and-answer section is provided at the end of each lesson to reinforce what you have learned. In addition, the lessons reinforce your learning further with quiz questions and exercises.

This 24-hour course also uses several common conventions to help teach the programming topics. Here is a summary of the typographical conventions:

- Commands and computer output appear in special monospaced computer font.
- Words you type also appear in a bold **monospaced** font.
- If a task requires you to choose from a menu, this book separates menu commands with a vertical bar. Therefore, this book uses File | Save As to indicate that you should open the File menu and choose the Save As command.

- When learning a programming language, you often must learn the syntax or format of a command. Lines similar to the following will be displayed to help you learn a new Visual Basic language command:

```
For CounterVar = StartVal To EndVal [Step IncrementVal]
Block of one or more Visual Basic statements
Next CounterVar
```

The monospaced text designates code (programming language information) that you'll enter into a program. The regular monospaced text, such as `For` and `Next`, represents keywords you must type exactly. *Italicized monospace* characters indicate placeholders that you must replace with your own program's values. Bracketed information, such as `[Step IncrementVal]`, indicates optional code that you can type if your program requires it.

In addition to typographical conventions, the following special elements are used to set off various pieces of information and to make them easily recognizable:

 The first time a *new term* appears, you'll fine a New Term icon and definition to help reinforce that term.

 Special notes augment the material you are reading in each hour. They clarify concepts and procedures.

 You'll find numerous tips that offer shortcuts and solutions to common problems.

 Caution sections warn you about pitfalls. Reading them will save you time and trouble.

Enough! Time Is Ticking

Want to master database construction? Turn the page.

HOUR 1

Database Basics

Learning how to create database applications with Visual Basic can be one of the most exciting types of programming that a developer can perform. Because standardized commercial applications for everything from word processors to spreadsheets have become so powerful, high-level custom programming has become almost exclusively concerned with database applications. Over the years, Visual Basic has evolved to become the perfect tool to effectively create these solutions.

Visual Basic makes it easy to program the connectivity to a database or use graphical controls to set up the data display and modification. In this hour, you will be using a wizard called the *VB Data Form Wizard* that is included with the VB system. The Wizard will quickly get you started in creating database applications by doing most of the work for you. The Data Form Wizard makes prototyping a database application a snap.

The highlights of this hour include:

- Using the VB Data Form Wizard to create a form for database access
- Learning the basics of database architecture
- Creating a VB application to access the sample Northwind database
- Looking through the Northwind database from your application

What Is Database Programming?

In this hour, you will learn how easy it is to use Visual Basic 6 to create applications that provide database access. Prior knowledge of programming Visual Basic and the fundamental programming environment is assumed. If you haven't learned general Visual Basic (VB) programming, check out the excellent book *Sams Teach Yourself Visual Basic 6 in 24 Hours*, also by Sams Publishing.

Database programming is really the process of storing a variety of information in a standard way so the data can be easily accessed and maintained. Information stored within a database, unlike a word processing document, usually follows a standard format. The data from these resources could be easily stored in a database:

- Phone book
- Address book
- Sales invoice
- Accounting information
- Library card catalog

Can you see the common thread running through all these applications? They all have many items that follow a standardized format. A phone book, for example, contains numerous entries that all contain a name, address (optional), and phone number. In the same way, items on a sales invoice would include the product number, description, cost, and quantity of each item sold.

In contrast, a word processing document follows a different form each time a new document is created. The database relies on a standard format similar to a standardized paper form with blanks to fill in specific information, such as an insurance form.

Database programming is the process of constructing a database file to hold information in a standard format. When the actual database has been constructed, a Visual Basic application is then constructed to allow the information stored in the database to be examined, modified, and augmented.

What Is a Database?

Programs that you might already be familiar with, such as a word processor, use a document metaphor. You load a document from the hard disk into memory for editing. When changes are made to the document, the changes occur in memory. When you save the document, changes are written to the hard disk.

A database is like a single file that contains numerous documents. Each database "document," actually called a database record, stores all the information concerning that item. For example, in an address book database, each record contains the information of a single individual (such as name, address, phone, and so on). Therefore, if the address book has the information for 100 people, the database contains 100 records.

NEW TERM   A *record* is the primary data unit of information contained in a table. In an address book database, each entry would be stored as a record containing name, address, phone, and so on.

The basics of using a database are already familiar to you. Even if you've never used an electronic database, you've probably used an address book, one type of database. An address book typically contains the names, addresses, and phone numbers of people or businesses that you know. Most often, this information is placed in alphabetical order so you can find it easily.

There are excellent reasons to store information in an electronic database so that it can easily be

- Searched for one or more items that match particular criteria
- Sorted in various ways
- Used to edit single or multiple entries
- Displayed in any order
- Used to generate reports from the information

The Parts of a Database

The database is actually the overall file that can hold one or more formats. Although the term is often used loosely, a *database* actually signifies the single file or structure that holds all the information for a process.

To simplify, imagine you are constructing an application for a small business. You want it to track customers, record financial information, keep track of inventory, and so on. Your application would most likely store all this information in a single database file.

NEW TERM   A *database* is the central structure that holds all the data relating to a particular
           area, such as storing information pertinent to a small business. A company data-
base can hold a list of customers, as well as the information for the sales invoices.

Within the database—usually a database file stored in Microsoft Access format—there
are a number of structures known as *tables* that actually hold the information in the various standardized formats. The records that contain information (such as individual people in a customer list) are stored within a customer table. The table is what defines the
structure of how the information will be stored.

NEW TERM   One or more *tables* within a database actually hold the data, with each table
           defining a particular structure. An address table might store the name, address,
city, and state of a customer. The invoice table, in contrast, can store the quantity,
description, and cost of each item in an invoice.

In Visual Basic, a sample database is included for an imaginary company called
Northwind Traders. In this database, sample data for the company is provided for the
company's customers, sales, and so on. The database itself is stored as the file
NWind.mdb. Within the database file are the following eight tables:

- Categories
- Customers
- Employees
- Order details
- Orders
- Products
- Shippers
- Suppliers

Each of these tables contains unique information in a format that is appropriate to that type
of data. You'll be using this sample database in this chapter to construct a simple database
application. Examining it will help you to understand how the database is organized.

A table contains structured information that is most easily visualized as a table or spreadsheet. In Figure 1.1, you can see the customers table of the NWind database displaying
common address book information in a spreadsheet layout. The headings of all the
columns (company name, contact name, address, and so on) appear in the first row of the
sheet. Each row after that contains the information for an individual person.

FIGURE 1.1

Customers table of the NWind database shown as a spreadsheet.

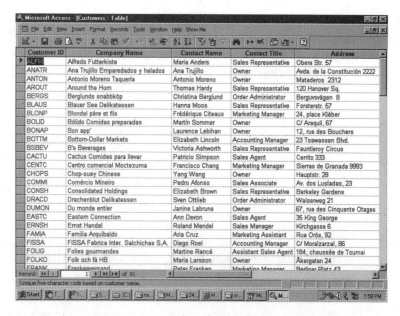

In the spreadsheet view, you can see that each row contains all the information that relates to a particular item. In this case, a row contains all the data related to an individual customer. Each row in a table is referred to as either a row or a record, which mean the same thing.

If you look at the bottom left of the window, you should see the number 91. This indicates there are 91 records or individuals stored within this table. Within each record, it is further broken down to the individual pieces of information that make up a record. These pieces are known as *fields*. In more advanced database construction, fields are also known as attributes or Data Elements.

NEW TERM A *field* is an element of a table record. The city field of a record would contain the city of that particular person. The state field would contain their state.

To understand how these terms are actually used, take another look at Figure 1.1. You can see that the first row of data contains the entry for a Maria Anders as the person to contact at the company named Alfreds Futterkiste. All the information in the table relating to Maria Anders is stored in record #1. Likewise, all the information for Ana Trujillo is stored in record #2.

The columns in a spreadsheet are referred to as either *columns* or *fields*. These two terms are used interchangeably and have exactly the same meaning. The various fields determine how the information will actually be broken down. As you will see later, the more precisely you can define the fields in a database, the more flexible the data is for any needed uses.

For example, if a single field contained both the name of the contact and the address of the contact, a search would result in dubious results. To find all the people with a last name of Jones, your search would return all those individuals with a name of *Jones*, as well as those who lived on *Jones Ave*. By having a separate field for the name and address, you can search the name field only. All returned entries will be names that contain the word Jones.

> For most of this book and other books related to Visual Basic databases or Microsoft Access databases, the terms field and record are used to denote the parts of a table. The terms row and column are typically only used for the more expensive and complicated database systems such as Microsoft SQL Server.

How Does Visual Basic Relate to All This?

Visual Basic 6 contains a complete database system that can be used to store and retrieve information quickly and easily. You've written VB programs before that stored information in memory variables and maybe even wrote this information to a disk file.

The VB contains a complete database engine, which is essentially a self-contained database application. In fact, the database engine used by VB6 is the same one that operates behind-the-scenes on Microsoft Access. For that reason, Microsoft Access and VB use exactly the same files (those with the .mdb extension) and file format. Also, an application created within Access can share the same file as a Visual Basic program, provided the access capabilities are set up properly.

NEW TERM   Unlike a word processor or other application with a user interface, a database typically operates behind-the-scenes. Any interface the user sees is most often constructed for a particular application. The functionality of the database is provided by a program called the *database engine*.

Although many programs can be written in Microsoft Access using the Visual Basic for Applications (VBA) language, the Visual Basic system is more powerful. It also allows a completed application to be compiled that can be installed on a machine without requiring the Microsoft Access foundation, which is fairly large, to execute.

Visual Basic is more powerful and contains numerous tools, essentially unavailable in Microsoft Access, to simplify creating a database application. Primary among them is the Data Control. The *Data Control* is a visible component that provides connectivity to a database file and the information it contains.

Visual Basic includes an ActiveX control known as the *Data Control*. It is a visible component placed on a form to provide database access.

Your First Database Project

Your first database project will consist of a single form that provides access to the customers table for navigation and modification. You will use the VB Data Form Wizard supplied with Visual Basic to create a form with controls to display and edit data stored in a table. When the form is created and working, you'll be able to examine it to see exactly what the Wizard did.

The simple project will access the sample NWind database. Microsoft included this database filled with data, which is convenient to use to demonstrate database concepts.

To begin, you'll need to load Visual Basic 6 now and begin a new project. The Standard EXE project type will be fine for the application. The Wizard will create an additional form that contains all of the necessary configuration and code to allow access to the NWind database.

VB Data Form Wizard

The VB Data Form Wizard is perhaps the most commonly used wizard included with Visual Basic. Given a database or other data source, the Data Form Wizard will construct a form containing a Data Control as well as all the other controls needed to display the information in the database.

Because the Wizard places all the controls and constructs the code with standard Visual Basic components, the form it creates can be easily modified. The Data Form Wizard is often used by programmers to create a quick prototype of the basic database screens. The forms that are generated are then augmented to include the required functionality.

The empty project that you should have opened in the Visual Basic environment contains a single blank form. This form will not actually be used because the wizard will create an entirely new form to hold the data access controls.

1. Select the Add Form option from the Project menu.

   This option will add a new form to the current project and will present a selection box to show all the possible types of forms that can be created. In a non-database application, you would probably select a blank form and begin adding controls to it. In this case, you need to select the VB Data Form Wizard.

2. Select the VB Data Form Wizard option and click the OK button.

   Selecting the Wizard will begin activating a seven-step process used to create a form patterned around a specific database table. The first screen simply explains the use of the Wizard (see Figure 1.2).

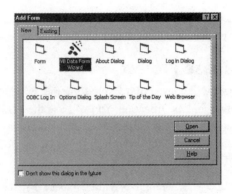

FIGURE 1.2

Adding a new data control form using the VB Data Form Wizard.

3. Click the Next button to advance to the type selection page.

   The Wizard first allows you to select a profile from which to load its settings. If you find you are creating many database forms based on the same selections made in this Wizard, you can save a profile with those settings so they don't have to be set each time.

   You don't have a current profile, so clicking the Next button will present the next stage leaving the (None) default profile in place.

4. Click the Next button again to accept the Access data source.

   This page of the Wizard allows selection of the access method or data source type that will be used by the form. Because the Northwind database is stored in Microsoft Access format, the default setting is fine.

5. Click the Browse button and select the NWind.mdb file. Click the Next button.

   The Northwind database sample is provided at the Visual Basic 6 root directory and contains a substantial amount of sample data. For the rest of this hour, you'll use the Northwind database (stored in the NWind.mdb file) to create several samples.

6. Enter frmCustomers in the text box for the name of the form and click the Next button. Your form will have this name set as the (Name) property.

> When programmers begin a project, it is often a temptation to ignore good programming practices and not name the objects and forms descriptively. Be aware that the little time taken in properly naming your objects at the start will increase the readability of your later code and save you a number of headaches.

The default form layout of Single Record will create a standard form that shows all the fields for a single record with navigation (forward record, back record, and so on) on the bottom (see Figure 1.3). There are five standard options for the default form:

- Single Record
- Grid (Datasheet)
- Master/Detail
- MS HflexGrid
- MS Chart

FIGURE 1.3

Selecting the name and type of form constructed by the Wizard.

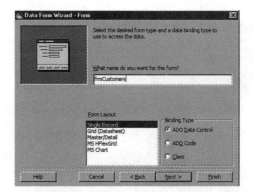

This step in the Wizard is the first page where you begin to make selections that will affect the final form. Selections from this screen forward, such as the type of controls to display your data, will affect how the form is constructed in VB.

The Binding Type selection provides selection of the type of form to be created. The default uses the Data Control for the central connection to the database. The other two options instruct the Wizard to construct a complete set of code to mimic the Data Control operations. Coded access to the database is more flexible but also more complicated than simply using the Data Control, as you will see in Hour 17, "Understanding ActiveX Data Objects (ADO)," where the ADO framework is explained.

7. Select the Customers record source.

The record source is the table within the database that contains the information that will be displayed from. Remember that the database file can contain numerous tables and that within each table the information is stored in individual records.

In the Northwind database, there are tables for every type of information that relates to the Northwind business. The Customers table contains contact and address information for every customer of the company.

Selecting the Customers table from the Record Source combo box will make the form that is created by the Wizard display record information for each customer.

8. Move all the fields from the Available Fields list box to the Selected Fields list box.

   Use the double arrow >> to move all the fields from the Available Fields list box to the Selected Fields list box (see Figure 1.4). Any fields that appear in the Selected Fields list box will appear on the final VB form.

9. Set the Column to Sort By to the CompanyName field and click the Next button

   In the combo box shown directly under the Selected Fields list box, you can select the Column to Sort By. Select the CompanyName field so all the presented information will be sorted alphabetically for display.

FIGURE 1.4

Move all the fields into the Selected Fields list box and select the Column to Sort By combo box.

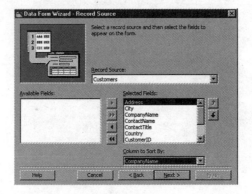

 When you add a new record, it is automatically added as the last record in the table. The sorting will not automatically re-sort the list to place the new item in the proper order. Not until the Data Control is refreshed will the new record appear correctly sorted.

10. Because the default condition contains all the buttons to be added to the form, click the Next button to accept the inserted buttons.

    Navigation buttons are built into the data control, but controls to add and delete records, as well as other functions, do not appear on the control itself. On this screen, the Wizard includes the option of automatically adding buttons and the necessary code to supply these functions. The available buttons include

> Add Button
>
> Delete Button
>
> Refresh Button
>
> Update Button
>
> Close Button

Leave all these buttons checked so that they will each be added to the form. The code for each button is added to the form and can be easily modified.

11. Click the Finish button to create the form.

After you click the Finish button to the Wizard, the form will be created and added to the Visual Basic project. You should see a form like the one shown in Figure 1.5.

FIGURE 1.5

The form automatically generated by the Data Form Wizard for the Customers table.

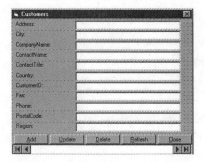

At the bottom of the form you'll see the Data Control. It has a set of arrows on each side for navigation through the records in the selected table. This control has been configured by the Wizard to access the Customers table of the NWind database. All the manipulation of the database will occur through the connection attached to the Data Control.

The control has four built-in navigation buttons that include Move to the Beginning of the Records, Move Back One Record, Move Forward One Record, and Move to the Last Record. Each of these buttons will change the record currently displayed in all the bound controls. In the next hour, you'll get a chance to closely examine the properties of the Data Control to see how it is configured.

Executing the Application

Before you execute the application to see how the Data Control works in action, you will need to set the project to execute the form you just created as the central form.

When the Wizard creates the data form, it is simply added to the current project. Because the new project already has a default form when it is created, the blank form is set to be shown when execution occurs. You'll need to select the new data form to have it displayed.

1. Select Project1 Properties from the Project menu.

2. On the General tab, locate the combo box for the Startup Object.

3. Select the frmCustomers form as the Startup Object.

   This will make your new database form display as the primary form.

4. Click the OK button.

Now execute the project. You will see a form like the one shown in Figure 1.6.

FIGURE 1.6

When you execute frmCustomers, the first record of the table will be retrieved and displayed in the text boxes.

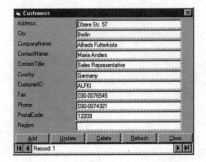

Use the navigation arrows on the bottom of the window to move through the records. The left and right arrows move backward and forward through the recordset, respectively. The arrows that appear with a bar at the point move all the way to the beginning or the end of the recordset, depending on the direction of the arrow.

Changing data in the text boxes will not be stored in the database until you either move to a different record or click the Update button. If you don't want to make any changes to the database, you can either make the dataset read only (a Snapshot) or you can make the individual controls read-only.

When you're finished looking through the customer data, close the form to halt execution. This will return you to the development environment where you will be able to look at the form and the controls stored on it to see how the application actually functions.

1

You've created a simple database application without doing any programming work. If you now examine what VB has constructed for you, it will be easier to begin to create your own applications or make necessary modifications to the forms created by the Wizard.

Summary

The VB Data Form Wizard can be used to quickly generate a prototype form that contains a Data Control connected to a specified database and table, as well as all the bound controls necessary to access that data.

The Data Control is an easy way to graphically create a connection to a database. In addition to connecting to the database, the Data Control must be set to reference one particular table within the database.

Q&A

Q After I've constructed a form using the Data Control, do I have to start from scratch to add more functionality?

A No, the Data Control uses the same technology that is used to program advanced solutions. By adding some additional code and removing the control from your form, the application that you created can be easily modified to use the more direct database technology.

Q Can I use the VB Data Form Wizard multiple times for a single project?

A Yes. Every time the Wizard is activated, it simply adds a new form to the existing project. To VB, a new form has been added, so there are no more restrictions than usual.

Q Should I make sure that I don't modify data in the Northwind database?

A The NWind database file is provided as an example, so you can freely modify it. If you want to get the original version back, all you have to do is reinstall it from the Visual Basic CD-ROM.

Workshop

The quiz questions and exercises are provided for your further understanding. See Appendix C, "Answers," for the answers to the questions.

Quiz

1. Can multiple tables be stored in a database?

2. What is a field? What is a record?

3. What is the purpose of the Data Control?

4. The database engine included with Visual Basic is compatible with what desktop application?

5. On the navigation bar of the Data Control, what functions do the four arrows perform?

6. Databases are sometimes described in terms of spreadsheets. What are the synonyms for fields and records?

7. What is a profile (used by the VB Data Form Wizard)?

8. When a new record is added to the database, will it be sorted in the correct order automatically?

Exercises

1. Create a new database form, only this time use the Biblio.mdb supplied with Visual Basic 6.

2. Using the Northwind database, create a form using the VB Data Form Wizard, only this time, select the Grid Datasheet type for the customers table. Run the application and examine the data in the grid recognizing how the columns and rows are related to the data stored in the table.

HOUR 2

Examining the Data Form Wizard Project

Applications created with the VB Data Form Wizard have a great deal of substance that is installed by the wizard. Not only does the wizard add the necessary controls, customized code to handle operations such as adding and deleting records is inserted into the form with proper data handling and error routines.

The highlights of this hour include:

- Examining the property settings made by the wizard
- Learning about bound controls
- Viewing the code placed in the buttons on the form

Opening the Project

Now that you've created a simple application with the VB Data Form Wizard, you can take a look at how the project actually provides the connection and database interaction technology. Most of the functionality of the program is provided by the Data control itself. However, the code included within the command buttons (such as Add, Update, and so on) activates methods within the Data control to provide functions not provided by the control.

Open the project that you created in Hour 1, "Database Basics." After the project has been opened, open and reactivate the frmDataEnv form that was created by the wizard.

You can begin examination of this project by seeing the data component itself that is used on the form. On the toolbox palette window, there is an extra icon added to the traditional controls. This icon represents the ADO Data control. This type of Data control is new to Visual Basic 6 and allows connections to be made between a data source and controls on the form through the ActiveX Data Objects (ADO).

If you look in the component window by selecting the Components option on the Project menu, you'll see the option Microsoft ADO Data Control 6.0 (OLEDB) option is checked. This component is the actual Data control that you've been using.

The growth of available data stores and increasing automation of almost every form of data acquisition has led to huge increases in the need to manage this information. Applications built with Visual Basic currently play a key role in maintaining and accessing all this information.

Although native support is provided for Microsoft Access databases, VB also supports a variety of other database formats to enable access to older data or information systems. Some of the database types that can be accessed natively by VB include:

- Access
- dBASE III, dBASE IV, and dBASE 5.0
- FoxPro 2.0–3.0
- Paradox 3.x–5.x
- ODBC

Dismiss the Components window and return to the form created by the wizard. Click on the Data control shown within the frmCustomers window. After it is selected, show the Properties window. You can examine the properties of the control and determine exactly how the data will be accessed when the application is running.

Examining the Data Control

At the bottom of the form you will see the Data control. This is the ActiveX control that is used to connect a database to user interface controls such as check boxes and text boxes.

Examining the Data control properties will show the settings that provide the access to the Northwind data source. The first thing you will notice when examining the properties is the Name property that is set to datPrimaryRS. The letters dat indicate that the control reference is to a Data control.

2

> You might have noticed that you placed the three-letter prefix dat before the rest of the title of the Data control. This is a naming convention known as Hungarian notation. Hungarian notation simply labels the name of the control with the first three letters that denote the type of object that is being named.
>
> Hungarian notation makes reading code much easier because when looking at a line of text, it is much easier to see that frmCustomers is accessing a form than if the name were just Customers. When you name your controls in the future, try to use the naming conventions to simplify your coding.

Here are some of the most common prefixes for controls:

Notation	Control
txt	Text box
lbl	Label
cmd	Command button
lst	Select list
rad	Radio control
chk	Check box
dat	Data control

The rest of the Data control name is short for "primary recordset." A recordset is a memory structure to hold all the records that were selected from the database on disk. In the example you created with the Data Form Wizard, there was no explicit record selection (such as "return only the customers located in California"), so the recordset contains all of the records in the current table.

NEW TERM A *recordset* is a memory structure designed to load information from a data source for querying, modification, and examination. A recordset contains all of the records that comply with criteria defined when the recordset is created.

To examine the properties that relate to data access, it is much easier to use the property category viewing option available in Visual Basic. In the Properties window, select the Categorized tab. It groups the properties by category, so all of the properties actually related to data access are grouped under the Data heading.

> Although the categories in the Properties window are very useful, they are not foolproof. Occasionally a property that directly affects the function of the control might be placed in a non-intuitive category. Therefore, it is often a good idea, when examining an unfamiliar control, to avoid this mode until you've examined the complete list of options provided by the All properties display tab.

To see what database is actually referenced, look at the ConnectionString property. In this property you will see the pathname to the Northwind database file, in addition to various parameters regarding the provider type (see Figure 2.1).

FIGURE 2.1

The properties of the Data control show a connection to the NWind.mdb file.

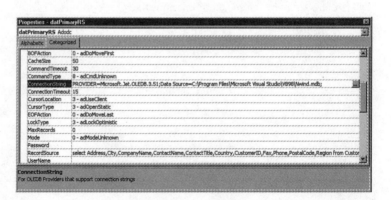

There is much more information in the ConnectionString than you need to know just yet. Visual Basic includes a helpful property wizard to aid you in creating this string even while not using the full Data Form Wizard. Therefore, you should have no trouble accessing any desired data source before you learn the meaning of each section of this parameter.

> By default, the entire pathname of the data source is stored in the RecordSource property. While excellent for testing, most applications you create need to be installed on machines for which you might not know the installation path at compile time.
>
> For this reason, you can delete the path information and only use the database name itself. This will make the Data control retrieve the data source from the default execution directory. During testing, this means you will have to locate your database at the VB6 root directory for it to be found properly.

The RecordSource Property

To see how the records are actually read, look at the RecordSource property. In this property, you will see a line that looks like this:

```
select Address, City, CompanyName, etc. from Customers order by
CompanyName
```

The RecordSource property contains the query to determine what information is retrieved and lists all of the fields to be included in the recordset. Although the query may look cryptic right now, in Hour 18, "Using SQL," you'll learn how to write your own queries using the Structured Query Language (SQL) that is used in this property.

If you examine the RecordSource property, you'll see that after the word from is listed the name of the table within the database. Because you selected the Customers table within the database file, this Data control will reference information stored in that table. One Data control must be added to a form for each table that needs to be accessed within the database.

The other properties are more complicated and can be left to their defaults for now. As you progress through the 24 hours, each of the properties will be explained. Let's take a look at the properties for the bound controls that attach them to this data source.

Examining the Bound Controls

Nearly any piece of information available in a database can be displayed in a control. Text, yes/no fields, and ranges of values all have available controls to represent them. These controls can include:

- Text boxes
- Check boxes
- Radio buttons

- List boxes
- Combo boxes
- Picture boxes
- Grids

Attaching any of these controls to the Data control is known as *binding*. When a control is connected to the Data control, it is said to be bound. Not all controls can be bound to the Data control. The Timer control, for example, has no binding properties allowing it to be attached.

| NEW TERM | *Bound* controls are controls that display information accessed by a Data control. The bound controls handle all of the behind-the-scenes work and can be easily graphically linked to the Data control. |

The VB Data Form Wizard automatically creates a number of controls on the form to represent all of the fields of the selected table. It then binds each control to the Data control (so data access can occur) and selects the appropriate field for the control to display (see Figure 2.2).

FIGURE 2.2

The bound controls are connected to the Data control with specific properties.

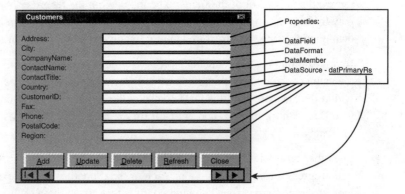

You can easily examine the properties used to connect the various controls to the data source. In the form window, click on the text box that displays the address and look at the Properties window again. The properties under the Data heading include:

- `DataField`
- `DataFormat`
- `DataMember`
- `DataSource`

You can see that only the DataField and DataSource properties are set. The other two properties, when left blank, automatically use the default settings.

In the DataSource field, you'll see the control name datPrimaryRS. This is the name of the Data control that appears at the bottom of the form. The bound control uses this Data control as the data source.

If you click on this property and use the combo arrow at the right of the box, you'll see a pop-up list of all the Data controls available on this form. Because there is only a single Data control, that name is the only one in the list.

The DataField property is the other key property that binds the control. In the DataField property, you'll see the listed field is Address. The DataField property determines what field of the current record will be displayed in the text box. If you click on the property and select the combo arrow at the right side of the entry, the entire list of fields available for each record is displayed (see Figure 2.3).

FIGURE 2.3

The combo box displaying all of the fields available from the database.

Moving to the next text box on the list (the one that displays the city), you'll see that the DataSource field is identical, but the DataField shows the field for the name of the city.

The fields available to the bound controls are set within the RecordSource property of the Data control. If the field does not appear in the field list, it cannot be used by bound controls.

That's all it takes to hook a data source to a Data control to a bound control. After the two properties (ConnectionString and RecordSource) are set for the Data control, each bound control must have the properties needed to direct it to the proper Data control and field (DataField and DataSource) to display.

Examining the Functional Buttons

Now that you've looked at the key properties of the controls and the property settings that link the control to the data connection, the work that the Data Form Wizard did should be much less mysterious. Most of the functionality is inherent in the Data control itself.

However, functions such as adding and updating records are not provided by the Data control. Instead, the wizard had to add extra code to the form to allow these to function correctly.

You can examine the code stored in the functional buttons. Double-click on the Add button to show the source code window with the associated VB code. It should look like this:

```
Private Sub cmdAdd_Click()
  On Error GoTo AddErr
  datPrimaryRS.Recordset.AddNew

  Exit Sub
AddErr:
  MsgBox Err.Description
End Sub
```

Aside from the traditional error checking routines, there is only a single command:

```
datPrimaryRS.Recordset.AddNew
```

This command references the datPrimaryRS Data control and the recordset it contains. Remember earlier when you learned that a recordset was a memory structure used to hold the records retrieved from the database? It is actually a completely programmable object. This command activates one of the functions that is built into the Recordset object.

After the Recordset object has been referenced, it issues a call to the AddNew() method to add the new record. If you examine the other buttons, you will see that they, too, have only one or two commands to fulfill their function.

The Data control is really only a simple user interface placed atop the powerful database engine. Therefore, to access the commands missing from the user interface component of the Data control only requires that the commands for the engine be activated directly.

Summary

Using the Data control is an easy way to graphically create a connection to a database. In addition to connecting to the database, the Data control must be set to reference one particular table within the database. Controls can then be bound to the Data control to display values held by the fields of the database.

The VB Data Form Wizard can be used to quickly generate a prototype form that contains a Data control connected to a specified database and table, as well as all of the bound controls necessary to access that data.

2

Q&A

Q Does the VB Data Form Wizard do anything I can't do myself?

A No, the Wizard simply automates tasks that would take you much longer to do yourself. In the example you created in Hour 1, the wizard essentially created a new form, placed and configured a Data control on the form, placed controls and bound them to the Data control, and added some buttons with code to activate them.

All of the settings on the form and all its controls can be changed by you at any time.

Q Can I change the field of a bound control?

A Yes, but realize that the label to the left of the control was created by the wizard. This means that changing the field will not automatically change the label title. You will have to change it to match the new field displayed in the bound control.

Q Are bound controls different from other controls?

A Yes, they are known as data-aware controls. Each data-aware control must understand how to read, write, and properly display data. Controls such as the `Timer` control are not data aware.

Workshop

The quiz questions and exercises are provided for your further understanding. See Appendix C, "Answers," for the answers to the questions.

Quiz

1. What is a bound control?

2. What is Hungarian notation?

3. Must ConnectionString contain the complete file path to the data source?

4. True or False: A recordset is stored on disk.

5. What properties on a Data control must be set to properly access a database file?

6. True or False: Double-clicking on the DataSource property of a bound control will automatically place the name of the first Data control in the property.

7. Which two properties are set on a bound control to reference a Data control and a particular field?

8. What functions are supplied by the Data Form Wizard through additional buttons and code?

Exercises

1. Open one of the sample Data control projects included with Visual Basic 6. Examine the settings of the Data control and the bound controls on the form.

2. Run the Data Form Wizard again and select the Biblio.MDB database. Select the Data control in the project and examine the RecordSource property to see how it differs from the same property in the first example.

Hour 3

Introducing the Data Control

Visual Basic makes it easy to program the connectivity to a database or use graphical controls to set up the data display and modification. In this hour, using one of the graphical components, the *Data Control*, will quickly get you started in creating database applications. The Data Control component makes prototyping a database application a snap.

The Data Form Wizard that you used to construct the sample database application from the Northwind database uses the Data Control to provide connectivity. Having examined the properties that connect the control to the data source, you will find it quite easy to construct a form manually.

The highlights of this hour include:

- Creating a form that uses the Data Control
- Programming the Data Control
- Binding controls to the Data Control

How Does the Data Control Relate to a Database Application?

The Data Control, as you have already seen, provides a crucial technology to simplify database connections within Visual Basic. The control provides the following advantages:

- Database connectivity with little or no programming
- Pre-designed database navigation allows the user to step through all the data
- Easy connectivity with controls (such as text boxes) make data instantly accessible
- Excellent upward compatibility for code retrofit to a more complex solution

All these capabilities are powerfully implemented in the component included with Visual Basic to provide a user interface to the database engine. Programming of the Data Control is really easiest to understand by using it. Therefore, let's create a simple application in Visual Basic 6 to display and navigate through some sample data.

Creating a Data Control Application

The Data Control is a component that provides data connectivity on a single form. It must be placed on a form and then attached to other user interface controls (see Figure 3.1). Any movement to show other entries in the database is automatically reflected in the controls that are connected to the Data Control.

FIGURE 3.1

The Data Control is connected to other user interface components for synchronized data display.

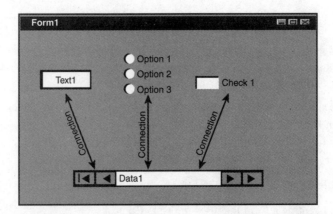

You will find that no matter how advanced you become with programming Visual Basic, you will continue to use the Data Control for quick prototyping of a data access form. The data control makes quickly attaching text boxes and other controls to specific pieces of data extremely effective for instant applications.

With the common install Visual Basic, the sample Northwind (NWind.mdb)database is automatically included in the VB6 folder. You'll use this data source again for the new Data Control project.

That's all it takes to hook a data source to a data control to a bound control. After the two properties are set for the Data Control (`ConnectionString` and `RecordSource`), each bound control must have the properties needed to direct them to the proper data control and field (`DataField` and `DataSource`) to display.

Using the Data Control from Scratch

Although the VB Data Form Wizard is excellent for constructing general data forms, there will often be times when creating a custom form is required. Additionally, modifications to the form after it has been created can be accomplished using the techniques you'll learn in this hour.

You'll create a form that contains a data control hooked to the Employees table of the Northwind database and contains bound fields to display two fields of the record information.

Configuring the Data Control

All the construction of this new Data Control example will occur on the original blank form that was created when you started a new project. If you removed this form from the project, simply add another blank form.

1. Open the original form.

   You can easily place the Data Control on the Form1 that was originally created when the project was first initialized. The bound controls can then be placed on the same form and attached to the data source.

2. Set the Name property of the form to `frmEmployees`.

   Remember that it is always a good idea to descriptively name controls and forms when you're beginning a project. If you wait until later to set them, you will probably not get it done.

3. Add the Data Control by double-clicking on the Toolbox icon.

   Double-clicking on the toolbar icon for the Data Control will add it to the form. You could alternatively draw the control on the form. The default placement and size is inappropriate for the application, so you'll have to move it.

3

4. Stretch and place the control at the bottom of the screen.

   Move and resize the Data Control to the bottom of the window, as shown in Figure 3.2. The standard placement of the Data Control is at the bottom of a form.

FIGURE 3.2

The Data Control is set to an appropriate height and moved to the bottom of the form.

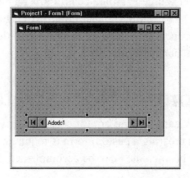

After the Data Control is placed on the form, it needs to be configured. After you set its two properties (`ConnectionString` and `RecordSource`), it can be used to bind controls on the form.

5. Double-click on the `ConnectionString` property.

   The `ConnectionString` property indicates to the Data Control where and what access method will be used to address the Data Source. The wizard takes care of this automatically, but setting it is a simple process. Double-clicking on the property will display the property wizard needed to set this property to the proper format.

6. Click on the Build button to the right of the Use Connection String selection.

   The Build button is used to show the Connection String builder window, which contains several tabbed pages allowing configuration of the data source.

7. Select the Microsoft Jet 3.51 OLE DB Provider option and click the Next button

   The Microsoft Jet engine is the database engine that is used by Visual Basic. Both Visual Basic and Microsoft Access use the Jet engine for database access.

8. Click on the Browse button to select the NWind.mdb file.

   After the NWind file is selected (see Figure 3.3), it will appear in the window with the full path name.

9. Click the OK button.

   You should now see that the `ConnectionString` property has been filled with a value very similar to the one set up by the Data Form Wizard.

   The data source points to the NWind database, so the `RecordSource` can now be used to select the table from which to read the data. In the Properties window, after the ConnectionString is set, accessing the RecordSource property will read the necessary information from the actual source file.

FIGURE 3.3

The NWind.mdb file selected as the database.

10. Select the RecordSource property and click the combo box arrow on the right.

    The Property Pages should be displayed for the RecordSource. From this property page, you will be able to set the type of data to be read in from the database.

11. Set the CommandType to the value 2 - adCmdTable

    Setting the CommandType determines how the recordset will be constructed for this Data Control. Because you want to view all the records in the table (rather than a selective search), the adCmdTable selection will provide a list of tables from which to select.

    Visual Basic will automatically read in all the available tables from the data source set in the ConnectionString. These will then be stored in the Tables combo box.

12. Select the Employees table from the list of tables.

    After the Employees table is selected (see Figure 3.4), bound controls can be attached to the Data Control. The two key properties of the Data Control have been configured.

    The Data Control is set to receive data and act as the connection to the data source. You will now need to add a couple of controls to display some of the field data available to the Data Control.

    The Data Form Wizard automatically added the necessary text boxes and labels for the fields. Here you will need to add them individually.

FIGURE 3.4

*The Property Pages
after the Employees
table is selected for the
RecordSource.*

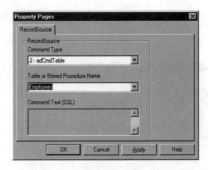

13. Add two text box controls to the form.

    Either click and drag the text boxes or double-click on the icons and move them
    about on the form. These text boxes will display the name (first and last) of the
    currently selected employee. To bind the text boxes to the Data Control, the
    DataSource and DataField properties will have to be properly configured.

> If you only have one data control on the form, double-clicking the
> DataSource property of a control to be bound (such as a text box) will auto-
> matically fill the property with the name of the primary data control.

14. Select the first text box and double-click on the DataSource property

    Double-clicking on the DataSource should fill it with the value of Adodc1, the
    default name of the data control that was added to the form.

15. Select the FirstName field into the DataField property.

    Clicking on the arrow to the right of the property will display a list of all the avail-
    able fields for this table. That is why it is important to set the DataSource property
    field first. If it was left unset, the DataField property would not know where the
    intended data was to be retrieved from.

16. Select the second text box and double-click on the DataSource property.

    Like the property in the other text box, this will contain the name of the Data
    Control.

> If there is more than one data control on the form, you can use the combo
> box for the property to select one or simply type the name of the control
> into the DataSource property. Double-clicking the property when multiple
> data controls exist will simply fill it with the first Data Control that was
> added to the form.

17. Select the LastName field into the DataField property.

18. Change the Startup object in the Project Properties back to frmEmployees.

    When the VB Data Form Wizard created the data access form, you changed the initial form to display it. Now you need to change it to execute the Employees form.

    Done! That was pretty simple. When you have completed all the steps, execute the application. You should have a form that looks like the one in Figure 3.5.

FIGURE 3.5

The completed form using the Data Control.

The Data Control allows you to connect controls to a database without writing a single line of code. It also provides a ready-to-use interface for navigating within the records of the database.

> You can use a data control on a form without having it displayed. If you set the Visible property to `False`, it will not be shown when the form is executed. However, it will still function normally and be available for use during design to bind controls. You can then create your own buttons to activate features such as record navigation.

Shortcomings of Bound Controls

Now that you have seen how to use the Data Control and how to bind other controls to a field within the data source, you might wonder why you shouldn't use bound controls all the time.

Bound controls have several shortcomings. First, they must be bound at design time. This means that a text field cannot take input and place it in a database field that is designated while the program is executing.

This capability is often needed when storing to a field that is created from one or more fields. For example, a `FullName` field might combine the `FirstName` and `LastName` fields after they have been entered.

Additionally, because the control itself handles all the updating of the data, there is only a limited amount of data checking that can be implemented before the update is written into the database. For example, if you wanted to write a small VB program to confirm that the data the user entered into the state field was actually valid, the opportunity to decide when this information would be checked is limited by bound controls.

Writing the information directly into the database, although more complicated, does not suffer from these disadvantages. For most simple solutions, however, the Data Control is perfect for creating a form that contains database access.

Because a data control resides on a single form, every time that form is loaded the recordset is initialized. Likewise, when the form is unloaded, so is the recordset. Also, the Data Control is linked to the form, so a global data source that is available throughout the application is difficult to accomplish.

If your application needs to frequently show and then eliminate a form or provide global access to a single source, it would be wise to make the database access available through the ActiveX Data Objects (ADO) detailed in Hour 17, "Understanding ActiveX Data Objects (ADO)."

Summary

Using the Data Control is an way easy to graphically create a connection to a database. In addition to connecting to the database, the Data Control must be set to reference one particular table within the database. Controls can then be bound to the Data Control to display values held by the fields of the database.

The VB Data Form Wizard can be used to quickly generate a prototype form that contains a Data Control connected to a specified database and table, as well as all the bound controls necessary to access that data.

Q&A

Q Does the Data Control have to be visible to function?

A No, you can easily set the Visible property to False and manipulate the control through program code.

Q If I have many bound controls on a form, is there an easy way to redirect them to a new Data Control placed on the form?

A Yes. You can select all the bound controls and then show the Properties window. If you change the DataSource property to your new control, it will be changed in all the selected controls.

Q After I've constructed a form using the Data Control, do I have to start from scratch to add more functionality?

A No, the Data Control uses the same technology that is used to program advanced solutions. By adding some additional code and removing the control from your form, the application you created can be easily modified to use the more direct database technology.

Q Can I have multiple forms access a single Data Control on a form?

A Although possible, this is not the best solution to the problem. If you need multiple forms to access a single recordset, it is usually better to use a global object defined as an ActiveX Data Object (ADO). This will be covered in greater depth in Hour 17.

Workshop

The quiz questions and exercises are provided for your further understanding. See Appendix C, "Answers," for the answers to the questions.

Quiz

1. What is the purpose of the Data Control?
2. Does the Data Form Wizard use a special form of database access?
3. What is the Microsoft Jet engine?
4. Why set the `DataSource` property on a bound control before the `DataField` property?
5. Why is the Command Type setting of the `RecordSource` property set to `adCmdTable`?
6. What are the limitations of using the Data Control?

Exercises

1. Create a new database form. This time, use the Biblio.mdb supplied with Visual Basic 6.
2. Place a second data control on the form and add fields that access one of the other tables included in the Northwind database.

Hour 4

General Database Concepts

The Northwind database that you used in the last hour provides a sample of a database that was already constructed by Microsoft. By examining that database, you learned the rudimentary concepts of what a database contains (such as fields and records). Rarely in your database projects, however, will a preexisting database fulfill the needs of your application.

This hour will focus on the various aspects of implementing your own database. So far in this book, you've spent most of your time actually implementing programs. For this hour, you will learn the important concepts used to outline and construct a database from scratch.

Like all skills, the more you practice creating databases, the better you get at it. Skill in creating a database translates into fewer modifications as the application is built around it, faster responses to queries, and a better fit to the final user's needs.

Learning to design the structure of the database to solve real-world problems optimally takes time. In this hour, however, you'll get a jump start on the process by seeing some of the decisions that must be made as the construction occurs.

The highlights of this hour include

- Learning the structure of a database
- Planning a database
- Relating tables to each other
- Using an index for fast access
- Defining the parts of a database

What Is the Structure of a Database?

To most beginning database programmers, it is difficult to understand how a database is structured. In many ways, it resembles writing when faced with a blank sheet of paper. Where do you begin? Any project really starts by creating the database file itself in order to place tables and data into it.

The database is a single file (in the case of Microsoft Access) that holds all the table definitions as well as the data stored into the database. Contained in each database are one or more tables, each structured to store information in a particular format. The structure of a table is defined by a series of fields that denote how the data will be recorded. The table definition acts like a template. The fields are described in this definition to determine the format of each record data. In Figure 4.1, you can see how the fields and table relate to the database that contains them. A database can contain one or more tables. Each table can contain one or more fields. The data for each table is stored in the format defined by the table.

Defining your database can be done either using the tools included with Visual Basic (such as the Visual Data Manager), using Microsoft Access, or through a database language known as Structured Query Language (SQL). In this hour, you'll use the Visual Data Manager to create the database. Before you begin defining it, you will learn how to think through some of the decisions that will determine whether your design is effective.

Importance of Planning

After the structure of a database is defined, it becomes more difficult to change. The tables and their definitions act as the foundation on which your application will be built. As the application framework becomes filled out, even a slight change in the structure of the database can cause a great deal of rewrites and modification.

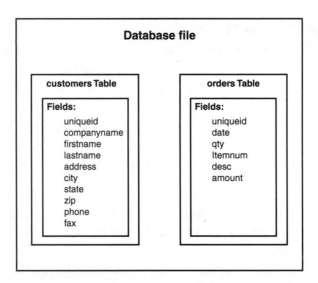

FIGURE 4.1

Database, table, and field structure.

For example, a table might originally be defined to contain an entire customer name in one field. If, half-way through the project, it is decided that both a first and last name field are required, any currently entered data will have to be modified or expunged. Coding for reports and forms will have to be recreated.

This example is one of the simpler situations that might occur. The most complicated one happens when a modification to the entire database structure is needed. For example, perhaps a table is created containing all the business information relating to a customer. Later it is decided that a different table is required to contain the information of individual contacts within the customer organization separate from the general business details (usually because many customers that work at the same organization need to be tracked). The wholesale changes that will be required to adapt an existing application to the new database model will be substantial. Schedules lengthen, deployment is delayed, and bugs are introduced. If the structure had been more clearly considered before the application was created, the project would be in substantially better shape. Often to accommodate late changes, inelegant solutions must be adopted just to allow the project to be completed in a reasonable amount of time.

By making the planning of a database a part of database application construction, you should be able to avoid most of the pitfalls of late changes. Planning simply requires thinking out the options that you will need for the database structure. In this hour, you will learn how to approach this planning.

Table Relations

Within the database, the information necessary for an application can rarely all be stored in a single table. For this reason, information is typically broken into more than one table, often with tables related to one another. Table relations enable one table to be connected to another via a common field.

The most common example of related tables is a customer table and an orders table. You don't want to duplicate all the customer information in each order record. Rather, the order record could point to a record in the customers table. Usually this is accomplished by placing a single field in the order to contain a reference number to the customer stored in the other table. In a simple example, imagine the customers table has every person stored with their Social Security number. When the order record is created, it only needs to store the Social Security number with the order to reference what customer placed the order.

Because you will not actually begin creating related tables until Hour 10, "Multitable Relations," this brief introduction is only to make you aware that the table breakdown is affected by the consideration of relationships. However, multiple tables in a database are rarely all related.

> If you break down the relations too much, the database can become too complex and slow. When many relations are used in a database, more processing overhead will be needed for a general query. Learning when to stop breaking down a table is more of an art than a science. During the 24 hours that you'll study database application construction, you will learn many rules of thumb to aid you in properly breaking down your tables.

Within a database, multiple tables are used to separate dissimilar data. Therefore, it is often the case that although multiple tables need to be kept in the same database for the application, they have no strict relation to one another. In this hour, you'll be creating a database that contains multiple unrelated tables.

What Is an Index?

Understanding some of the technology that can make the tables you construct effective to use is a highly important part of effective database design. Chief among these technologies is the table structure known as the index. An *index* is a list of record numbers in a predefined order that point to records, enabling quick searching and sorting.

NEW TERM   An *index* is a list of record pointers in a presorted order.

In the last hour, you saw the customers table that had a companyname field. In an application using a database like Northwind, you will often want either to search for a particular company name with great speed or display a sorted list of the names in proper alphabetical order.

When databases were originally created, records in a database were sorted and stored in a defined order. Every time a change was made to a record or a new one was added, the entire list had to be resorted. Although it wasn't a good solution, it was the best one known at the time.

What happens if you need to display the data sorted in several different orders? What if you insert a new record? These actions require a great deal of processing power because the entire data set must always be in proper order. Constant resorting is a time-consuming process and also requires a great deal of memory to accomplish properly.

Another problem appears when searching a table. How quickly can the computer locate a particular record in the list? When the data isn't properly sorted, it could take quite a deal of time to search a database with 40,000 records. If the desired record is record number 5,000, the computer has to search through each one of the records that precedes the desired record to find the right one!

Instead of living with these limitations, database architects invented a new method called an *index*. In a book index, each index entry indicates that a term can be found on a certain page. For databases, an index entry points to a record number. Rather than sorting all the individual records, the index list of record numbers is sorted. The actual data is rarely moved around (a processor- and disk-intensive task), but instead simply stored in the order it was added to the database.

In Figure 4.2, the left box shows a box containing single-letter records stored in the order they were entered. They are obviously not in alphabetical order. This is the way the Visual Basic database engine stores records.

FIGURE 4.2

This shows the structure of an index and how the sort affects the results.

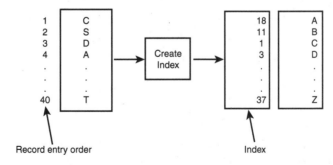

From these records, an index is created. The index is a long list of record numbers in the proper sorted order. When a list of the records in alphabetical order needs to be displayed, the database engine simply accesses the list and displays the records in the order shown by the index. The index also vastly expedites searches. When a new record is added, it is simply added to the end of the table. Then the database engine determines where the new record number should be inserted into the index list. To make the insertion, it only has to rearrange the list of numbers, rather than all the records in the table.

> Every time a record is inserted or an index field is modified, the change must be sorted into the index. This adds processing time and reduces user responsiveness. Therefore, try to be slightly conservative with your use of indexes and limit your application of them to fields that will be frequently searched or sorted.

To add an index to a table, you simply selected the fields that need to be indexed and execute the create index function either through Visual Basic or using a utility like the Visual Data Manager. After it is created, the database automatically maintains the index for you.

How Do I Decide What Goes in My Database?

Now that you have a general overview of the structure of a database, the presence of multiple tables (related or not) in the database, and the function of an index, you need to begin examining how a new database is actually designed. Because database planning is one of the most central aspects to create a database, it will be important to having a standard way to approach the task. You can establish a methodology of database design using these five steps:

1. Decide what the database needs to do
2. Determine what tables you need
3. Define the fields within each table
4. Test sample inputs
5. Begin refining your design

Each of these steps involves a varied amount of work. Realize that when a database project is complicated, more people than usual will be involved in approving it. Therefore, if the database application you are designing will be used by others as well as yourself, these five steps can also be used to guide everyone who needs to cooperate to complete the project.

Step 1: What Does the Database Need to Do?

Defining the purpose of the database can be one of the most difficult tasks. As with any plan, after the general direction is chosen, all the other choices become easier. Don't rush to make a decision, however. Unless you know the exact limits of the database you want to create, there are a few considerations you should examine.

Very rarely when creating any type of database is there not some sort of existing data that will make for data overlap. There are probably already several applications that are at least slightly related to the new one you will make. For example, what if

- You are creating sales lead tracking software, but the organization already has all the contact information in Microsoft Outlook?
- You need an expenses application for tracking hourly billing, yet you already track overall expense information in QuickBooks?
- There is a custom inventory database application you want to create, but all the inventory is stored in a mainframe application used by the whole company?
- You want to make a database of your new DVD collection that will complement the video collection list you already have entered in a shareware application?

When considering a new database, your first task will be to attempt to allow as little overlap with existing applications as possible. The more you minimize duplication of information, the better off you are. Who wants to maintain three different data sources containing virtually the same information? This only creates confusion as to which contains the most accurate information.

Therefore, one of the primary decisions you need to make when creating the database is "What DON'T I want the database to contain?"

If all your contacts are stored in Outlook, you might be able to access this information from the VB program itself so you won't need to duplicate the information. Similarly, Symantec's ACT program stores the data in a dBASE format file that is accessible from Visual Basic.

If you can't reference the other database directly, can you use a reference number or keyword (such as last name) so as to avoid duplication? Or can your new database completely take over the operations of the older one?

4

Before you've finished determining the overview of the database, write down a list of questions the information in the database must answer. If it were a sales database, common questions would might include:

- How many units of each item were sold?
- What was the top seller last month?
- What was the margin for each product type sold?

Asking such questions will help you make sure that the information that is actually needed for the database. The whole reason for a database is the information that you'll retrieve from it, not enter into it.

After you have a better idea of what is to be contained in the database, define it on paper. Simply stating in a sentence or two what is and isn't included in the database will help you a great deal. In the next hour, you'll be constructing a database that keeps track of to-do lists and projects. Here is a simple paragraph outlining the purpose of the database:

This database should be used to track projects and individual to-do items. The information contained within it should be able to individually list projects that are complete, projects in progress, items that must be done today, and the number of days unfinished items are overdue.

Step 2: Determining the Tables You Need

Figuring out what tables you need is difficult because it requires deciding how data will actually be broken down within the database. Deciding on the breakdown for the tables is also an area where you probably have the least experience. The final output, reports, and windows will probably not reflect the exact table definitions. This means that the experience you have using available data-driven programs doesn't translate toward understanding of table selection.

The determination of what tables to place in your database should take place by task. Some of the tasks for the Northwind database might appear like this:

- Track customer information such as name, address, and so on.
- Keep employee information for billing, title, and so on.
- Record individual orders.
- Track inventory and enable subtraction.

To create your list of tables, figure out what you need the database to do. For example, if you wanted to track names, addresses, and other general information, one table could be created named Addressbook. If you needed to track multiple types of people (for example,

Northwind has separate needs for employees and customers), then you will need to create multiple tables.

The list of tables can be simple. For the database you will create, the table might look like the one shown in Table 4.1.

TABLE 4.1 THE TASKS REQUIRED OF THE TABLES IN YOUR DATABASE

Table Name	Description
todo	Track individual to-do items while recording such information as the begin and end dates, percentage complete, and priority.
projects	Record each project to be tracked. Include information to determine the in progress conditions.

The table list will be your guide before you actually execute Visual Basic. By considering exactly what tasks the database will need to perform, you will have a sharp conception of the tables needed in the database.

Step 3: Define the Fields Within Each Table

When the tables are selected, you have the difficult task of choosing the fields, their names, types, and sizes. Leaving out a field is not as much of a problem as setting the field up improperly. As soon as the deployment begins on an application, making changes to core fields is difficult.

You already have your list of fields to use. Write a table name on a sheet of paper and begin writing down the types of information that are needed in the table. Exact field definition can wait for a moment. A list for the todo table might look like this:

Name of item

Description (optional)

Create date

Due date

Percentage done

Priority

Done or Not done check box

Take some time making this list. Usually the best way to accomplish it is to build it over a couple of days. Sit down with the actual task that needs to be done. Can it fit into the field framework you've created? Is there some important information that has been left out?

Be sure you don't set aside a field for derived or calculated data. In the projects table, both the begin date and end date are stored. Creating a field to hold the total number of days for the project would be a waste of space and would require additional programming. It is easy within a query to calculate the difference between the begin and end dates. Therefore, placing this information in a separate field would be redundant.

Additionally, it creates another possibility for the table to contain bad data. If the user were to alter the end date, the number of days would change. Either extra programming would be required to monitor and update the number of days field, or that field would become inaccurate as each change is made.

It is often difficult to resist placing a massive number of fields into a single table so the information is kept together. It also makes access easier from the application—either through the Data Control, or directly through the database objects.

Although you should resist placing too many fields in a single table, sometimes it is unavoidable. It is only a problem if the fields are not directly related to the task set for that table.

Imagine a table where each record contained not only all the customer information (name, address, and so on) but also individual purchase items. Because the task of a customer table would be to record the customer information, adding ordered item information would be a violation of this task.

If the database will be deployed where it is difficult to update the database structure (such as an older database server), it is a good idea to add a few empty fields of various types labeled miscFloat, miscText, and so on. If you ever need to alter an application to store data not originally foreseen when the database was created, one of these fields can be used.

After you have created your list of fields, you need to start defining how they will actually be stored by the computer.

Choosing the Field Type

In a database, each field must have a data type. The data types used by a table are very similar to the ones you're already familiar with from programming Visual Basic. When you dimension a variable, you typically set a type:

```
Dim myStr As String
```

In VB, actually setting the type is optional because an undeclared type will simply become a *variant* type. That is not allowed in table definition. Each field within a table must have a selected type. Table 4.2 shows you the basic types available for definition.

Most of the field types that you use with a VB database will be exactly the same when accessing almost any database. Often, however, the names will change. For example, Memo fields will often be called Text fields. When accessing a new database type, simply be aware that there might be a difference in terminology.

TABLE 4.2 FIELD TYPES AND THEIR DESCRIPTIONS

Field Type	Description
Variable-length Text	For most strings, the variable string is perfect. It uses NULLs to indicate when no value is present and essentially takes up the amount of space for the string as required.
Fixed-length Text	The fixed string will always take up the amount of space defined by its size.
Date/Time	This field type will store a combination date and time. It can also be used to store one or the other.
Integer	A integer type that can store any integer value between +32,768 and −32,768.
Long Integer	A long type that can store much larger integers than a standard (or small) integer type.
Single	A single precision floating point number.
Double	A double precision floating point number.
Currency	The Currency type will store the numbers with two decimal places.
Boolean	A Boolean value is a Yes or No/True or False value.
Memo	These fields are catch-alls that can store tremendous amounts of information (such as the full text of a book). By their very nature, queries against Text fields tend to be slower when compared with other traditional data types.
Binary	This type will store binary objects such as OLE objects, image data, sound data, and so on.

When making choices about the data types, realize that moving up from a smaller data type to a large type will not result in any loss of data. For example, if a database contains a number of Single type fields, modifying the Single fields to Double fields will result in no data loss. Changing from a Double to a Single or Integer, however, might result in data loss.

Make sure when you create the database that you have a "notes" or "memo" field in the most common user input table. For example, when a user is recording customer account information, the customer might indicate that all shipments should be made through Federal Express with the customer's airbill number. Although there might be no dedicated field to contain this information, it should be kept with the customer record.

Providing an information space for unintended data recording can be one of the most important additions to the table. When no place is supplied for critical general information, users will often begin a separate paper reference file, sometimes defeating the purpose of the application in the first place.

One of the best methods of determining what field types to use in your table is to examine existing tables such as those included with VB or other existing systems. If many of the other databases that you use define a last name field as a variable string field with a 40-character limit, it is usually a good idea to match this standard. If data ever needs to be exchanged, it is a simple process and no information needs to be lost.

Be sure to consider carefully before limiting a particular field to a type or size. For example, often table designers make a ZIP code a number or a 5-character length text field. This makes recording ZIP + 4 codes impossible in the field. Likewise, often telephone fields are defined such that entering telephone extensions is difficult. Consider some of the possible variations of the data that will be stored in the table.

Step 4: Test Sample Inputs

After the database has been constructed, you should attempt to enter some of the information that will be stored into it. Real data is the best because it will immediately indicate possible shortcomings.

Sit down and enter a complete test record, filling every field. This process alone can save many hours of difficulty because problems are very easy to correct at this point. The sample records can be deleted later.

If the database will be used by someone other than yourself, have them attempt to enter the information. Often the data that appears on a form or in a list of samples will work, but there might actually be changes that the

> users need made. Simple field additions such as an extended ZIP code or the capability to enter a specific phone extension might make the final application far more useful.

Step 5: Begin Refining Your Design

No table design is ever perfect. When you are doing your design, you will find yourself making many trade-offs. Determining the tables to use and the fields within them, not to mention choosing the correct fields types, can often be very trying. Needless to say, no matter how rigorously your initial design stage is planned, there will be some mistakes or misjudgments made. As the project is heading toward the final milestone, re-examine the design decisions you made earlier. Could minor changes be made that would significantly increase the usefulness of the data later?

The most important time to refine your design is *before deployment*. After the system is deployed and users are regularly entering data, changes become much more expensive. Therefore, try to schedule some hands-on testing before the system is actually deployed to determine the changes that must be made.

Summary

Creating a proper database is the cornerstone to creating an effective database application. If the structure of the database is not set up properly, the application built on top of the database might require either extensive additional programming or might not be able to fulfill some of the processing or reporting functions.

By considering what shouldn't be in the database in the beginning, a big step will be taken toward eliminating duplication of information storage. The tables and fields within the tables can then be defined.

Q&A

Q Why do I need to take so much time designing my database?

A Modifications to the structure of the database are more expensive in time and resources than almost any other change during development. After data has been placed in the data file, even slight changes to the structure of a table or type of a field can cause tremendous problems and can require manual re-entry of data.

4

Q How important is defining the proper field type in the beginning?

A As long as a data type can be easily converted, finding the exact type is not tremendously important. For example, defining a field with the type Single can easily be converted to Double later or vice versa. Simply try to make sure that the proper general type is selected, such as a numeric type (Integer, Single, Double, and so on) or a string type (Variable Length or Fixed Length).

Q After I've created a table, can I later add indexes to additional fields?

A Yes. Indexes can be added at any time. In fact, often indexes are added later when it is known what are the most accessed and sorted fields. Note that when more data is stored in the current table, it will take more time to initially create the index because all existing data must first be processed for indexing.

Q What is a "flat-file" database?

A The databases that you have created so far are essentially all "flat-file" databases. This simply means that the tables are not directly related to one another. For example, if you had created an address table separate from the customers table and connected them, it would be known as a *relational* database. When there are no connections between tables, the database is said to be flat. In Hour 10, "Multitable Relations," you'll learn all about relational databases.

Workshop

The quiz questions and exercises are provided for your further understanding. See Appendix C, "Answers," for the answers to the questions.

Quiz

1. Why is planning in the beginning so important?

2. How do you decide how to separate data into tables?

3. What are the primary purposes of an index?

4. What is a key question you should ask yourself when beginning design of a new database?

5. When is the proper time to add an index?

6. True or False: Adding many indexes to a table can slow down record additions or updates.

Exercises

1. Consider how you would create a database for an application you need (for example, group list, address book, and so on). What fields would you choose? How many tables would you need? Which fields should have indexes?

2. In your sample database, what would you leave out? What type of information would be best left in a general notes field? What type of fields would you combine (fullName) or keep separate (lastName, firstName)?

4

Hour 5

Constructing Databases

The database concepts that you learned in the last hour will crystallize into useful knowledge as you actually begin to construct database files. For this reason, you need to become familiar with the Visual Data Manager included with Visual Basic to complete this task. The Visual Data Manager is really a tool that provides all the basic functionality of database creation and maintenance.

By learning to create a database and tables contained in it, you will be learning a necessary skill for database programming. Constructing a database from scratch is easy given the tools provided with Visual Basic 6. This hour will focus on the various aspects of implementing your own database.

The highlights of this hour include:

- Creating a custom database
- Adding two tables to the database to contain information
- Setting a Primary key field to each table for unique record references
- Adding indexes to the tables

The Visual Data Manager

The Visual Data Manager is a complete database construction utility included with Visual Basic. Accessible through the Add-Ins menu of Visual Basic 6, the Data Manager gives you the ability to

- Create a database
- Construct and design tables within the database
- Gain complete access to the data contained within the tables
- Import and export various data types
- Compact an existing database

The Data Manager can access a number of database file types including Access, dBASE, FoxPro, Paradox, text files, Excel files, and ODBC data sources. However, in this hour you will only need to edit Microsoft Access format databases.

Introducing the Data Manager

The Visual Data Manager is actually a separate program from Visual Basic, although it is only accessible through it. To activate it, go to the Add-Ins menu and select the Visual Data Manager option.

When the Data Manager is displayed, it does not automatically open any databases. Under the File menu (see Figure 5.1), you can open a database, create a new one, set up a workspace, and compact or repair an existing database. The Data Manager itself does not have many options until you actually open a database.

FIGURE 5.1

The File menu enables the opening of a variety of different databases.

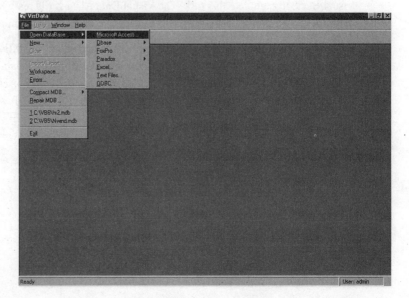

The Importance of NULLs

The more database programming that you do, the more you will encounter all the special considerations you will have to make in your code for a value known as a NULL. A NULL is not the same as an empty string (" "). A NULL means that there is literally no value stored in the variable.

NEW TERM   When a field in a record is completely empty and does not even contain a blank value (such as an empty string), it is known as a *NULL*. A NULL essentially identifies that there is currently no value stored in the field.

It's easy to understand why NULLs are used when you realize how much space they can save. In the case of a database, imagine that a string field is setup to hold 255 characters. If the field is set to an empty string (" "), the 255 characters of disk space in the database must be allocated. However, if the field contains a NULL, there is no space allocated.

It is not difficult to imagine a database of 40,000 records where each record contains two strings. If these two strings were empty for half of the records, the NULL value would save almost 10MB of disk space! This makes the advantages of using NULLs clear.

As you will see more extensively in Hour 17, "Understanding ActiveX Data Objects (ADO)," when ADOs are covered, fields that might contain NULL values require special handling. When a program attempts to manipulate a NULL value, the program can generate an error.

NULLs are important to recognize when you begin database construction. The Visual Data Manager enables you to set a field to not accept NULL values. Although this will tend to make a database larger, it can also avoid errors when creating more advanced solutions.

5

Creating Your First Database

After covering the basic aspects of database design, you need some experience actually constructing a database. The Visual Data Manager can be used to easily construct some simple tables and provide all the accessory technologies (such as indexes) that are used by the database engine.

In the last hour, you learned that before you begin database construction you should have a simple description of what should be contained in it. Here is a paragraph outlining the purpose of the database:

This database should be used to track projects and individual to-do items. The information contained within it should be able to individually list projects that are complete, projects in progress, items that must be done today, and the number of days overdue unfinished items are.

You can use this as a guide to understand the overview of the database as you follow the individual construction steps.

1. Select New, Microsoft Access, Version 7.0 MDB

   When earlier 16-bit systems such as Windows for Workgroups and Windows 3.1 were the standard, the Access 2.0 format was popular. For compatibility reasons, Visual Basic and the Data Manager can still address these file types. If a client application needs to be deployed on both 16- and 32-bit systems (such as Windows NT and Windows 95/98), the older data format must be used for both systems to address the same database file.

   However, any newer database files, such as the one you're creating now, should be in Access 7 format. This format provides a variety of new features and is also much faster than the older version.

2. Name the file hr5.mdb.

   The database file in Access format should have the .mdb extension. Here, you're simply using a filename that complies with the current hour of learning.

3. Expand the properties in the Database Window.

   The database itself, when created, has a number of default properties (see Figure 5.2) that determine how it functions. Because you are just constructing a simple sample database, all the defaults work fine.

FIGURE 5.2

Default properties of the newly created database.

4. Right-click the mouse within the Database Window and select the New Table option.

5. Type in the name of the table as todo.

6. Click the Add Field button.

7. Type the Field name as uniqueid.

8. Select the Field type as Long.

   The data type Long stands for long integer, which can be any number between –2,147,483,648 and 2,147,483,647. Each table should have a uniquely identifying number so it can be referenced, particularly from another table.

Setting the type to Long versus using a smaller number type ensures that there will be enough unique identification numbers for most any project.

When the Long type was selected, you might have noticed that one check box in the lower part of the window became highlighted, whereas another became dimmed.

The first check box, labeled AutoIncrField, makes the database automatically increment the number to be placed in the field every time a new record is added. Therefore, the value in the very first record of the database will be set to 1, the second to 2, and so on. Using the automatic increment ensures that the number in this field is always unique. If records are deleted, it does not affect the current count.

The second check box is AllowZeroLength, which means that NULL values are allow for this field. Because an empty field for a number type field wouldn't save any disk space, there cannot be a NULL value for any of the set size data types. Because the option is not available, it dimmed when the Long data type was selected.

9. Check the AutoIncrField check box.

You should now have a field dialog box that looks like the one shown in Figure 5.3. From now on, every new record placed in this table will automatically be assigned a number when this field is left blank.

FIGURE 5.3

Check AutoIncrField to complete the definition of the current field.

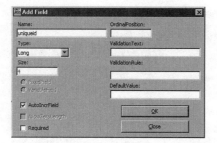

5

The automatic increment only sets this field when a new record is created. The number stored in this field for a particular record can be changed after creation if that is necessary.

10. Click the OK button to accept the field.

The field will now be added to the list box in the window behind. Because the Data Manager assumes you will want to enter multiple fields at one time, the window does not actually close. All the values that had been present are now cleared and you can begin the creation of a new field.

11. Type the Field name as itemName.

12. Set the Size of the field to 20.

13. Click the OK button to accept the field.

14. Enter the rest of the fields shown in Table 5.1.

    The fields shown here will define the data that will be accepted into the table. The done field is a Boolean that can only accept TRUE or FALSE values. That way, for a to-do list, you can locate only those items that are complete or those left undone.

TABLE 5.1 FIELDS FOR THE CUSTOMERS TABLE

Field Name	Type	Size
uniqueid	Long	n/a
itemName	Text	20
itemDesc	Text	120
beginDate	Date/Time	n/a
endDate	Date/Time	n/a
done	Boolean	n/a

When all the fields are entered and you close the Field Definition dialog box, your table structure should look like the one shown in Figure 5.4.

FIGURE 5.4

The fields have been inserted into the table definition.

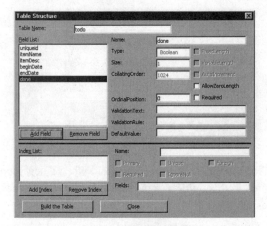

15. Click on the Build the Table button to create the table.

Your first table will now be created in the database. The customers table will appear in the Database Window list. You can expand the properties of the table to see all the parts of the table.

Now that the basic construction is complete, you will need to learn a little bit more about the Visual Data Manager to enhance the database and enter initial information. The next hour will provide a complete overview of the features included in the Data Manager.

Summary

The to-do table you just constructed is your first exposure to building a database from scratch. You will see as your knowledge and understanding increases that most of the databases you will create in the future will not greatly differ from this one.

As covered in Hour 4, "General Database Concepts," the planning of the database takes far more time and consideration than the actual implementation. With this simple database, you have only used the most basic capabilities of the Visual Data Manager. In the next hour, you will use this same database to explore other features of the application.

Q&A

Q If I set the field to not accept NULL values, will each record take up more disk space?

A Yes. The NULL helps prevent fields that are empty or undefined for a particular record from setting aside the field space on the disk. By preventing the use of NULLs, the space will have to be allocated for the record whether the field is empty or not.

Q Why isn't it possible to change the field size when the type is set to Long, Integer, and others?

A Certain data types, particularly numeric data types, have a set size in memory and on the disk. If the field containing them were expanded, the space would be simply wasted.

Q Will I use the Visual Data Manager a lot or is there a more powerful tool included with Visual Basic?

A Although there is a more powerful tool, the Visual Modeler, included with Visual Basic, you probably won't use it any time soon. The Visual Modeler is for complex business system deployment and primarily used during a team development project. Learning the Visual Data Manager will facilitate most of the work you will ever need to do.

5

Workshop

The quiz questions and exercises are provided for your further understanding. See Appendix C, "Answers," for the answers to the questions.

Quiz

1. What program is used to construct a table?

2. Can the Visual Data Manager open Microsoft Access database files?

3. What is a NULL value?

4. Can the value stored in a field that is set to AutoIncrement be changed?

5. How is a Primary key set?

Exercise

1. Create a database for a collection that you own (videotapes, stamps, albums, and so on). Include such information as location, quantity, value, and so on. The variety of items to be found in most collections will provide some of the best experience you will encounter when trying to make a standardized database, yet still provide enough latitude to account for the different items.

2. Examine the Northwind database and consider the decisions made by its creator. For your application, would you need to make the database accommodate the international aspects included with NWind.mdb? What fields would you add? Would you include a secondary address table?

Hour 6

Visual Data Manager

The Visual Data Manager, first introduced in the last chapter, will become one of the most useful tools in your database arsenal. Like the Notepad application included with Windows, the simple functionality and fast execution make it excellent for the most common tasks that it was created to handle.

In this hour you'll learn all about the Data Manager and use it to augment the database that you created in Hour 5.

The highlights of this hour include:

- Using the feature set of the Visual Data Manager
- Using the Data Form Designer
- Examining the features of the Query Builder
- Adding an index to the todo table
- Entering information into a table

Visual Data Manager Overview

The Visual Data Manager is an application made to allow database creation, table creation and modification, and data entry. Because it is easy to access from within Visual Basic, even if you use another database application (such as Access) for most of your database needs, the Data Manager will be excellent for use as a handy general tool.

To display the Visual Data Manager, you can select it from the Add-Ins menu. If you look in the Visual Basic folder, you can also activate it by executing the VisData.exe program.

 Although the Visual Data Manager is extremely powerful and convenient, you might also consider using Microsoft Access to construct your databases. Because the files are entirely compatible, Access provides a friendlier construction environment.

From the Data Manager, you've already created a database with basic capabilities. For maintenance of a database after it has been created, the Visual Data Manager also provides the capability to repair a damaged database file or compact it for reclamation of disk space unused by the database.

When you load a database into the Visual Data Manager (see Figure 6.1), there are three basic windows that you will normally see. The Database Window displays all the items contained within the database file. The query window enables you to enter SQL code and execute it against the data source. Finally, the Edit window can be used to edit or examine data from a table or query.

Editing the database file loaded into the Data Manager is not the only functionality included with the application. Under the Utilities menu are a number of features that are useful for managing a database system (see Table 6.1).

TABLE 6.1 UTILITIES INCLUDED WITH VISUAL DATA MANAGER

Utility Name	Description
Query Builder	Displays a visual window that helps construct a SQL language query
Data Form Designer	A miniature version of the VB Data Form Wizard
Global Replace	Makes a replacement across global fields and tables that match particular criteria
Attachments	Enables attachment links to other databases to be contained within the current database

Groups/Users	Provides for definitions of users and groups that can be used to restrict access to particular parts of the database
System.MD?	Set the system security file used to define security levels
Preferences	Such as timeout values (query and login), open database settings, and included system tables

SQL window

FIGURE 6.1

The three primary windows available in the Visual Data Manager.

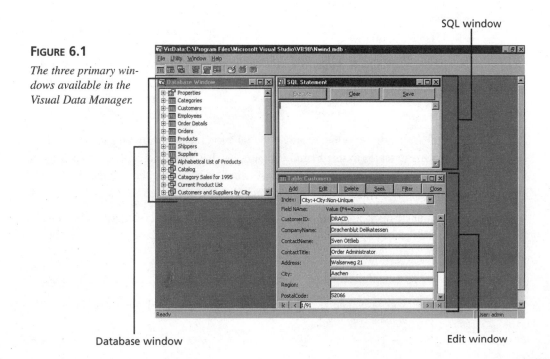

Database window

Edit window

The utilities provide the occasional use functionality for maintenance on the current database. However, most of the routine work that you will need to accomplish with the Data Manager will occur in one of the three primary windows.

6

The utilities that enable you to set security for the database should be left alone until you understand the complete security setup. This information is covered by Hour 22, "Database Security."

If you make a mistake with the security setup to the database, you could lock yourself out! Therefore, it is not recommended to experiment with security until you have covered the workings of it.

Database Window

The primary window (the Database window) in the Visual Data Manager display contains all the primary information concerning the database. Three primary categories of information contained in a database are shown in this window:

- Properties
- Tables
- SQL language queries

The properties define the general characteristics of the database file. Each property is a single-line value. Double-clicking an individual property will let you modify the value it contains. Right now, most of the properties are a little advanced and should be left to their default values.

The tables displayed in the window are all the tables contained within the database file. You can expand to tables to see the individual fields that they each contain. No editing of the table actually occurs in the main Database window, but rather through the right-mouse button menu as you saw in the last hour.

The SQL language queries enable a set of database record selection criteria to be imbedded within the database. By adding the selection code to the database, it can be treated by a program as if it was a table.

If you haven't added any SQL queries, this category will not appear in the Database window.

The Database window is not really used for any type of modification. It allows for selection and examination of the structural items that are contained within the file.

Edit Window

The Edit window, unlike the Database window, will enable you to examine and edit the actual data contained in the tables of a file. This window does not provide any type of advanced error checking for data entry (for example, to stop entry into an AutoIncrement field that will cause an error), so it is used primarily by a developer and not a novice user (unlike Access).

Double-clicking on a table in the main Database window will display the Edit window for the selected table. The buttons displayed along the top of the Edit window show the functions available for use within this window.

In Table 6.2, you can see a list of the buttons that appear at the top of the Edit window. Although most of these buttons are pretty self-explanatory, the functions of some might not be as readily apparent.

TABLE 6.2 THE BUTTONS OF THE EDIT WINDOW

Button Name	Description
Add	Adds a new record
Edit	Edits the current record
Delete	Deletes the current record
Close	Closes the current window
Filter	Filters records to a set that matches specified criteria
Move	Performs a "goto" operation that jumps to a particular record for display
Seek	Searches the recordset for a record that matches criteria

In Figure 6.2, you can see the Seek button function. The Seek function will locate a particular record within the current table.

FIGURE 6.2

Using the Seek button to locate a record.

The Seek command can be set to locate the first record, last record, or other specifications to find the record that matches the set criteria.

SQL Statement Window

After a database is filled with information, you can retrieve any information that you have the rights for using the Structured Query Language or SQL. SQL is the common way that all information is retrieved out of all relational databases. You might need to find all the people with the last name of Smith in the address book. Or you might want all the addresses of the people sorted by their ZIP code.

Searching the database to return an ordered set or subset of the data is called querying the database. The RecordSource property in the Data Control is actually a query used to select all the fields and all the records contained in the Customers table.

6

NEW TERM   A *query* is a set of instructions that dictate how data will be filtered when read
           from one or more tables.

The simple query that is currently used by the data control accepts all the records stored
in the table. Queries can, however, be far more focused and, when used for an explicit
data selection, usually include the name of a field that is to be searched. This is a sample
query (in the SQL language) that reads all the records where the state field is set to
California:

```
select * from Customers where state = 'CA'
```

Although you won't be doing a selective query soon, you can now understand how a
query can be one of the core pieces of technology that makes a database application perform as needed.

A query such as the preceding one can be entered into the SQL Statement window while
the Northwind database is opened. After the Execute button is pressed, the query will be
executed and the results will be displayed in a window similar to the Edit window.

Because the Northwind database has a number of SQL language queries included in the
database, try double-clicking on one to execute it. For example, double-click on the item
labeled *Alphabetical List of Products* and this will be displayed in an Edit-like window.

In the window, you can see most of the functions available in the Edit window (when a
table is opened directly). There is also the Sort button that sorts the records by a specified field name. In Figure 6.3, you can see the sort being activated to sort the records by
the ProductID field.

FIGURE 6.3

*Sorting records by the
ProductID field name.*

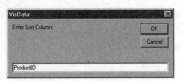

A Filter within a query enables you to further refine the records that will be displayed.
For example, you could display only those products that have fewer than 15 units in
stock (see Figure 6.4). On the Northwind database, running such a filter would leave 13
records remaining after the filter is activated.

FIGURE 6.4

*Using the Filter button
to isolate some
records.*

Note that each time you activate a filter, it further refines the displayed
records. Therefore, for best results, only use the filter command when while
the Edit window is open. Closing the window and re-executing the query
will restore the data set to the complete number of records.

The Find button mirrors the functionality of the Seek button available in the Edit window. In Figure 6.5, you can see an attempt to locate all the records in the ProductName
field that begin with the letter B.

FIGURE 6.5

*Find a record that
begins with the letter B.*

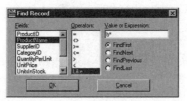

In the text box of the field, you might have noticed that the letter B was followed by an
asterisk (*) symbol. The asterisk in queries is known as a wildcard. The wildcard symbol
(*) is inserted into a search string to specify that any records that match the other criteria
should be used.

For example, placing the wildcard after the B and not following it with any characters
makes it search for any words that begin with the letter B.

If a wildcard was enclosed between letters, it would take any values that began and
ended with the specified letters. For example, if searching a first name field, the criteria
T*M could return

> Tim
>
> Thom
>
> Tom
>
> Traimm

In hours that follow, you'll encounter much more information on using wildcards for
searches.

6

Within the Find window, you might also have noticed that the = option in the list box wasn't selected. Instead, the Like command was used. The Like command acts much like the equal command, but in the case of strings, it ignores case-sensitivity. That will enable the search to find both BEN and ben.

Compacting a Database

The one option on the File menu of the Visual Data Manager that you might not recognize is the Compact Database option. For reasons of speed, when a record is deleted from a table, it is only marked deleted within the database file. This means that if you had an Access database that was 11MB in size and deleted every record, the file would still be 11MB in size.

Only after the database was compacted would the space be reclaimed. You can notice the Compact Database file command in the Visual Data Manager. Using this function will create a new file that contains only the data that is still valid.

It is usually a good idea to schedule how often the database will be compacted in an organization. The relative size of the database has an effect on performance, so occasional compaction will keep your database speedy and clean. For average database usage where records are not being constantly deleted, biannual compacting should be fine.

Data Form Designer

Within the Visual Data Manager, the Data Form Designer utility is included. This utility is a quick and less powerful version of the VB Data Form Wizard. From this utility, you can select a table or query (see Figure 6.6) and the fields to include to create a form.

FIGURE 6.6

Creating a form from the Products table.

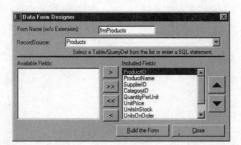

Clicking on the Build Form button will actually add this form to the currently active project. While this utility is useful, it is recommended that you use the full wizard included in Visual Basic. It is more powerful and uses a more updated version of the form construction code.

Query Builder

Constructing queries can be extremely complicated. For this reason, the query builder is included as a utility within the Data Manager. From combo boxes and lists, you can select the criteria to be used to create a SQL language query. You can see in Figure 6.7 that clicking the Show button will actually display the SQL query that will be used.

FIGURE 6.7

Clicking the Show button after selecting some options.

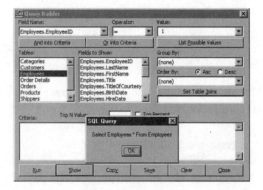

The Show button at the bottom of the builder will display the data set that will be generated when the query is activated.

Clicking on the Save button will store the query in the database itself. After you've given it a name, it will appear in the query list in the Database Window.

Entering Initial Information

6

You have mostly seen the capabilities of the Visual Data Manager that affect the structure of an open database file. However, it can also be used to enter information.

To enter some sample data, you will need to re-open the HR5.mdb file that you created in the last hour. After it is open, follow these steps:

1. Double-click on the todo table in the Database window.

   This will show the records that are contained in the table. If you look at the bottom of the window, you'll see some text that says BOF/0. The text means that you are at the beginning of the file and the number zero (0) represents the number of records stored in the table at this time. Now you'll add a record so the table won't be empty.

2. Click on the Add button.

3. Enter some of the information shown in Figure 6.8.

   In the figure, you'll see some general data, but you can enter whatever you want for the first record. Be sure to leave the uniqueid field empty so it can be filled with the automatic increment number.

FIGURE 6.8

The information is entered into the first record of the table.

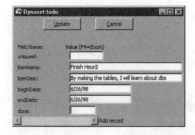

4. Click the Update button to save the modifications.

   The Update button will write all the changes into the table and display the browse window again (see Figure 6.9).

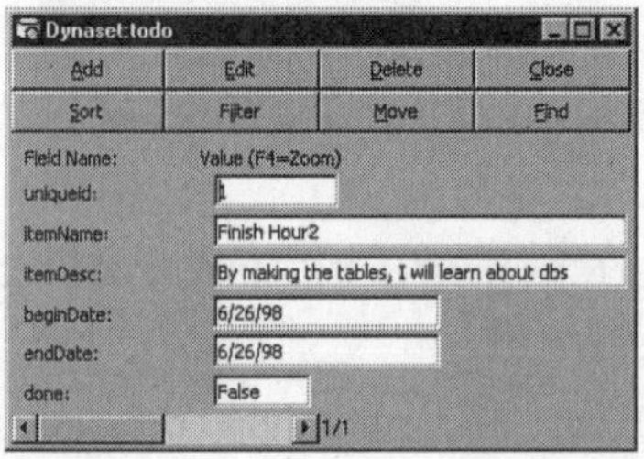

FIGURE 6.9

After the record has been stored to the database.

With the modifications saved, you will see that two of the fields filled in automatically. The uniqueid field should contain the number 1. Also, the done field is a Boolean type that cannot be left empty, so the default of False was automatically set.

You might also notice that the number of records is now set to 1. The text at the bottom reads 1/1, which means that you are looking at the first record out of one record.

Creating an Index for the todo Table

To create an index for the todo table, you'll need to use the design window that was used when the table was initially created.

1. Right-click on the customers table and select the Design... option.
2. Click on the Add Index button at the bottom of the screen.

   This will show the Add Index window.
3. Enter idxItemName as the name of the index to create.
4. Click on the itemName field in the list of available fields.

   By default, both the Primary and Unique check boxes are checked. The Unique setting requires that no two records contain the same value. Because the itemName field can contain more than one item with the same name (for example, more than one Take out trash), you need to clear this setting.

   The Primary box relates to the central default index that will be used by the table and makes the current field a way of referencing the table (known as the Primary key). In the case of this table, the Primary index will be the index used for the uniqueid field. Therefore, you need to make sure that this field is not selected as the primary field.
5. Uncheck the Primary and Unique boxes and check the Ignore Nulls box.
6. Click the OK button.

   You should also create a uniqueid index in case the field is used from another table.
7. Click on the Add Index button.

   You need to add another index, this time to the central uniqueid field. Creating this index will speed the lookup of this unique field and enable the table to be connected to other tables.
8. Enter idxUniqueID as the index name.
9. Click on the uniqueid field for the selected index.
10. Leave the Primary and Unique boxes checked.
11. Click OK.
12. Close the Design window.

6

Now you can expand the Index heading in the Database window and you will see both of the indexes properly listed. The table is all set up now. As new records are added, they will automatically be indexed by the database engine.

Because there was almost no data stored within the table, the creation of the indexes was almost instantaneous. However, creating the indexes involves sorting all the records in the table so if there are many, it can take several minutes for the initial sort.

Creating One More Table

When the primary table is completed, you can easily add one more table in the same manner. This new table will be the projects table that will be used to watch an entire project. Because it has different requirements (such as the subtasks and milestones fields), it will be created as a table separate from the todo table.

Click the right mouse button in the Database window to create another New Table. Name the table projects and create the fields shown in Table 6.3. Although there are some of the fields that are identical to the ones used in the todo table, because this table is used for a completely separate task, it is created separately.

TABLE 6.3   FIELDS FOR THE PROJECTS TABLE

Field Name	Type	Size	Index?
uniqueid	Long	n/a	Yes
projectName	Text	20	Yes
projectDesc	Text	120	No
beginDate	Date/Time	n/a	Yes
endDate	Date/Time	n/a	Yes
numSubTasks	Long	n/a	No
milestone	Boolean	n/a	No
teamName	Text	20	Yes
done	Boolean	n/a	No

After you complete construction on the table, click the Build the Table button. The constructed table can be used to track projects including team-based ones. Notice that only the fields that searches are likely to occur upon have been indexed. Because it is unlikely anyone will ever need the project description sorted quickly, it is left without an index.

Your Database window should now show both tables (see Figure 6.10). If you need to make any modifications to either of the tables, right-clicking the mouse on the desired entry provides the menu option labeled Design. This option returns you to the table construction window.

FIGURE 6.10

The Database window after the new table is added.

You now have a complete database. These tables were created simply to enable you to understand how the Visual Data Manager can be used to define an entire database. Throughout the next 18 hours, you will occasionally use the Data Manager for table construction and simple data entry.

Summary

Using the Data Control is an easy way to graphically create a connection to a database. In addition to connecting to the database, the Data Control must be set to reference one particular table within the database. Controls can then be bound to the Data Control to display values held by the fields of the database.

The VB Data Form Wizard can be used to quickly generate a prototype form that contains a Data Control connected to a specified database and table, as well as all the bound controls necessary to access that data.

Q&A

Q Can the Visual Data Manager be used when Visual Basic 6 is not being executed?

A Yes, executing the VisData.exe application will display the Visual Data Manager whether or not VB is launched. However, the Data Form Designer, which relies on VB to be present to construct the form, will not function properly without VB loaded.

Q Can a link to another database be added within the database without importing the data?

A Yes, it is stored as an Attached database. This method is perfect for files that must reside outside the Access file (such as a shared dBASE file) while making it appear to your VB application that it is really an Access table.

6

Q Is there anything in an MDB file that I can't access through the Data Manager?

A The MDB file is the native file format for Microsoft Access. Numerous items such as reports, forms, VBA code, and anything else from an Access application can be located in the MDB file. These cannot be accessed from the Data Manager.

The Data Manager makes it possible to access tables and queries. All the other information contained in the MDB file is transparent to the Visual Data Manager.

Workshop

The quiz questions and exercises are provided for your further understanding. See Appendix C, "Answers," for the answers to the questions.

Quiz

1. What three categories are displayed in the Database window?
2. What is the wildcard character?
3. True or False: No problems will occur if the security for the database is set up improperly.
4. What function does the Like keyword serve in a query?
5. Why bother compacting a database?
6. Should indexes be added to every field?
7. How is a query used?

Exercises

1. Create a sample table within the HR5.mdb that contains fields of every data type. Then open the table for data entry and see the types of information that can be entered into each data type.
2. Use the Query Builder to find records that match criteria you choose. After the query is refined and the data returned matches your expectations, save the query into the database file.

HOUR 7

Data Environment

So far, all the connections you have made to a data source have been created by individually setting the properties such as the `ConnectionString` and `RecordSource`. In Visual Basic 6, new technology has been added to simplify connection creation—the Data Environment.

A Data Environment is added to a VB project just like a form or a module file. The connections and recordsets defined within the Data Environment are now available from any code to access a data source. They can also be bound to data-aware controls.

Creating a Data Environment produces a sharable and reusable connection file that can be used not only in your current project, but also on later projects. The Data Environment is a key to automating the expanding number of technologies used to connect to data sources. It provides a simplified programming environment used to connect to data sources.

> If you've used Visual Basic 5 in the past, the new Data Environment
> supercedes the less powerful UserConnection designer. Although the
> UserConnection designer could only use ODBC data sources, the Data
> Environment can connect through OLE DB data sources as well.

The highlights of this hour include

- Creating a Data Project
- Using the Data Environment within a project
- Programming to manipulate the Data Environment
- Using the drag-and-drop features to populate a form
- Understanding the structure of the environment

Data Environment in the Project Window

In Visual Basic 6, a Data Environment is a file where all connections and events related
to the connections can be stored. By centralizing the connections in the data environment, the information for a project can be kept in one place.

You are already familiar with other files such as forms, modules, and class files that are used
in a project. Like these files, the Data Environment appears in the Project window under the
Designers folder (see Figure 7.1). Like these other items that are part of the project, the Data
Environments can be easily managed as files and even added to other projects.

FIGURE 7.1

*The Data Environment
item shown in the
Project window.*

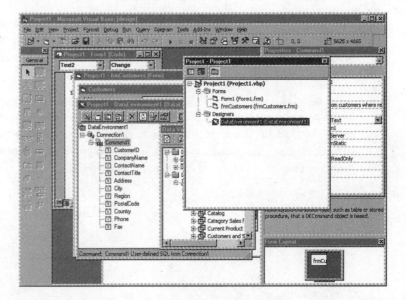

A Data Environment file can include

- Data Links and Connections
- `Connection` objects
- `Command` objects
- Event code for ADO events
- Hierarchical grouping and aggregates of Command objects

All the connections created within a Data Environment file are sharable and reusable. Each Data Environment supports multiple connection objects sources within a single Data Environment.

The Data Environment is an object framework available through ActiveX support. Using the References option under the Project menu, you can select the Data Environment 1.0 item and check it to make it available to the current project.

Because in the previous hours you have used the Data Control to provide the connection to the data sources, this will be new to you. However, because you will again be using bound controls, the configuration of the Data Environment will be the primary difference.

Creating a Data Project

There are many data controls and object model references that need to be added to a project in order to take advantage of all the database capabilities of Visual Basic. To simplify beginning a database project, VB includes a template project that contains all the major pieces needed for a complete database application. Called the Data Project, it is a template option available when a new project is defined.

When you start a project with the Data Project template, the project automatically includes

- One blank form
- All the available Data Aware controls
- One data report file
- A Data Environment

Although none of these items are configured, it provides the perfect starting environment to begin constructing a database application. Any controls or object models that you don't want to use can be removed before you ship your application.

7

To demonstrate the Data Environment, the Data Project provides the perfect starting point to construct a simple application that connects to the Employees table in the Northwind database and enables navigation through its records.

To begin with, you will only need to configure the Data Environment to provide a connection to the employees table. When you drag and drop three fields from the environment onto the default form included in the project, you will see how the controls are connected, as opposed to the data control you've previously used.

By following the creation of a simple database project using the Data Environment, you will have a clear picture of how it can be used.

1. Create a New Project and select the Data Project template.

   Using the File Menu, select the New Project option. From the list of project templates and wizards, select the Data Project.

   This adds form, all the Data Aware controls, a Data Report, and a blank form.

2. Double-click on the DataEnvironment1.

   From the Project window, double-clicking on a Data Environment item will open it in a window. For this window, you see the Data Environment and the Connection1 because there is a single connection added by default to the environment.

   The default Connection object that is added is not configured in any way. In order to properly point it at the Northwind database, you're going to have to set properties that determine the data access type as well as the location on the intended database.

3. Right-click on the Connection1 and select the Properties option from the context menu.

   The Connection object must be configured before you can add an active table. The Properties option on the context menu (see Figure 7.2) will display the wizard required for configuring the ConnectionString property of the connection.

   Selecting the Properties option will display the Data Link properties window. In this window, the Connection object can be set to interact with any data source available to the ActiveX Data objects.

4. On the Provider tab, select the Jet 3.51 OLE DB Provider and click the Next button.

   You need to select the type of driver that will be used to address the Northwind database. Selecting the Microsoft Access database engine, also known as the Jet Engine, will enable the connection to access an MDB format file.

5. Select the NWind.mdb file using the Browse button and click the OK button for the Properties window.

FIGURE 7.2

Configuring the Connection1 *item in the Data Environment.*

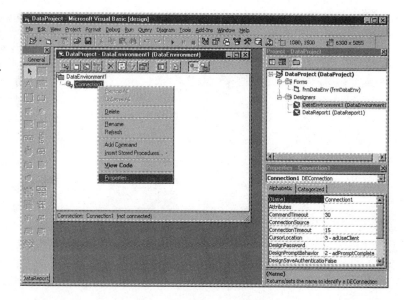

You can either type the path or use the browsing button to select the Northwind database file. After you have selected it, the name and path should appear in the proper text box.

Because you have set the driver type and directed the driver where the MDB file can be found, accepting the setting by clicking the OK button on the Properties window will finish the configuration of the connection.

With the Connection object configured, you will need a Command object added to the connection to actually access a table within the database. The Command object can then be used as a data source by any bound controls.

6. Click the Add Command button on the toolbar of the DataProject - DataEnvironment1 window.

   Clicking the Add button will add a Command object (explained later in the hour). Whenever a new Command object is added, it will be added underneath the item currently selected in the environment window. Because you were earlier adjusting the property settings of the Connection object, it was already selected.

   The new object will appear as a child of the Connection object. This Command object will be modified to point to one of the tables within the database.

7. Right-click on the Command1 item (see Figure 7.3) and select the Properties option.

   The Properties dialog box for the Command object enables you to configure how it will appear and the basic functionality of this object.

7

FIGURE 7.3

*Selecting the
Properties option for
configuring the*
Command1 *item.*

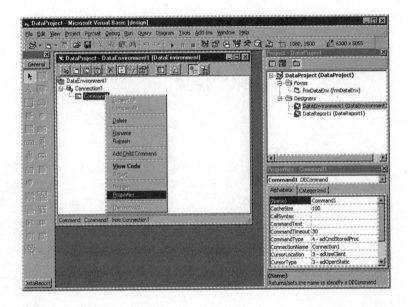

8. Set the name of the Command1 to tblEmployees.

   The Command object will be the primary connection to an individual table within the database. It will use the Connection object to provide an access path to the proper database.

   As with any other control used on a form, setting the name defines the control and how it will be addressed within code and other property references. Setting the name properly will help you when setting the proper references among the bound controls on the form.

9. Set the Database Object to Table.

   A Command object can actually represent one of several different types. It can represent a SQL query that returns particular data, an advanced database construct, or a simple table reference.

   By setting the database object to a table, all the records in that table will be available for access and modification. There is no query used to selectively present only some of the records.

10. Set the Object Name to Employees.

    From the list of possible tables and queries, select the Employees table (see Figure 7.4). In the previous step you told the Data Environment that the Command object would be of a table type. This setting enabled Visual Basic to retrieve the names of all the tables available in the database.

    The Object Name defines what table will be used as the Command object's data source.

FIGURE 7.4

Setting the employees tables as the accessed object.

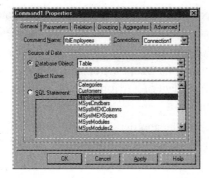

11. Click the OK button.

    The Data Environment will now show the Command item with a table icon. The icon of a Command object changes to represent the type of access method that will be used. The generic icon that was shown before represented the Unknown type that was being used. Setting the type to table enabled it to use the table icon.

12. Expand the table item.

    By expanding the table item, you will be able to see all the fields available within the table (see Figure 7.5). Not only can these fields be examined, they can also be used with the drag-and-drop interface to aid in constructing a data form.

FIGURE 7.5

Displaying all the fields contained in the table.

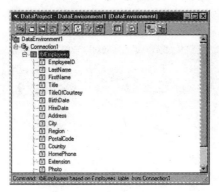

13. Open the frmDataEnv form of the project.

    By default, a new Data Project includes a default form that can be used as the primary form. By adding a few of the fields from the Command object to it, you will be able to see how the Data Environment is used in contrast to a data control.

7

In addition to the added flexibility (such as shared connections) provided by the Data Environment, it also has a design-time user interface feature that makes database application construction much simpler.

Fields can be dragged from the Data Environment window onto a form. Because the environment is independent of any form (unlike the Data Control), the fields can be displayed on any form.

When the field is dropped, the appropriate bound control to express the field (such as a text box) is displayed on the form. Additionally, a label that contains the name of the field represented by the new bound control is also created.

14. Reactivate the Data Environment window and use the shift key to select the EmployeeID, LastName, and FirstName fields.

   You will create bound controls from three of the fields of the table. In the Data Environment window, you can click on one of these fields and then use the SHIFT or CTRL keys to select the other two fields. This will enable all three fields to be dragged onto the form at once.

15. Drag and drop these three fields onto the form.

   When you drag the cursor over the form, the cursor will turn into a small icon representing the control to be created. Upon releasing the button, the bound control and the matching label for the dragged field will appear on the form. After you have completed this process with a few fields, your form should look like the one shown in Figure 7.6.

FIGURE 7.6

Drop the three fields on the supplied form.

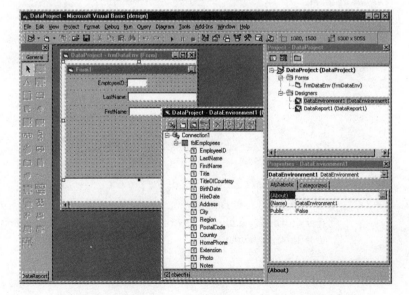

When you drag fields onto the form, the Data Environment automatically follows the control naming conventions. All the text box controls begin with the prefix *txt* followed by the name of the field. Likewise, the labels use the *lbl* prefix.

16. Execute the application.

    You now have an application that connects several bound controls to a Data Environment. You can create a second form that points to the same environment and the two forms can simultaneously display data from the same data connection.

You might have noticed that although the application runs well, only the information from the first record is displayed. To correct this problem, you will need to add some code to access the recordset itself.

Adding Forward and Back Buttons

Although you have a simple application constructed, it can only display the first record contained in the table. The Data Control that you used previously had the advantage of providing instant navigation buttons for use with the data set.

Using the Data Environment, you'll have to program these yourself. Luckily it is not very difficult to manipulate the data set. In this example, you'll add to the form two buttons that will enable movement forward and backward through the data set.

The Data Environment is perfect to advance projects already built with the Data Control. The control can even remain on the form. Simply point the bound controls to the DataEnvironment object in the DataSource property.

1. Add two command buttons to the form.

    On the form, place two buttons at the bottom of the window. These buttons will be used as navigation buttons.

2. Name the first command button cmdPrevious.

    You need to name the button something descriptive because a button with the default name makes code written to that button more difficult to read.

3. Set caption to Previous.

The user will be able to click this button to move toward the beginning of the recordset. Because the controls are bound to the Data Environment, executing this method will automatically update the displayed controls.

4. Name the second one cmdNext.

5. Set caption of the button to Next.

   This button will be used to advance to the next record.

   As a Visual Basic programmer, these steps should be straightforward and clear. With adding just a small amount of code, you will be able to use your two new buttons for record navigation.

6. Add the following code to Previous button. The code will access the recordset of the Data Environment and move the pointer one record backward using the MovePrevious() method.

```
Private Sub cmdPrevious_Click()
  ' Setup an error catching/reporting routine
  On Error GoTo MoveErr
  ' Check if the current record is the beginning
  ' of the file
  If Not DataEnvironment1.Recordset.BOF Then
    ' Move the displayed record to the previous one
    DataEnvironment1.Recordset.MovePrevious
  End If

  Exit Sub
MoveErr:
  MsgBox Err.Description
End Sub
```

   Before the code actually executes the movement method, the Beginning-Of-File marker is checked. Attempting to move backward when the pointer of the database currently sits at the beginning will generate an error.

7. Add code to Next button.

   This code mirrors the code used for the Previous button only it uses the MoveNext() method to step forward through the database. It also uses the End-Of-File (EOF) property to make sure that the attempt is not made to move beyond the final record.

```
Private Sub cmdNext_Click()
  On Error GoTo MoveErr
  If Not DataEnvironment1.Recordset.EOF Then
    DataEnvironment1.Recordset.MoveNext
  End If

  Exit Sub
```

```
MoveErr:
  MsgBox Err.Description
End Sub
```

After you have entered the code, the application is ready to be run.

8. Execute application

You'll now be able to page back and forth through the recordset for the table.

> If you want to further investigate the code you would need to manipulate
> the Data Environment. Use the VB Data Form Wizard to create a form.
> Instead of using the Data Control, select the option to generate ADO code.
> You can then examine this code for a complete example of all the basic com-
> mands used with the recordset.

Adding Data Environments to a Project

Just like a form, Data Environments can be added to a project using the Project menu. However, from the Data View window, you can also add a new Data Environment simply by clicking on the Add Data Environment icon.

Although a Data Environment can hold more than one connection, you can also add multiple Data Environments to a single project.

Data Environment Project Item

The central feature of the Data Environment is the Connection object. The Connection object contains all the parameters, such as the path or location used to actually connect to the data source, and required logins and passwords.

Selecting a Data Environment item in the Project window will display the properties of the primary connection object (see Table 7.1) contained within it. If there is more than one connection object in the Data Environment, the properties of the environment are displayed. There are only two properties: the Name string and Public Boolean field.

7

TABLE 7.1 DATA RELATED PROPERTIES OF THE DATA ENVIRONMENT ITEM

Property	Description
Attributes	Stores any additional connection string properties that are passed to the Connection object.
CommandTimeout	Holds the time in seconds that the server will wait for a command to return a reply.
ConnectionSource	Complete ConnectionSource string that describes the path to the data source connection.
ConnectionTimeout	Holds the time in seconds that the server will wait for a connection to open on the destination server.
CursorLocation	Determines the location of the cursor engine to use for the connection. Supports two options: use server-side cursor (2) or use client-side cursor (3).

You can see that all the properties are available either by selecting the Data Environment item in the Project window or by opening the Data Environment window and selecting the Connection object. In Figure 7.7, you can see the Connection1 item selected.

FIGURE 7.7

Selecting the Connection in the Data Environment window displays the appropriate properties.

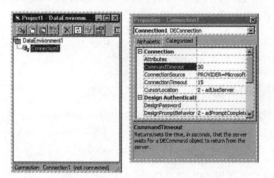

From the Data Environment window, you can

- Add new connections
- Add new commands
- Insert a stored procedure
- Add or edit Data Environment event code
- Set Data Environment options (including drag-and-drop selections)

Although the Connection object should be somewhat familiar because configuration of it matches the Data Control and wizard configurations you've done in the past, the Command object can seem foreign.

Command Objects

Command objects are used to define what data will be retrieved from the database when a query takes place. Command objects can be based on a database construct (such as a table or a view) or on a query written in SQL (see Hour 16 for more information on SQL). Command objects can also be used to define relations between tables (see Hour 6, "Visual Data Manager").

Like a Recordset object, although the Command object can be created using the New command, it will not be valid until it is connected to a Connection object.

A Command object might return a recordset. If it does, the object is said to be recordset returning. At runtime, a recordset returning Command object can be accessed as either a method or a property through the DataEnvironment object. If it doesn't return a dataset, it can only be accessed as a property.

NEW TERM   A Command object can be a table, view, or SQL statement that is executed. If the object will return a recordset on execution, it is said to be *recordset returning*.

Most of the technical details of dealing with the Command object are handled by the Properties window. However, the Command object will be the door through which more advanced database access is possible in the future.

> In the Data Environment Designer, you can ignore the recordset that is returned by a recordset returning Command object. In the Properties window for the Command object, clear the check box for recordset returning on the Advanced tab.

Although you've already created one Command object, this time you'll create one that is a little more advanced using a specific query rather than simply pointing at a table.

To set up a Command object, create a new connection to the Northwind database. Using Northwind, you will create a selective query to only include customers located in Oregon. The actual command will be written using the SQL language.

7

1. Select the `Connection1` object in the Data Environment window.

   By having the `Connection` object selected, the `Command` object will be created hierarchically under the connection (see Figure 7.8). That way you will need to make no special reference to the connection to have it properly access the data source.

> It is also possible to create a `Command` object that is not directly related to a `Connection` object. However, at runtime, you will need to define a connection or one will be dynamically assigned.

FIGURE 7.8

The new Command *object created directly under the* Connection *object.*

2. Select the `Command1` object and display the properties window.

   The `Command` object properties will let you define what type of object it will be. Earlier, you made a `Command` object into the type to directly access a table. In this instance, you will need to set the properties of the `Command` object for it to execute your SQL query statement.

3. Type the query text into the `CommandText` property.

   Type the following query text:

   ```
   select * from customers where region = 'OR'
   ```

   This code is a SQL query command that searches the Customers database to return all entries that have the abbreviation OR (for Oregon) in the region field. The `Command` object will then have a child recordset that contains only the records that match the conditions of the query.

4. Set the `CommandType` property to 1 — adCmdText

   In this case, your `Command` object will not be a table or stored procedure. The `adCmdText` option will enable SQL language code to be entered.

   Just like the last time you selected a type, when you modify the type, it will be directly reflected in the icon shown in the Data Environment window.

5. Expand the Command1 in the Data Environment window.

You might have noticed that after you entered the command in the last step, the icon on the Command object changed to a SQL icon. When you expand the Command1 object, you will see all the fields contained in the query (see Figure 7.9).

The Command *object has become an object to execute your SQL query.*

Within the Data Environment, you can add a child Command object to an existing Command object. Simply right click on the Command object and select the Add Child Command from the context menu.

Binding the Data Environment to a Control

The two main properties available for the bound control are the DataSource and DataMember properties. The DataSource is used to point to the Data Environment item. Any Data Environment included in the project can be used as a data source.

The DataSource property can be used to point to either a Data Environment or a Data Control. Both types of data sources will appear in the property list. If the Data Control is selected, clear the DataMember property to avoid confusion.

The DataMember property is used to select from the command objects within the Data Environment. In the example you created, there is only a single Command object. However, within a single connection you can create as many Command objects as you need.

7

Data View Window

In addition to the Data Environments, there is one other similar data technology provided in Visual Basic. The global Data View window can be displayed from any project.

The Data View window is really a data connection management interface. There are two primary items that can appear in the Data View window: Data Environments and Data Links.

From the Data View window, you can

- Drag and drag objects into a Data Environment
- Create and modify tables
- Program stored procedures and triggers
- Construct database diagrams

The Data View window provides access to the Microsoft Visual Database Tools that are included with Visual Basic 6. These include two utilities: the Database Designer and the Query Designer.

Adding Data Links

The Data Links are similar to connection objects, except they are available through the Visual Basic environment.

Although both the Data Links and the Data Environments appear in the Data View window, only Data Environments are added to the current project. The Data View window actually displays all the data access of the currently running VB 6 system. Therefore, although the creation of Data Links is global and therefore always displayed, the Data Environments displayed will be determined by the currently opened project.

If you click on the icon to add a new Data Link to the project, you'll see the window shown in Figure 7.10.

FIGURE 7.10

Creating a new Data Link is the wizard window used when creating connections.

After the Data Link has been created, you can use it to examine the structures contained in the data source that the link points toward. Because a simple Data Link can be created to access the Northwind database, expanding the link will show folders containing the tables and views of the database. Opening the table folder will display all the structures contained within the source (see Figure 7.11). Within each table item, you can examine the fields that make up the table.

FIGURE 7.11

Expanding the Tables folder in the Data Link.

Double-clicking on the table entry within the Data Link will display the table in a spreadsheet form.

7

Summary

The Data Environment is a new and easy-to-use way to maintain data connections for an entire project. By providing a simple way to central data access connections, Visual Basic simplifies database project management.

Q&A

Q Can the connections created in the Data Environment be used with the Data Control?

A Yes. You can create a connection to a data source for a Data Control using the connections that you've created in the Data Environment.

Q Can multiple Data Environments exist in a single project?

A Yes. There can be many Data Environments within a single project. However, because multiple connections and commands can exist within a single Data Environment, this will not occur often.

Workshop

The quiz questions and exercises are provided for your further understanding. See Appendix C, "Answers," for the answers to the questions.

Quiz

1. What type of objects can be used within the Data Environment?
2. In what way does the Data Environment support drag-and-drop insertion?
3. What is a Data Link?
4. Are Data Links shared by multiple projects?
5. True or False: Each Data Environment in a project can support more than one connection.

Exercise

1. Establish a Data Environment that includes Command objects to three of the tables within the Northwind database. After the objects are created, make a single form that displays some of the field record information from each of these four tables simultaneously.
2. Create a connection within the Data View window. Use the drag-and-drop interface to move the connection to a Data Environment.

Hour **8**

Data-Aware Controls

Although you have seen the most basic data-aware bound control (the text box), now is a good time to be exposed to the great breadth of controls included with Visual Basic. Most of the common user interface controls such as the check box, radio buttons, combo box, and so on, can be easily bound to a data source.

You'll create a sample project that uses these controls with the help of the Data Environment. Then you can advance beyond the standard user interface controls and be exposed to the powerful table or grid controls.

The highlights of this hour include:

- Reviewing the data-aware controls
- Creating a project with data bound controls
- Hooking up a DataCombo or DataList to two tables
- Configuring a DataGrid control for recordset display
- Using the HFlexGrid control

Data-Aware Controls Overview

Visual Basic includes a number of common data-aware controls (see Table 8.1). Most of these controls are added automatically when the new project type of Data Project is used. Data-aware controls that can be bound to a data control or environment include

- Traditional controls (Textbox, Checkbox, OptionButton, Picturebox, Label, Image, OLE)
- Advanced controls (DataCombo, DataList, DataGrid, and HFlexGrid)
- Data Repeater
- Other controls (Date Picker, Calendar, RichTextBox)

TABLE 8.1   COMMON DATA-AWARE CONTROLS IN VISUAL BASIC

Icon	Name
	Picturebox
	Label
	Textbox
	Checkbox
	OptionButton
	Image
	OLE
	Data Repeater
	DataGrid
	DataList
	DataCombo

Icon	Name
	HFlexGrid
	MonthView
	Date Picker
	RichTextbox
	Calendar

The traditional controls are bound with the properties `DataSource` (that is, Data Control or Data Environment), `DataMember` (that is, `Command` object within a Data Environment), and `DataField` (the field to bind to the control). All these controls are very easy to implement and for most uses, the VB Data Form Wizard creates a form that uses them.

The advanced controls, such as the DataCombo and DataGrid, have more complex interactions with the data source. The DataCombo can use more than one data source to both display a list of items and write the selection into a separate table. In this hour, you will use the advanced controls to create some sample solutions to familiarize yourself with their workings.

The Data Repeater is a control that displays other bound controls. Hour 9, "Creating an ActiveX Control and Using the Data Repeater," contains a complete explanation and sample construction of a Data Repeater control. Because you need to actually create an ActiveX control to hold the bound controls, it requires its own dedicated hour.

The other controls are not automatically added by the Data Project because not every project will need their features. The Calendar and Date Picker are both included in the Microsoft Calendar Control component. The RichText control, which functions essentially like the Textbox control except it can contain rich text (multiple fonts, styles, sizes in the same text area), is located in the Microsoft RichText control component.

You already have a fair amount of experience with the traditional controls from the past hours. The advanced controls, some of which you will probably use in any medium-sized database project, require some special explanation. To that end, you'll construct several samples in this hour giving you a working knowledge of how these controls are configured.

Setting Up a Test Environment

To begin the exploration of the data-aware controls included with Visual Basic, you will need a new project. For this project, you'll once again use the Data Project Wizard to automatically add the most common required aspects such as the data controls, a form, and a data environment.

For the Data Environment, you'll set it up to reference the Northwind database and access two of the tables (customers and orders) within it.

 Because you have already created a project using the Data Environment that points to the Northwind database in the last chapter, you might simply want to augment that project. If you open the Data Environment from the last project, you can then skip to step 8.

1. From Visual Basic, create a new project of type Data Project.

   The Data Project type is set up in Visual Basic as an instant project creation used to include an empty form, all the primary data-aware controls, a data environment, and a data report (that you won't need for this project).

2. In the project window, double click the Data Environment item to display the DataEnvironment1 window.

3. Right-click on the Connection item in the window and select the Properties option.

   Before you add the tables that you need (via Command object), the connection itself must be configured to address the Northwind database file that contains the tables.

4. On the first tab of the properties, set the provider to Microsoft Jet 3.51 OLE DB Provider.

5. On the second tab, set the connection to point to NWind.mdb.

   Selecting the Northwind database (see Figure 8.1) will provide the connection with the necessary data source. The data source will be used as the path through which objects that are added below the connection access the data.

6. Click the OK button to finalize the new configuration.

   Now the connection has been configured. You need to add the objects that will be used by the data-aware controls to display current record information.

7. Select the Connection item in the Data Environment window.

FIGURE 8.1

The connection in the Data Environment should point to NWind.mdb.

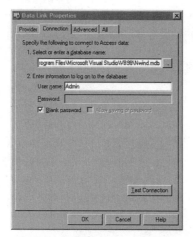

8. Click on the Add Command icon to add the first Command object.

   The Add Command icon is located on the Data Environment window toolbar. It will add a generic Command object under the selected connection. The object then needs to be configured to point at a table accessible through the Connection object.

9. Open the properties of the first Command object (through the Properties option on the context menu using the right mouse button).

   You need to configure the Command object as you have in the last hour. The Properties window will enable you to make modifications to the Data Environment items at any time without reprogramming the objects that are connected to it. This is one of the primary advantages to using the Data Environment.

10. Set the name of the Command object to Customers, the type to Table, and select the customers table in the Provider Source combo box.

11. Add another Command object to the connection.

    You need another object for the Orders table. Make sure that you select the Connection object before you click on the Add Command icon on the toolbar. Remember that the object will be added hierarchically under any selected item. If the Customers item were to be selected, the orders table would be added to it rather than the connection.

12. Set the name of the Command object to Orders, the type to Table, and select the orders table in the Provider Source combo box.

    This Command object will now be recognized by Visual Basic as a table access object.

When you've added the two command objects, your Data Environment window should appear like the one shown in Figure 8.2.

Figure 8.2

The Data Environment when it is property configured.

With the connection and the two tables configured, any code throughout the project can address this data source. The data environment can be used to bind data-aware controls to a data source or manipulate directly with Visual Basic code. In this hour, you'll be attaching numerous controls on different forms to the same environment.

Using the Bound Controls

Now that a data environment has been created to properly access the Northwind database, you can connect some of the data-aware controls to various fields within the table. You can begin by using the Data Environment as a drag and drop source.

Remember that any settings within the Data Environment will affect what can be done on the form by the controls. By default, the Command objects and the connection itself that you just created are set to read-only mode. You will have to change these properties if you need to edit values within the bound controls.

Simple Bound Controls

To demonstrate the simple bound controls, you'll need to open the default form (frmDataEnc) that was added to the project by the Data Project Wizard. Make sure to leave enough room on the screen so that the Data Environment window is still visible.

The drag and drop environment automatically uses the specified data type to create the appropriate control. If you drag the Yes/No field onto the form, a bound check box will be created. Because the field is a Boolean data type, Visual Basic is set up to use the check box control by default for this field type.

The Textbox, the Label, and the Checkbox are the only primary controls that are created by default. The other controls must be specifically configured because their implementation's need for a particular data type is less implicit.

> If you right-click on an item in the Data Environment window and select the Options... menu selection, you can alter the default drag and drop controls. In the Field Mapping tab, the type of control created on the form for any given field type can be set.

1. Expand the Orders table in the Data Environment.

   The Orders table item in the Data Environment will have all the fields that are present in the table. You're going to use the drag and drop functionality of the Data Environment to create bound controls that are attached to field in the table.

2. Drag the fields OrderID, OrderDate, and ShipName from the orders table onto the frmDataEnv form.

   From the orders table, drag the field onto the Visual Basic form. A text box and label will automatically be created to reflect that field. The ShipName field is a string type.

3. Add a command button at the bottom of the form.

   Because you're using a data environment instead of a data control, the navigation user interface is not automatically created. Therefore, in order to move forward through the records, you'll create a button that advances the data displayed to the next record in the recordset.

4. Set the command button Name to cmdNext and Caption to Next.

   When the Next button is properly placed and configured, it should look like the form shown in Figure 8.3. The control is placed at the bottom of the form so additional room is available for adding a list box control in the next section.

FIGURE 8.3

Order fields on the form.

5. Add the following code to the button's click event:

```
Private Sub cmdNext_Click()
    DataEnvironment1.rsOrders.MoveNext
End Sub
```

This code simply executes the MoveNext method of the recordset that is stored for the Data Environment. Any of the ADO methods related to a recordset can be used through this Data Environment reference.

ADO is the advanced programming object model for accessing databases. If you will be doing a great deal of database coding, you will need to use ADO. By the time you reach Hour 17, "Understanding ActiveX Data Objects (ADO)," which provides an explanation and some examples of ADO, you will understand how commands such as MoveNext are used.

6. Execute the application.

The application will display the first record in the Orders table (see Figure 8.4). When the Next command button is clicked, the recordset will advance through all the available records.

FIGURE 8.4

The application exe-cuting and displaying the first record of the Orders table.

You've mastered a majority of the concepts that were used in constructing this form in earlier hours. Now you'll expand this form to access the second table (the Customers table) to provide a reference list for the value stored in the Orders table.

DataList and DataCombo Controls

The ListBox and ComboBox are excellent controls for presenting lists of information. In their data-aware incarnation, these controls are known as the DataList and DataCombo, respectively.

These controls can be used to simply bind to a field within a single table, but without a source for list values, they are not very useful. For example, the orders table contains a field that holds the ID number of the customer that placed the order. Wouldn't it be help-ful if, instead of simply displaying the ID number, the name of the customer (retrieved from the customers table) was displayed?

> The ability to attach two tables to a combo box or list box is a feature that
> is new to Visual Basic 6. Previously, the lists to be displayed in these controls
> had to be added with custom programming code.

The DataList and the DataCombo can be configured to access two different tables to provide a single control reference display of a field. You'll just need to add a DataList control to the current form.

1. From the control palette, select the DataList control and add it to the form (see
   Figure 8.5).

FIGURE 8.5

*The DataList control
added to the
frmDataEnv form.*

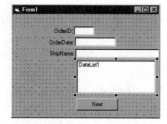

After the control has been added, the properties must be set to address the data
environment and the two tables within it.

> When you configure data-aware controls, try to start from the foundation
> up. This means that the source properties should be set before the field
> properties.
>
> Because some of the properties add to the definition configured by earlier
> properties, setting them out of order can result in some of the earlier prop-
> erties being reset. In these examples, the properties should be set in the
> order that they are described.

2. Set DataSource and RowSource to DataEnvironment1.

   Both the data source table that will be used to read the primary records (the orders
   table) and the reference table (customers) are stored in the primary data environment.

3. Set DataMember to Orders.

The DataMember property specifies the primary recordset that will be used. Think of the DataMember as the behind-the-scenes table. Although values for this table won't be displayed directly, it will affect what entry in the reference table is displayed.

4. Set RowMember to Customers.

The RowMember field is used to select the reference table that will be used for display in the list box.

5. Set ListField to CompanyName.

This property determines what field from the Customers table will be displayed in the list box. In this case, it will display the name of the company.

This field was chosen because the ShipName field will already be displayed on the form for the current record. In most cases, this referenced name will match the one stored in the ShipName field.

6. Set DataField to CustomerID.

This property specifies what field from the source table that will be referenced for display (input).

7. Set BoundColumn to CustomerID.

This property specifies what field from the source table that will be returned from the selection (output). If you were to write the data selected by the user back into the orders table, this property determines what value from the reference table will be returned.

8. Execute the application.

When the application is executed (see Figure 8.6), the current record will be displayed and the DataList will automatically show the customer name selected for the current order.

FIGURE 8.6

The DataList control executing on the form.

If you click the next button to advance through the records, the item highlighted in the list box will change with each change of the CustomerID field.

Data Bound Grid Control

Although most of the data-aware controls so far have only been able to display a single record at a time, the DataGrid control can display numerous records simultaneously. The DataGrid control is one of the most powerful data-aware controls included with Visual Basic.

The multiple records are presented in a spreadsheet-like interface for browsing and editing. By simply setting two properties, you can create a quick and simple table access tool.

1. Add a new blank form to the current project.

   Because you will still want to use the data environment for the data source, simply add an additional form to the current project.

2. Stretch the new form for more screen space.

   Because many records will need to be displayed, it is a good idea to increase the size of the form before you insert the grid.

3. Select DataGrid control and draw it on the form.

   Make the control fit the entire form, like the one shown in Figure 8.7. Because the scroll bars will be used to navigate through the recordset, there is no need to leave additional room for forward and backward navigation controls.

FIGURE 8.7

DataGrid placed on the form.

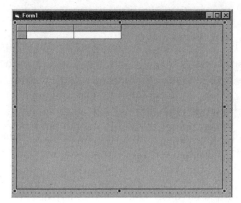

4. Set DataSource property to DataEnvironment1.

   Because you have already customized the Data Environment and added the Command objects for both the orders and customers tables, the Data Source property on any data-aware control can be pointed to this environment.

5. Set `DataMember` property to Customers.

The DataGrid control is ready to go! However, to execute properly, you will need to set the new form as the form that will be launched when the project is executed.

6. In the Project Properties under the Project menu, select the new form to be the Startup Object.

7. Execute the application.

When the application is executing, the rows and columns of the customers table should be displayed (see Figure 8.8). Clicking in individual cells would normally enable editing of the record information.

FIGURE 8.8

DataGrid executing on the form.

Be aware that the sources that you created in the data environment are set to Read Only by default. Therefore, to allowing actual editing of the data within the records, you will need to reset this property in the Customers command object.

MSHFlexGrid Control

The DataGrid control is excellent for providing full editing features in a spreadsheet-like solution. However, the DataGrid is fairly memory-intensive and not incredibly fast with large data sets.

The HFlexGrid control, on the other hand, is extremely fast and contains a number of features such as hierarchical organizations and multitable related data not included in the DataGrid. The HFlexGrid, however, is only for displaying information and does not enable the data bound to it to be edited.

When looking through the HFlexGrid properties, one thing that you will notice immediately is the number of variations of the display that are allowed. Although the DataGrid only offers the most rudimentary changes, the HFlexGrid enables you to change the

8

color and style of nearly every piece of the grid (gridlines, bound columns, selection, and so on).

To use the HFlexGrid, you can easily create a new form that will display the records stored in the customers table in the Northwind database. You might notice that the operation of the FlexGrid is faster than the traditional DataGrid. Because the data set is read-only and there are no editing capabilities in the FlexGrid, the performance is better.

> Using the hierarchical capabilities of this control requires the creation of hierarchical recordsets that are fairly complicated. Creating these types of recordsets is beyond the scope of this book. For more information on creating hierarchical recordsets, see your Visual Basic manual.

1. Add another form to the project.

2. This new form will have the FlexGrid to stretch the form for additional space to display the Customers table information. Although you could place this control on the form with the DataGrid, performance would suffer.

3. Select the MSHFlexGrid control and draw it on the form.

   Make the grid wide so that you can see as many of the fields in each record as possible.

4. Set the `DataSource` property to `DataEnvironment1`.

5. Set the `DataMember` property to `Customers`.

   The FlexGrid is more flexible in display and general user interface than the DataGrid. It can easily be configured for such complex needs as full row selection, automatic cell merging, and drag and drop interfaces.

   In this example, you can configure the grid to select the entire row when any item in the row is clicked upon.

6. Set the `SelectionMode` to `1 — flexSelectionByRow`.

   With this property set, a click on any cell will select the entire row. Like Excel, however, the FlexGrid has a focus rectangle. This means that the first selected cell has a special border to make it stand out.

   Because this example is trying to show an entire selected row, the focus rectangle can be distracting to the user. By modifying the `FocusRect` property, you can turn this selection off.

7. Set the `FocusRect` property to `0 — flexFocusNone`.

   The control is now ready to be used in the application. Because there are multiple forms in this project, you will have to first select this form to load when the application executes.

8. In the Project Properties under the Project menu, select the new form to be the Startup Object.

   Although in this book you have been modifying the Startup Object for each new form, you can alternately place a command button on a central form and use the `Show` method in the Click event to display others.

9. Execute the application.

When the application executes (see Figure 8.9), you can click on any row and you'll see the entire row is selected as if it was a list box. To really access the power of the FlexGrid, you'll need to do some programming. It can be used to individually color cells or even display pictures within each cell. Check the Visual Basic manual for more information.

FIGURE 8.9

DataGrid executing on the form.

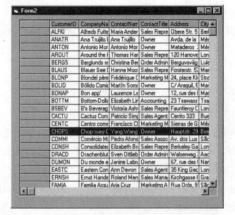

Summary

There are a number of bound controls that can be used to provide nearly any type of data display. The simple bound controls such as the Textbox or Checkbox can be used to quickly create a database solution.

The more complex controls such as the DataList or DataCombo can be used for advanced multitable solutions including invoicing and others.

Q&A

Q **Can the connections created in the Data Environment be used with the Data Control?**

A Yes. You can create a connection to a data source for a Data Control using the connections that you've created in the Data Environment.

Q **Does the reference table used to supply the lists for the DataList or the DataCombo have to be located in the same data environment?**

A No. Because the DataSource and RowSource properties can be set separately, there is no need to locate both tables in the same data environment.

Q **Can the DataGrid be used for read-only data sources or must I use the HFlexGrid control?**

A The DataGrid can be used with a read-only data source without any problem. However, because the HFlexGrid is smaller, faster, and more powerful for read-only display and manipulation, it is usually a good idea to use it instead for read-only applications.

Workshop

The quiz questions and exercises are provided for your further understanding. See Appendix C, "Answers," for the answers to the questions.

Quiz

1. What items are included by default when a new Data Project is created?

2. True or False: A data environment can be accessed from any form, class, or code module in the project.

3. How can you change the type of bound control created by default when using the drag and drop interface?

4. What two properties must be set in the DataGrid for it to display a recordset?

Exercise

1. Create a new form that contains all the records from the Orders table except the CustomerID field. For this field, create a DataCombo to display the Customers reference table.

2. Reconfigure the Customers table object in the Data Environment so that it will no longer be read-only. Try modifying a record, closing the application, and re-executing it. Was the change made to the Northwind table?

HOUR 9

Creating an ActiveX Control and Using the Data Repeater

The Data Repeater is extremely useful if you want to display more than one record in a window without resorting to the spreadsheet or grid format. The Data Repeater enables you to place controls inside a frame-like container that can display multiple times within a window.

The highlights of this hour include

- Creating an ActiveX control
- Exposing properties within the control
- Binding the control to the Data Repeater

How Is the Data Repeater Used?

In programming Visual Basic projects, you might have created your own user controls for use in multiple projects. You might have taken the extra step of compiling the user control as an ActiveX control or OCX.

Visual Basic provides the capability to create an ActiveX control. You have been using the ActiveX controls (such as the Textbox, Data Control, Command Button, and so on) supplied with VB already. From within VB, you can create your own controls that can be inserted into other projects (including VBA or Microsoft Office applications).

To use the Data Repeater control, you will need to create an ActiveX control containing other controls (such as text boxes, check boxes, and so on) to display the information for a single record of the table. This new control will then be repeated within the space allocated for the Data Repeater control (see Figure 9.1).

FIGURE 9.1

Final Data Repeater.

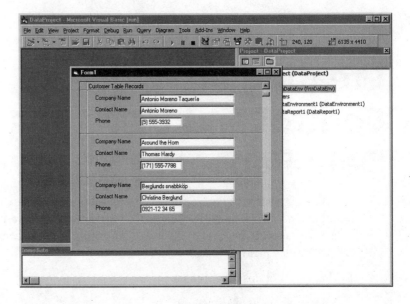

The Data Repeater has an entire user interface including scroll bars. It also accepts the arrow keys, Home, End, Page Up and Page Down keys for movement through the records.

Creating the ActiveX Control

Creating an ActiveX control is not much more difficult or different than creating an application. Because a control must be registered in the registry, it cannot be simply executed and tested. Instead it is compiled into an OCX control.

The best method of developing an ActiveX control is to start by creating a User Control in a Visual Basic project. As a User Control, it can be inserted on a form and debugged within the same project. An ActiveX control is more difficult to construct because it must be compiled every time and loaded into a separate project.

For a user control, features can be easily added as the control becomes more stable. After debugging is complete, all the code and controls can be converted into an ActiveX control for use in other programs and control reuse.

9

In this section, you'll create a control that contains three fields from the customers table of the Northwind database. When the control is added to the Data Repeater, the properties representing the controls will be bound to data fields.

You'll need to begin a new ActiveX control as a completely new project within VB.

1. Create a new project by selecting the ActiveX control type.

2. Name the project vbdbControl.

   Setting the Name property of the project is important on an ActiveX control because it will become the prefix to the control name in the OCX list.

3. Name the control ctlCustomers.

4. Add three labels and set the captions to Company Name, Contact Name, and Phone (see Figure 9.2).

5. Add a textbox control and set the Name property to txtCompanyName.

6. Add another textbox control and set the Name property to txtContactName.

7. Add a third textbox control and set the Name property to txtPhone.

8. Resize the control so it is only little bigger than the control space (see Figure 9.3).

You have to add some interface code so the control values can be set through the binding that occurs when the control is bound to the Data Repeater. Controls cannot be directly exposed outside a control. Instead, property functions are exposed that can be bound to values.

9. Open the code window for the form.

10. Under the Tools menu, choose the Add Procedure option.

11. Set the Type to Property, the Scope to Public, and the Name to CompanyName.

FIGURE 9.2

Add three labels to the control.

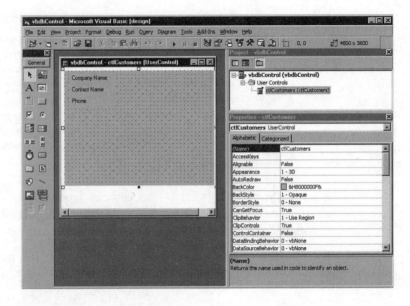

FIGURE 9.3

Resize the control to fit the displayed controls.

12. Create two other properties using the same method: `ContactName` and `Phone`.

    If you look in the code window, you will see `Property Get` and `Property Let` statements for each of the new properties (see Figure 9.4). Because the `Property Let` definition is used to set the value of the property and the `Get` is used to retrieve it, you need to create some code to accomplish these functions.

    As you can see in the figure, the `Get` and `Let` statements default to passing a `Variant` data type for all the variables. You'll need to modify these in the next step to pass and return `String` data type variables.

FIGURE 9.4

The Property Let *and* Get *structures have been created for the properties.*

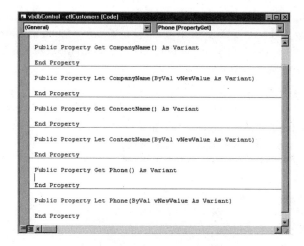

13. Modify the Get and Let statements to match the following code:

```
Public Property Get CompanyName() As String
    CompanyName = txtCompanyName.Text
End Property

Public Property Let CompanyName(ByVal inputStr As String)
    txtCompanyName.Text = inputStr
End Property

Public Property Get ContactName() As String
    ContactName = txtContactName.Text
End Property

Public Property Let ContactName(ByVal inputStr As String)
    txtContactName.Text = inputStr
End Property

Public Property Get Phone() As String
    Phone = txtPhone.Text
End Property

Public Property Let Phone(ByVal inputStr As String)
    txtPhone.Text = inputStr
End Property
```

As you can see, this code simply bridges the Let and Get statements to the Text properties of each text control. These properties will then be exposed for access outside the control.

With the Get and Let functions created for the properties, you will need to attach them to the controls. All the data input controls (such as textboxes) have an event known as the Change event that activates when the user has made a change to the data in that control.

By adding a few simple lines of code to the Change event of each control, the properties settings will automatically be updated to reflect the new information.

14. Add the following code to the Change events of the text box controls:

```
Private Sub txtCompanyName_Change()
    PropertyChanged "CompanyName"
End Sub

Private Sub txtContactName_Change()
    PropertyChanged "ContactName"
End Sub

Private Sub txtPhone_Change()
    PropertyChanged "PhoneName"
End Sub
```

This code will flag a change to any of the text boxes so that the controls that are bound to the text boxes (that is, the Data Repeater) are notified of the change.

15. Under the Tools menu, select the Procedure Attributes option.

16. Click on the Advanced button to expand the window.

17. For all three properties, check the Data Binding attributes Property Is Data Bound and Show in Data Bindings Collection at Design Time (see Figure 9.5).

FIGURE 9.5

Setting the Data Binding attributes of the properties.

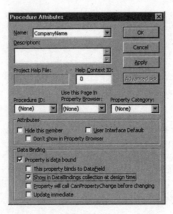

18. Save the project.

19. Compile and register the OCX control by using the Make vbdbControl option on the File menu.

> Any time you create a control, it must be registered in the registry for use by other programs. Visual Basic automatically registers the control when you make the OCX. Be aware that it will be registered on your hard disk where you compile the control from VB.
>
> If you want to move the control later, you will want to unregister it, move it, and then reregister it. This can be done with the regsvr32 utility executed at the command line.
>
> The regsvr32.exe program can be found in the Windows\System directory. If you execute regsvr32 at the command line without any parameters, a help screen will be displayed. You can use the -u switch to unregister the control.

You now have a complete ActiveX control! You can insert the control into any application that is enabled for OCX controls. For example, you could place this control on an Excel spreadsheet.

More importantly, the control is now data-aware. Therefore, you can bind the control to the Data Repeater to have it display multiple records in a window.

Setting Up and Binding the Data Repeater

You can add any OCX control to the Data Repeater.

1. Create a new Data Project.
2. Open the Data Environment and configure the connection to point to the Northwind database (NWind.mdb).
3. Add a new Command object to the connection.
4. Using the context menu (right-click) on the Command object, open the Properties window.
5. Set the Command Name attribute to comCustomers.
6. From the Database Object type combo box, select the Table option.
7. Select the customers table from the combo box list.
8. Click the OK button to accept the Command object changes.

You have configured the Data Environment to hold a connection to the Customers table. Now you will have to set up the actual form that contains the Data Repeater.

Adding the Data Repeater to the Form

1. Open the frmDataEnv form.
2. Expand the form and place the Data Repeater control on it (see Figure 9.6).

FIGURE 9.6

*The Data Repeater on
the expanded form.*

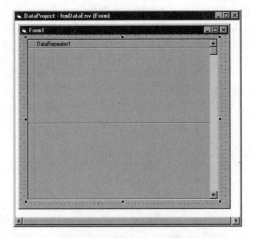

The Data Repeater control is automatically added to the Tools palette for use in a
data project.

3. Set the `RepeatedControlName` property to `vbdbControl.ctlCustomers` (see Figure
9.7).

FIGURE 9.7

*Setting the
RepeatedControlName
property to the control
to repeat.*

This `RepeatedControlName` property has a combo list that contains all the qualifying
controls registered on the current system. You can select the control that you just created
to bind it to the Data Repeater.

As soon as you select a control from the list, the Data Repeater is automatically populated with the control on the form.

Binding Individual Properties to the Controls

With the Data Repeater bound to the ActiveX control, you will need to bind the individual properties exposed (through the Let and Get commands) to fields on the data source.

1. For the Caption property, set the title of the Data Repeater to Customer Table Records.

2. Set the DataSource property of the Data Repeater to the DataEnvironment1.

3. Set the DataMember property to the comCustomers object.

4. Right-click on the Data Repeater control and select the Properties option from the context menu.

> You can also access the Properties window by using the (Custom) property row in the traditional docked Properties Window.

5. Select the RepeaterBindings tab.

6. From the PropertyName combo box, select the CompanyName property.

7. Select the CompanyName field in the DataField combo box.

8. Click the Add button to add the binding to the list box.

9. Use the same method to create bindings for the ContactName and Phone fields.

   When you're finished binding the three fields, the window should appear as the one shown in Figure 9.8.

FIGURE 9.8

Adding the three bindings to the Data Repeater.

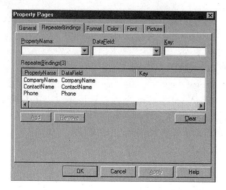

10. Click the OK button to approve the bindings.

    After the bindings have been approved, the application is ready to execute. The Data Repeater will automatically handle binding the values within the control to the data source.

11. Execute the application (refer to Figure 9.1).

The Data Repeater will now display the number of controls that can be shown in the space allocated for it. Properties such as the Scrollbars property enable you to fine-tune the appearance of the Data Repeater.

Summary

The Data Repeater is a convenient way to display aspects of multiple records without resorting to using a grid-like presentation. In order to use the Data Repeater, you must initially create an ActiveX control to contain controls that could be bound to the desired properties.

After the ActiveX control is completed and the properties exposed using the Property Let and Property Get statements, it is bound to the Data Repeater by setting a single property. The configuration is complete when a data source and particular fields are bound to the Data Repeater.

Q&A

Q Can the Data Repeater control be used without creating a custom ActiveX control?

A Although it is not impossible to create a generic OCX, most applications will require that a custom control is created to address desired bound fields.

Q Do I have to ship the OCX control with my application?

A Yes, and it must be registered on the client system when the application is installed. Luckily, the Application Setup Wizard included with Visual Basic automatically takes care of these details.

Workshop

The quiz questions and exercises are provided for your further understanding. See Appendix C, "Answers," for the answers to the questions.

Quiz

1. What two properties determine how an ActiveX control is listed on the system?

2. How can properties be exposed from within an ActiveX control?

3. What property is used to bind an ActiveX control to the Data Repeater?

Exercises

1. Create an ActiveX control that addresses a table you've created (such as the todo table in Hour 5, "Constructing Databases").

2. Modify the project that you created so it is bound to a Data Control rather than a Command object in the Data Environment.

9

Hour 10

Multitable Relations

Although the terms data and information are often used interchangeably, there is an understanding in the database community that the term information really means *organized data*. Data is raw and unusable. The more organized that data is, the easier it is for a computer to manipulate it. When it is organized so you can get the answers you need, it has become information.

You have already seen that a database is far more organized than a word processing document. Instead of being a simple beginning-to-end structure, a database has information broken down by table and field. By creating relations between multiple tables, the information is further organized.

In this hour, you'll learn how to connect two or more tables within a database together and how this creates a much more flexible and powerful information system.

The highlights of this hour include

- Understanding multiple table design
- Learning how a primary key and foreign key are used in concert to create a relation

- Modifying the todo and Projects table from previous hours to create a relational database
- Understanding the process of normalization and bubble diagramming

What Is a Relational Database?

Relational databases are truly at the center of any modern information system. The ability to keep data separated among various tables and yet allow the tables to be connected provides flexibility, speed, and expandability.

Most databases contain multiple tables within a single file. Up until now, you've created tables where each table was independent. In Hour 6, "Visual Data Manager," you were first introduced to the idea of multiple tables within a database. The tables you created in that hour resulted in a flat-file database. This means that none of the tables were interdependent.

Flat-File Northwind Database

To understand the need for relational tables, it is generally easiest to begin with an exact case that shows the disadvantages of a flat-file system to solve a particular problem. Imagine you were designing the Northwind database from scratch. When someone bought an item from Northwind traders, you would have to generate an order record. What fields would have to go into this order record?

Right now, you know how to create only a flat-file database (the hr5.mdb database). This means that each table is independent of the others. In a flat-file database, a single table must be constructed to accommodate all the needed functionality within that table.

For each order, you would need to record:

- The customer and all the related customer information (name, address, tax status, contact person, and so on)
- The primary ordering information such as shipping address, date of invoice, salesperson, and so on
- Each item ordered including description of product, cost, quantity, and so on

Try to imagine generating the record to fulfill all these needs. Each record would be immense with probably hundreds of fields. Just to record each order item, you would need a separate field. To be able to record just two order entries, you would need these fields:

ItemNum1

ItemDesc1

ItemQty1

ItemTaxable1

ItemNum2

ItemDesc2

ItemQty2

ItemTaxable2

If you needed the capability to potentially record 10 sales items on an invoice, in this example, you would need to dedicate 40 fields just for the order items! This system also requires vast duplication of information. In the preceding example, the item description would have to be entered in each record allowing for a large number of potential errors.

Using related tables solves these problems. A single table is broken down into two or more tables that interconnect. Instead of storing all the information in one table, it can be stored in a table that focuses on each particular aspect of the data being entered.

In this case, there could be one table that contains the general information on the order and another table that stored all the details for each item for the order. In fact, this is exactly the method actually used by Northwind.

Related Tables within the Northwind Database

The Northwind database is created as a set of related tables that contains everything from ordering information to supplier records. You can see in Figure 10.1 that there are connections between all the tables stored in the database. The relations enable particular fields within each table to connect to other tables, providing the structure to connect one record to another.

FIGURE 10.1

The relationships between the tables in the Northwind database.

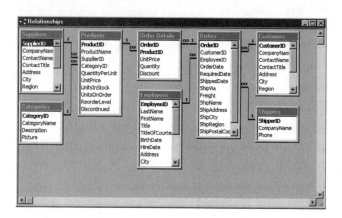

In the figure, you can see that the table labeled Orders is connected to the table labeled Order Details. This relation solves the problem you faced when trying to keep track of all the order items in the flat-file database.

Rather than having a single table hold all the information, the Orders table holds the primary information related to the order (that is, ShipName, OrderDate, and so on). The Order Details table holds the Products #, the quantity ordered, and so on.

Because many Order Details records can be created to connect to a single order record, a simpler and better organized solution than an ever-expanding flat-file database is found.

In database terminology, this relation is known as a one-to-many association. That means that a single order record can be connected to many different records in the Order Details table.

In Figure 10.1, you can see that the line that connects the two tables has the number 1 on the side that enters the Orders table and the symbol for infinity(∞) on the side that enters the Order Details. This indicates that for one Orders record, there can be an infinite number of Order Details records.

NEW TERM   When one record can relate to multiple records in another table, the connection is said to be a *one-to-many* relation.

On the link between the Orders table and the Customers table, you can see exactly the opposite. For this association, there is only one customer allowed per order. You might think this is a one-to-one relationship, but if you look at Figure 10.1, you will see that it is really another one-to-many.

> In any database relationship, recognize that although the relation might be present, that does not necessarily mean that there is an connected record in the adjoining table.
>
> For example, an order might be created in the Northwind database, but no customer is specified. Although there is a relation between the two tables, it does not necessarily mean that for each record a reference actually exists.

So far, you have looked at the connections with the Orders table as the starting point. If instead you consider starting at the Customers table, you'll see that each customer can have many orders, whereas only one customer is specified per order.

In the Northwind database, all the table relations have a one-to-many connection. There are two other types of connections that are not present in this database: one-to-one and many-to-many.

One-to-one connections only allow a single record to be connected in each table. An example of this would be a salary table related to the Employees table. Each employee would have one and only one salary. Each salary record would be directly bound to each individual employee.

NEW TERM In a *one-to-one* relation, one record in one table is linked to only one record in another table.

The many-to-many connections become fairly complex and are the least common type of relation. In the Northwind database, there is one supplier for every product. This creates a one-to-many relation when referencing the product supplier. But what if there were multiple suppliers for a each product?

This would create a situation where multiple suppliers could be connected to each product and multiple products to each supplier. Under these conditions, a many-to-many relation is needed.

10

NEW TERM In a *many-to-many* relation, multiple records in the first table are linked to multiple records in the second table and vice versa.

Considering what type of relations will be used in your database during the design phase can help you understand how the database will be structured. Unless referential integrity is used (see the section "Referential Integrity" later in this hour), the type of relation is not actually codified in the database, but simply understood.

> Sometimes designers who have never created a relational database tend to go "hog-wild" after they learn the basics, breaking down every piece of information into its own related table. This can be worse for performance and functionality than a poorly designed flat-file database.
>
> Just remember that for all the complexity of the Northwind database, it is still only comprised of eight related tables. Use moderation when making design decisions.

Multiple Tables

You can use the Visual Data Manager to create tables and table relations. In order for tables to be related, they must contain fields that enable the relations to occur. Using the fundamental table created in Hour 6 you can augment it to contain additional related information.

Right now, the todo table contains individual todo items stored as records. Instead of leaving these tasks as individual items, you can modify the table known as Projects that will correlate the tasks.

Bubble Diagram

To design the new table and the relation to the table, it is best to use a type of diagram known as a *bubble chart*. A bubble chart shows individual fields within a table and their relation to fields in other tables.

In Figure 10.2, you can see two samples of fields in bubble chart format. The first example shows a simple one-to-one relationship, whereas the second chart is a one-to-many relationship.

FIGURE **10.2**

*The bubble chart rela-
tionships between
fields.*

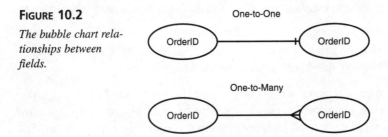

The one-to-one relation has a single crossed bar on the destination side of the link to indicate which table holds the primary key (source table) and which holds the foreign key (destination table).

The one-to-many shows the source table with a single line out. On the destination, you can see the multiple lines that go into the destination table, indicating multiple records connecting to a single record in the source table.

By diagramming the connections that you will need to make for the database, an abstract concept can become much more concrete. In the following sections, you will see bubble charts to demonstrate how the new Projects table will be linked to the existing todo table items.

Normalization

The process of breaking down tables is known as *normalization*. Simplifying a large singular record into multiple related tables makes the entire data system more flexible and stable for expansion.

NEW TERM *Normalization* is the process of simplifying a complex data structure by breaking it down into simple connected parts. In the case of database design, this means constructing simple related tables.

You might already have created databases that are stored in a flat-file format. Or you might have created a relational database but realize that the records must be broken down into further tables. The process of normalization is recognizing what data should be separated into smaller related tables.

How Is a Relational Database Constructed?

In Hour 5, "Constructing Databases," you initially created a database with the name hr5.mdb. This database held only a single table, the todo table. By Hour 6, "Visual Data Manager," you had added a second table known as the Projects table. Until now, these tables, although located in the same database, are completely separate and individual.

By making a few slight modifications to each table, you can associate them. First, it would be a good idea to review the structures of these tables.

In both tables, the uniqueID field provides a distinct ID number for each item. The database can use this field as the table's primary key. When used in a relational database system, a *primary key* is the field that uniquely identifies each record so it can be referenced from a related table. If you needed to reference a task from another table, this key would be recorded in a field in the other table to provide the connection.

NEW TERM A *primary key* is the field that uniquely identifies each record so it can be referenced from a related table.

In the Projects table, this key won't be useful for any relating. This project requires a one-to-many relation with the todo table. If the todo table stored the uniqueID number to a common project, such a relation could be created.

A field added to the todo table to store the Project identifiers is known as a *foreign key*. A foreign key is a field that stores the value of a primary key from another table.

NEW TERM A *foreign key* is a field in a database that holds id values to relate records stored in another table.

You might have noticed that within the Northwind database, both the primary key in the source table and the foreign key field in the destination table have the same name. This makes it easier to identify exactly what purpose the field serves.

For this same reason, you will need to modify the name of the uniqueID field in the Projects table in order to provide a clear reference within the todo table. When examining the table individually, it is much easier to see to which table the field is connected.

10

It is easiest to remember the difference between a primary key and a foreign key by recognizing that a table can only have ONE primary key, whereas it can contain many foreign keys.

The bubble chart for the todo and Projects tables will look like the chart shown in Figure 10.3. With the bubble chart, you can see the types of connections between the tables much more clearly than a text description.

FIGURE 10.3

The bubble chart relationships between the todo and Projects tables.

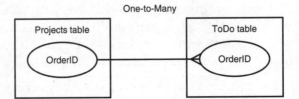

A bubble chart takes only a few seconds to sketch, but will aid you when you actually have to modify the tables because it is very easy to become confused as to the direction of the relation between tables.

Modifying the Tables

You will need to modify each table in the hr5.mdb in order to allow them to relate. Begin the process by executing Visual Basic 6 in order to provide access to the Visual Data Manager in order to make the necessary changes.

1. Open the Visual Data Manager.

2. Open the hr5.mdb that you created in Hour 5 and modified in Hour 6.

3. Right-click on the Projects table and select the Design option from the context menu.

   The modifications you will need to make will affect the structure of the database. Therefore, if you constructed any projects based on these tables, you might need to reformat them so that the bound objects will reference the field changes.

4. Change the name of the uniqueID field to read projectid (see Figure 10.4).

   Because you originally created the uniqueID field with all the attributes of a primary key (that is, auto incrementing, unique, indexed, and so on), there is no need to alter any of these characteristics.

   From the Visual Data Manager, it is difficult to modify anything by the name of a field. If you need to make more comprehensive changes (including data type), use Microsoft Access on the table because it includes this functionality.

FIGURE 10.4

Changing the primary key of the Projects table to a more descriptive name.

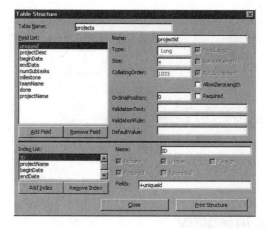

When creating a key field, try to use a numeric data type for the field. Although text fields can be used, they are much slower and larger than numeric fields. Although sometimes you might not have a choice (in Hour 20, "Accessing Outlook," you will learn that the Outlook item primary key is a string), try to use numeric types.

5. Close the table definition window.

   This will store the change to the field name. If you right-click on the Projects entry and select the Refresh List option from the menu, you will see the change of the name of the field.

   Now that you have that field in place, the foreign key field must be added to the todo table to provide a connection.

6. Right-click on the todo table and select the Design option on the context menu.

7. Click on the Add Field button.

8. Enter the field name as projectid and set the type to Long (see Figure 10.5).

   Unlike the primary key, the foreign key is recorded in this field when a project is selected—there is no need to make the field auto-increment.

9. Click the OK button to accept the added field definition.

10. Close the Design window.

11. Close the database.

After all the references are constructed, you can place sample data in the fields to provide a connection between some of the records.

10

FIGURE 10.5

*Adding the Foreign key
of the todo table to
hold the relational
link.*

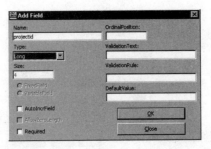

In Hour 12, "Multitable Forms," you'll use the tables that you've modified to actually display the records and their related information.

Referential Integrity

Earlier in the hour it was noted that just because a relation exists, it does not necessarily mean that an associated record exists in each table to fulfill the relation.

Although you have constructed the fields in the tables to create the relations, you haven't codified the connections within the database. Creating the relational objects is not absolutely necessary. The database can be used relationally in its current form. Placing the relational rules within the database ensures that there is *referential integrity* between the tables.

Referential integrity is the technology built-in to the VB database engine that can ensure all related tables contain the correct partner records. In the Northwind database, this makes it impossible to record an order without specifying a customer for the order.

By enforcing this integrity in a relational database, many problems (such as incomplete query results) can be avoided. It also means, however, that there cannot be floating or unattached records. In your existing table, existing records already probably violate this condition.

Unattached records in existing databases make upgrading difficult. This problem is often solved by having a default or miscellaneous record in the primary table that all unassigned related records point towards.

Referential integrity is the technology that forces all related tables to keep consistent records for relations, so the database is said to have integrity.

After the referential integrity rules are placed within the database, the burden of tracking data consistency is largely removed from your program. It must only track errors that occur when the consistency is violated.

Referential integrity can be added to the table using the Database Designer included with VB 6 Enterprise Edition, directly through code using the DAO objects, or via the capabilities of Microsoft Access.

The complications introduced by adding referential integrity are beyond the scope of this book. For more information on this topic, see *Sams Teach Yourself Database Programming with Visual Basic in 21 Days*.

Summary

To organize information effectively, most databases require that a group of related tables are used for each piece of information. By separating the record information into tables that focus on a particular aspect of each entry, the database system becomes much more flexible and expansive.

Creating a relation merely requires having a primary key in one table and storing the appropriate key in a foreign key field in another table. The process of normalization helps you figure out how the data should be divided. By adding one field, you modified the hr5.mdb database to relate the two tables.

Q&A

Q Does a primary key need to be of any particular data type?

A No, but it must contain a unique value for each record within the table. If there are duplicates of the same value, the relation will be corrupted.

Q How important is making a bubble chart for a database?

A Very important. When the relations get beyond a simple two-table relation, it is extremely easy to become confused with how the tables interconnect. Simply drawing the charts will clear up most misconceptions and planning inaccuracies during the design phase.

Q Is referential integrity on a database required?

A It is not required between related tables, but it does keep the rules stored within the database rather than having the rules individually coded in every application that uses the tables. This means that no special coding is required to enforce them, especially if an ODBC connection is placed to the data.

10

Workshop

The quiz questions and exercises are provided for your further understanding. See Appendix C, "Answers," for the answers to the questions.

Quiz

1. What is a table relation?

2. How is a relation created?

3. Explain the meanings of the primary and foreign keys and how they are used together.

4. True or False: Database normalization is the process of breaking down tables to minimize duplication of information.

5. In what way does database normalization provide extra expandability when storing information?

Exercises

1. Examine the Northwind database and study the one-to-many relations exposed in Figure 10.1. Do you understand why the tables were normalized?

2. Draw a bubble chart of the various tables in the Northwind database. How many tables contain more than one foreign key?

HOUR 11

Creating a User Interface

An effective user interface is truly the key to a successful program. Unless you're creating a program only for yourself, making the interface intuitive for the end users (whether that includes one or a thousand people) should be high on your list of priorities.

In a database program, this is especially important because information entry might occur in an unfamiliar format. Unlike a word processor or spreadsheet, which have well-understood interfaces, a data-intensive program interface can be constructed in numerous ways.

> In many ways, the user interface can be even more critical in a database program than traditional applications. Database programs traditionally must access and manipulate information accurately. A poorly designed user interface can cause information to be incorrectly entered, compound mistakes leading to flawed data, or facilitate critical data loss or deletion.

The highlights of this hour include:

- Learning the interface design process
- Effectively planning your application interface
- Special considerations for creating database applications
- Emulating user interface features of popular programs
- Guidelines for interface challenges

Interface Design Process

Creating a good interface requires adoption of two important practices: forethought and feedback. You should carefully think about what the program is made to do and who will be using it. Additionally, it is very important to give the end users an opportunity to contribute suggestions and information that should be included in the design.

Realistically, people seldom reference manuals. This means an intuitive interface and online help might be the only methods a user will have to find out about features and processes.

Designing the interface before the program is actually implemented can save you a great deal of time. If the interface is added after much of the coding is complete, making necessary additions or changes can be cumbersome. By examining what the program needs to do and how it will be presented to the user, a project can be implemented properly in less time.

Write a Feature List

The first step to be taken when you begin creating a substantial database program is the creation of a list of features that need to be included in the program. By clearly describing the features, you will have a good idea of the scope of the project and the technologies necessary to complete it.

The feature list will also help create the general layout and organization of the program to be created. For example, if you were going to build a simple address book application, your feature list might look like this:

- Entry Input—Allow entry and modification of fields: FirstName, LastName, Company, Address1, Address2, City, State, Zip, HomePhone, BusPhone, and Notes.
- Searching—Ability to search all the fields, including wildcards.
- Deleting—The program should allow a single record to be deleted or multiple records from a list.

- Sorting—For viewing and printing, a sort should be available on LastName, Zip, State, and Company fields.
- Printing—Printing should be available for both a single record and multiple records in spreadsheet format.

You can see from this list that the printing, searching, sorting, and deleting will require special programming not included by any of the wizards. By creating this feature list, you will be able to explicitly consider what is involved in creating the project.

Most Used Features

The importance of a particular feature does not necessarily determine how often that feature is used. For example, in an accounting program, the balance sheet report might be the most important document generated by the program. However, each transaction must be entered correctly, so the transaction entry feature is used hundreds of times before the important report is generated.

You will need to consider how the program will be used to determine which features are the most used to make them quickly accessible.

Start by considering who the most common users will be. Maybe salespeople have to use the program every day, but management use it once a month. The entire presentation of the application should then be slanted in the direction of the most frequent users.

11

Step-By-Step Operations

After the most-used features are determined, the order in which they are used is the next item for consideration. This can be one of the difficult parts of the user interface to construct because everyone uses a program in a slightly different manner.

The easiest way to outline this problem is to create a simple flowchart. A flowchart describes the order in which operations take place and can provide conditional branches. In Figure 11.1, you'll see a flowchart for a sample accounting situation.

As you follow the flowchart through the process, you can begin to see where problems might occur. What if the user doesn't select the customer before entering information? How comprehensive will you make the product additions window? Examining the important processes of the application will allow you to plan for many of these contingencies.

The drawing tools included with Word 97 are fantastic for quick flowchart creation. If you make the Drawing toolbar visible within Word, you'll see that the AutoShapes menu contains all the basic symbols you'll need. There is even a Flowchart submenu in the AutoShapes list for detailed flowchart shapes.

FIGURE 11.1

*Simple invoice pro-
gram flowchart.*

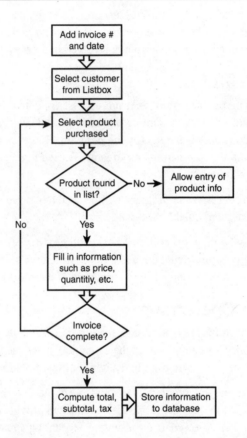

The flowchart should also tell you what forms need to interact. In the example above, the user might need to add a product that is not currently in inventory. Is this appropriate for a sales associate to do? Should this part of the program be limited only to the personnel in the warehouse so inventory can be more accurately tracked?

For day-to-day operations, does entry in one window require information from another? Looking at all the operations, you should be able to determine what data is interdependent and requires simultaneous access.

After you've created the operations flowcharts, try to keep them with the project. If revisions ever need to be implemented on the program, it is a good idea to re-examine the processes that were initially important during program construction. If they are still valid, make sure the new features don't interrupt the process flow.

Add, Test, and Redesign

Long before the coding is complete, you should demonstrate the application to the people who will be using it. Visual Basic is ideal for creating a rapid prototype of a finished program. Prototyping provides you with important feedback as to what should be changed.

Have a list of operations you want the user to complete. If you ask a person, "Will you try this out?", the user won't know where to begin. Instead, create a list of common operations that will be required by the person and have him provide feedback on the difficulty of completing these tasks. For example, for a sales application, you might ask the user to go through the process of selling two widgets. Note any difficulty encountered while the user attempts this common process.

After you have a list of problems or possible improvements, prioritize the most important changes. This should be accomplished by checking the feedback list against the most important features list you made before. There is never enough time to make all the desired changes. This fact should help you prioritize.

Visual Basic makes constructing forms so easy that you can often do the layout directly on the form without much forethought. It is often a good idea to draw a rough layout of the form and then print it out. From the printed copy, consider how fields should be organized or placed within frames.

Organization is usually easier to consider objectively when you're not moving around controls, stretching boxes, and modifying labels on the screen. The paper copy can also be left with users so they can even fax you desired form layout changes.

Database Specifics

Database program development presents unique challenges for user interface design. Because the design of the database itself is flexible and its design strongly impacts the presentation to the user, structuring of both the database and the interface should be done cooperatively.

The two primary questions with each aspect of data display in a database application are

- Do multiple records need to be displayed at once?
- What type of editing control is required on a form?

Multiple record display creates special problems that must be resolved in each application. Likewise, editing abilities will determine what type of interface can be used effective for an operation.

> If you are building a database program for your own use, keep in mind that perhaps others could use the same program type. If the interface is understandable to the layman, it might have broader use than you originally suspected.

Database Structure

The tables contained within a database can provide numerous complicated relations. For example, the invoice application shown in Figure 11.1 might need information from four tables on a single form: the customer table, the product table, the order table, and the order items table.

All these tables will have to be used for a single order. It is not difficult to see how complicated a database application can become. If you have the structure already established, recognize that the greater number of tables required for each form, the more difficult the information management can be.

Multiple Record Display

Multiple record display is usually a complicated problem. If a spreadsheet-like display is appropriate, the Data Grid control will solve most of the problems required. Otherwise, special measures might be required.

The VB Data Form Wizard is used primarily for single record display forms. If single record display will provide the functionality required by the application, choose it; it simplifies numerous other issues.

The most common way to determine if you need to display multiple records is ask:

Do two or more records need to be compared simultaneously?

Comparison between records is usually the primary reason for displaying multiple records. Displaying a single record is more intuitive for the user and much faster because only a single set of information must be retrieved from the data source.

Using the Data Repeater control is often one of the most effective ways to present multiple records if this is necessary. In Hour 9, "Creating an ActiveX Control and Using the Data Repeater," you learned how to use the Data Repeater on a form.

Editing Problems

Editing records complicates an application dramatically. With read-only display, navigation can be easily created using typical data-aware controls. Editing adds data validation routines (for example, was a valid state entered into the state field?), edit mode selection, multi-user issues, and data decay.

NEW TERM When data is loaded into an application in a multi-user setting, that data might be subject to *data decay*, or relevance decay. If other users are actively modifying the data, the information you have in memory can become outdated and irrelevant.

In Hours 19, "Database Application Deployment," 21, "Sharing the Database," and 22, "Database Security," you'll learn how to address these problems. For now, recognize that when designing your user interface, all editing requires additional coding and windows (such as "Do you want to save these changes?").

Operational Passwords

11

To safeguard against deletion by untrained employees, many database programs feature operational passwords in particular areas of the program. An *operational password* requires the entry of a simple password to complete a particular operation.

Simple code like this can be used to display an input box:

```
tempPassword = InputBox("Please enter the delete password.")
If tempPassword <> "DCOM" Then
    MsgBox "That password is invalid.",16,"Invalid Password"
Else
    ' Complete operation
End If
```

This type of implementation is not meant for intensive security, but rather as a basic block to prevent accidental or untrained access to particular areas. It operates as an effective fail-safe block.

Use operational passwords with discretion. If too many are used in various areas, someone is bound to make a list or "cheat sheet," which will nullify the original intentions of the block. Also, if a common operation requires a password entry every time, users will become frustrated with your program.

Other Interface Guidelines

Following are a few of the most important aspects of design for the type of programming and designing you will be doing for Visual Basic database applications. Remember that although these are just guidelines, the more of them you follow, the more likely your program will be a hit with the people who use it.

Copy Other Programs

One of the best ways to create a program others can use is to examine the programs they are already using. Unless your program is doing something radically new, it is best to build on the interfaces people are already familiar using.

It is always tempting, when creating a new program, to invent new ways of interacting with it. Try your best to resist this urge. Making your program evolutionary rather than revolutionary will, in most cases, make it far more successful.

If your program will be used in an environment dominated by WordPerfect, try to emulate the icon style and the general look and feel of that program. If a vertical market application is what users are accustomed to, model your interface upon it.

NEW TERM Most popular applications have a broad or horizontal appeal. Specialized applications (such as dental accounting, real estate tracking, and so on) have a selective or *vertical market* appeal.

Features to consider include:

- Menu organization
- Keyboard shortcuts and function keys
- Window organization
- Icons and toolbar styles

Make Deleting Information "Appropriate"

One of the most difficult problems faced by a database interface program designer is how to safeguard against unintended deletion of data. It is difficult to decide whether protection is enough or too much.

When deleting information is too easy, mistakes will lead to a large amount of information lost. On the other hand, if multiple safeguards are in place for simple operations, the user will feel harassed. Especially if the operation must be done repeatedly.

The easiest way to make a decision on the number of delete dialogs (for instance, "Are you sure you want to delete this?") is to consider the harm the loss of that particular data will cause. Ask yourself this question:

"How hard is it to replace this data?"

A record detailing the statistics of an individual product, if deleted, can be re-entered. An order printed on an invoice can also be recovered. Notes on a customer available only through the database might not again be available if lost.

 Asking your users which safeguards should be in place should also be considered, but not taken as law. Don't forget that a user might find a safeguard a hassle, but might not be ultimately responsible if the data is lost.

Function Keys or Popup Menus

Function keys or keyboard shortcuts can be one of the most effective ways of making a program more useful for intermediate users. After the program is learned, users can usually use the function keys as a method of increasing the speed required to complete an operation.

Programs should provide context-sensitive help and ToolTips to note the possible function key alternatives. If your program will be available for a wide number of users, functionally disabled individuals will benefit greatly by making everything that can be accomplished with the mouse available with a key command.

Although in some programs (such as drawing programs) providing function keys for everything is impossible, most database programs can be readily configured for such functions.

Over-reliance on function keys, however, can make the program difficult to use by a beginner or someone who has not used it in a while. Function keys should be used as an addition to common interface functionality (such as menus and buttons), rather than instead of it.

Much like pressing a function key, right-clicking the mouse in a particular context will often display a program menu. Also like function keys, these can be abused by overuse. All functions available on the context menu should also be available in the central menu or through a toolbar button. Users don't automatically use the context menus, but tend to use them as their experience with the program increases.

Consistency

Although it appears last in the list, consistency is central to any interface. If the key combination of Alt+O approves an item on one form, it should do the same on all forms.

11

Some of the most popular programs do not provide uniformity in particular places to the persistent frustration of their users.

Microsoft has increasingly targeted consistency in its applications such that most Microsoft programs use the Ctrl+F (Find) and Ctrl+H (Replace) standard as well as the fundamental menu structure. Following this model will help users master your program.

> If your program will be used by many users, it is a good idea to consult Microsoft's Windows User Interface Guidelines, which is available free on the Microsoft Web site. Search for User Interface Guidelines to locate it.

Summary

Paying attention to the user interface can be crucial to enabling your intended audience to use the program effectively. By following some of the suggestions in this hour (such as creating a feature list, prototyping, modeling other programs, and so on), you will greatly increase the chances the users will enjoy working with your application.

Q&A

Q Is Microsoft Word the best way to create operational flowcharts?

A It depends on the needs of your application. Because the diagrams can be included in a normal Word document and a majority of the computing world uses Word as its word processor, it is convenient. More powerful programs such as Visio should be considered if you need to do a great number of these diagrams.

Q I don't like most of the interfaces to popular programs. Why should I copy them?

A If you're designing the program for your own use, you should use the methods that best serve your program. If others will be using your application, consider the amount of training and specialized knowledge required to operate your program if you break the mold.

Ask yourself the question, "Does a unique interface provide multiple times the functionality of existing conventions?" Unless the answer is yes, you should reconsider your pioneering features.

Q What is the easiest way to make my program more user-friendly?

A Add online help. A help file (.HLP) can be accessed in context within a Visual Basic program. Examine almost any control and you will find the HelpContextID property. This property enables you to associate a unique number with a topic section in your help file. When the focus is on that control or form, hitting the F1 key will load your help file and display the related topic.

To create a help file for your application, buy one of the programs that help automate the task, such as RoboHelp. Check out one of the major vendors such as VBXtras (www.vbxtras.com) for programs that range from inexpensive to professional production packages.

Workshop

The quiz questions and exercises are provided for your further understanding. See Appendix C, "Answers," for the answers to the questions.

Quiz

1. True or False: The most-used features are also the most important features of a program.
2. What common program provides flowchart symbols?
3. How do you choose whether to display multiple records on a form?
4. Why shouldn't operational password dialogs be used as often as possible?
5. What question should be asked to determine how difficult deleting particular information should be?

Exercise

1. Examine two of your favorite applications. How do they present data? What user interface conventions do they support? Can these elements be used in your program?
2. Look at Microsoft Word or Excel and examine the function, control, and Alt key combinations. Does your program have similar functions? Can you use these established standards?

11

Hour 12

Multitable Forms

Now that you have constructed a relational database and understand some of the important concepts in user interface design, you can construct a sample application that connects to multiple related tables. This sample application can contain all of the important data technology included in Visual Basic and at the same time create a general solid user interface.

Using the Hr5.MDB database, the interface will allow a project to be added, as well as individual tasks for the project. In the application, the ToDo task items are linked to the projects, providing a basic project planning system.

The highlights of this hour include:

- Creating a form that accesses two tables
- Using a data environment with the Data Form Wizard
- Setting up a hierarchical Command object
- Editing and updating records from code
- Selecting a record to display on another form

Constructing a Two-Form Application

Most databases contain multiple tables within a single file. Up until now, you've mostly used tables as if they were independent. However, in the Northwind database, all the tables are actually interconnected.

In Hour 8, "Data-Aware Controls," you linked a combo box to two tables. The method you used was a very simple way of creating the necessary relations between the two tables. Now that you understand relations between tables, it will be easier for you to see the connections between the keys held in the various tables.

This application will mirror many of the operations you will undoubtedly have to implement in your own database solutions. You will be using a form that will display two interconnected tables on the same form (see Figure 12.1).

FIGURE 12.1

An example of the Project application executing and displaying information from both the Projects and ToDo tables.

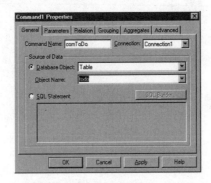

Some of the operations demonstrated by this application include:

- Handling multiple tables on a single form
- Using a selected record to edit on another form
- Editing a database record
- Storing updates to multiple tables
- Handling two Command objects
- Coordinating updates between two forms
- Providing an accessible user interface

The application itself will be a simple project tracking application. The two related tables that will be used interactively are the ToDo and Projects tables that you modified in Hour 10, "Multitable Relations."

The final application will contain:

- Main form
- Task detail form
- `Command` object in the data environment connected to the Projects table
- `Command` object in the data environment connected to the ToDo table
- Hierarchical `Command` object connected to a subset of the records contained in the ToDo table

Creating the Main Form

The central form of the application will allow you to look through and modify Projects table records. You going to use the VB Data Form Wizard to generate the basic code necessary to control the user interface.

However, although the code generated by the wizard uses a custom connection initialized when the form is loaded, you're going to modify this code so that the data environment is used instead.

The recordset will be retrieved from the data environment so it can be shared across the whole project. This ability will be critical to you in the future as you design multiple form projects that need to share database references.

Because the data environment is being used, you can easily add additional bound controls to any form by the drag-and-drop interface. These instances can be made to share common data resources.

12

 Although many programmers in the past have used global variables to make recordsets available throughout a project, using the data environment is preferable. The fact that it is stored in a single centralized, reusable file is a compelling reason to change from earlier habits.

Configuring the Data Environment

You will need to add three `Command` objects to the data environment: two that access the ToDo table and one for the Projects table. In this section, you will create a hierarchical `Command` object, something you haven't done previously.

1. Start a new Data Project.

The Data Project will add all of the user interface elements you will need for this project. You will be using the bound controls, the HFlexGrid, and the data environment.

2. Configure the Data Environment Connection object to connect to hr5.mdb.

   Use the standard Microsoft Jet 3.51 OLE DB Provider and browse to select the database.

3. Create a Command object attached to the ToDo table and name it comToDo.

   You have by this time configured many Command objects so the process should be straightforward (see Figure 12.2).

This Command object will be used to display specific ToDo items in the ToDo Edit window. It will be used almost as a scratch recordset that will need to be opened and closed as specific records need to be targeted.

4. Click on the Advanced tab and set the Lock Type to 3 - Optimistic.

   The default setting (1 - Read Only) has been fine for most of the table connections that you've needed so far. This Command object must allow for editing. Setting the type to optimistic locking allows the table to be edited.

5. Select the Connection1 object again and create another Command object.

6. Configure this Command object to be attached to the Projects table and set the name to comProjects.

7. On the Advanced tab, set the Lock Type to Optimistic.

   You have the two primary Command objects created. In this project, a slightly more advanced use of the Command object will be required. The application needs to display all of the ToDo items related to the currently selected project record.

   The data environment provides a simple way of accomplishing this by allowing for hierarchical Command object definition. Just like folders on a hard drive can be placed one inside another, Command objects can be used hierarchically.

Unlike folders, Command objects can be set to relate to the parent objects that contain them and are directly affected by the information selected there. To define a Command object under another, you simply need to select the object under which it will be inserted.

8. Select the comProjects Command object and click on the Add Command toolbar icon.

   If you expand the comProjects object, you will see the new Command object at the bottom of the list.

9. Display the Properties window of the new Command object.

10. Name the object comToDoView.

11. Click on the Relation tab.

    You will now see all of the properties used to create the connection between it and the parent object.

12. Check the Relate to a Parent Command Object box and select comProjects as the parent from the combo box.

13. Make sure both the Parent and Child fields read ProjectID and click the Add button.

    You have now added a connection between the two objects (see Figure 12.3). This means if a project with a ProjectID number of 3 is being displayed, all of the associated tasks (ToDo items with the ProjectID number 3) will be stored in the recordset for the comToDoView object.

FIGURE 12.3

The relation created in the comToDoView *object with the* comProjects *object.*

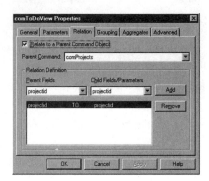

14. Click the OK button to accept the configuration.

    When you have finished the table configuration, the Command objects should look similar to those shown in Figure 12.4. You can see how the two Command objects (comProjects and comToDo) are directly added under the Connection object, whereas the comToDoView object is a child of the comProjects object.

FIGURE 12.4

*The data environment
after all three* Command
objects are configured.

Setting Up the Form

You now have the data environment configured as it needs to be. The primary form must be added to display all of the information for the Projects table. The VB Data Form Wizard will add all of the core bound controls.

After the wizard has completed the form, it will be the basis for the enhancements you will add to see the project details.

1. Add a new form and select the VB Data Form Wizard for the form type.

    The wizard will create all the central code you'll need in order to allow for the editing and updating of individual records.

2. In the Data Form Wizard, select the Access database format and click the Next button.

3. Using the Browse button, select the hr5.mdb file and click the Next button to advance to the next screen.

4. Name the form frmMain, select the Binding Type as ADO Code, and click the Next button.

    Rather than using a Data Control, the wizard will write code to simulate all of the functionality of the Data Control. You'll then modify this code to access the data sources from the data environment.

5. Select the Projects table as the record source, add all the available fields to the form, and click the Next button.

6. Accept all the code for the available controls by clicking the Next button.

   As you work with this project, you'll modify the existing wizard code that was created. The code gives an excellent starting point including all of the required error checking routines.

7. Click the Finish button to construct the form.

   The form will now be stored as part of the project. Like all project structures created by a wizard, this form is meant as a starting point. The presentation of the form is currently not very effective with the fields displayed in no particular order or size.

8. Set the Alignment property of both the picButtons and picStatBox controls to 0 - None.

   Right now all the simulated Data Control items appear at the bottom of the screen and are kept there by the alignment control setting. Setting it to none will allow these controls to be moved around the screen.

9. Format the form as shown in Figure 12.5.

FIGURE 12.5

The reformatted main form.

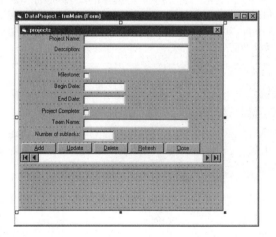

This window appearance is just a general suggestion to make the layout more attractive. You can choose any layout you find appropriate.

Notice the bottom of the form has been dragged downward and the space left blank. This is the area where you will place the connected ToDo items that relate to the currently displayed project.

Also notice that the ProjectID field was eliminated. Because this field is filled in by the database itself, eliminating it cuts down on the confusion to the user.

12

10. Change the `Name` property of the text box bound to the description field to txtDesc.

11. Clear the `Index` property.

    By default, the `Index` property was likely a number such as 5. Clearing the `Index` property will make this control independent of the other text controls.

    This text box is unique because it will need to display multiple lines of the description.

12. Set the `MultiLine` property of the txtDesc control to `True`.

    Because a description often needs to be much longer than other entries, it is a good idea to provide the appropriate space.

13. Set the `TabIndex` properties to reflect the new data field order on the screen.

    After the controls have been rearranged, be sure to set the `TabIndex` properties so when the user hits the Tab key, the cursor advances to the next logical control.

> Often after rearranging a form, modifying these properties is forgotten. Often this is the first problem users notice when presented with a new application. To save yourself numerous headaches (and user complaints), go through the entire application and check the tab order before your first deployment.

14. Set the `ToolTips` property of each control to an effective description of the field.

    In the hour on constructing a user interface, you learned that making the application intuitive is a big part of an effective application. Because few people consult the manual for a program, the ToolTips are an ideal method of providing immediate online help.

> By having ToolTips for each control, more complete information can be explained without cluttering the screen with explanatory text. An experienced user can easily ignore the tips.

15. Modify the code in the `Form Load` event to match the code shown below.

    The code generated by the wizard opens a connection and a data source. You already created these connections in the Data Environment. Therefore, with only slight modification, the form can be changed to address the data environment.

If you open the Load event, you will see code very similar to this code. The big exception is that the first six lines of this code have been commented out with an apostrophe (') and three lines of code have been inserted after those lines.

You should be able to see that the line that begins with DataEnvironment1.comProjects and the three lines that follow it are new. Insert this new code in the proper place and comment out the old code.

```
Private Sub Form_Load()
    'Dim db As Connection
    'Set db = New Connection
    'db.CursorLocation = adUseClient
    'db.Open "PROVIDER=Microsoft.Jet.OLEDB.3.51;Data Source=C:\Program
Files\Microsoft Visual Studio\VB98\24hr12\hr5.mdb;"

    'Set adoPrimaryRS = New Recordset
    'adoPrimaryRS.Open "select
projectName,teamName,projectid,projectDesc,numSubtasks,milestone,endD
ate,done,beginDate from projects", db, adOpenStatic, adLockOptimistic
    ' Initialize the Command objects
    DataEnvironment1.comProjects
    DataEnvironment1.comToDo
    ' Set to recordset used by the form to Projects
    Set adoPrimaryRS = DataEnvironment1.rscomProjects

    Dim oText As TextBox
    ...
```

After this new code is in place, the form will work as if no changes were made. In fact, you just redirected all of the controls on the form to use the comProjects object in the data environment.

16. Alter the Startup object in the project properties to execute frmMain.

17. Execute the application to test the data source and ToolTips.

    If you haven't added any Projects so far, make it a point now to add some new project records. Soon you will be able to link individual tasks to these projects.

The form should correctly initialize the data environment and display the primary records. Now that the core form has been added, you will augment it with the additional controls needed to show the details attached to the project.

Adding the ToDo Task Display

With the data source working and the data environment objects activated, you will need to display the task items held in the ToDo list relevant to the project. The form will use the hierarchical recordset to obtain the records in the ToDo table attached to the individual Project item records.

12

You will also need a few buttons to Add, Edit, and Delete task records. Because you don't have a form for the editing yet, these buttons will at first be left inactive.

1. Add a Frame control to the bottom of the form and set the Caption property to Relevant Tasks.

    A Frame control provides a good user interface item to indicate the function of the controls contained within it, and at the same time to separate the controls from the others on the form. All the controls added now must be placed inside the Frame control.

2. Add an HFlexGrid control and set the Name property to flxToDoItems.

    This bound flexgrid will be used to display all of the items connected to the currently displayed project.

3. Add three buttons and name them cmdToDoAdd, cmdToDoEdit, and cmdToDoDelete.

    Your form should now look like the form shown in Figure 12.6. With only another few modifications to the Form Load code, it will properly display the tasks.

FIGURE 12.6

The main form with the Frame containing a flexgrid and three buttons.

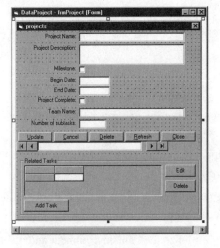

To begin, you won't have any linked tasks. However, you can use the Visual Data Manager to add a few. Simply add records to the ToDo table and make sure the value in the ProjectID field matches a ProjectID of one of the available projects.

4. Add the following code to the General Declarations area of the form:

```
Dim myRS As Recordset
```

This statement defines a recordset that will be used to connect the comToDoView recordset to the flexgrid control.

5. Add the following code after the code you added earlier in the Form Load event.

```
' Create recordset for connected ToDo items
Set myRS =
DataEnvironment1.rscomProjects.Fields("comTodoView").Value
' Configure flexgrid
flxToDoItems.FixedCols = 0
flxToDoItems.SelectionMode = flexSelectionByRow
flxToDoItems.FocusRect = flexFocusNone
flxToDoItems.ColWidth(0) = 200
flxToDoItems.ColWidth(1) = 1000
flxToDoItems.ColWidth(2) = 3000
flxToDoItems.ScrollBars = flexScrollBarVertical
' Link flexgrid control to ToDo items
Set flxToDoItems.DataSource = myRS
```

This code creates a recordset, configures the appearance of the flexgrid, and sets the DataSource of the flexgrid to the new recordset.

6. Execute the application.

Unless there are some entries in the ToDo table, nothing will be displayed in the flexgrid. You can see, however, the formatting that occurs to the grid. To continue, you will need a form to accept and edit ToDo record entries.

You now have a perfect application for viewing the primary project data as well as the ToDo items attached to each project. If you had added any attached items in the Visual Data Manager, they would be displayed in the flexgrid.

The program can still not add, edit, or delete items from the ToDo table. To add this capability, you will need to create an additional form.

12

Creating the ToDo Entry Form

The original form will display all of the Projects table records, but the second level of the application, the ToDo items, requires an additional form.

The VB Data Form Wizard can be used again to create the foundation for the form. After this is created, you can add the code to accept either inserts or edits of new ToDo records. This form will be displayed by the buttons on the primary form.

1. Add a form to the project using the VB Data Form Wizard.

2. Configure the new form to point to the ToDo table and set the same parameters that you did creating the Project form.

You can use the wizard to automatically create the code in the form that will be used for the ToDo entry. This form will require more substantial modification.

3. Add the following code to the Form Load event:

```
Private Sub Form_Load()
    'Dim db As Connection
    'Set db = New Connection
    'db.CursorLocation = adUseClient
    'db.Open "PROVIDER=Microsoft.Jet.OLEDB.3.51;Data Source=C:\Program
    ➥Files\Microsoft Visual Studio\VB98\24hr12\hr5.mdb;"

    'Set adoPrimaryRS = New Recordset
    'adoPrimaryRS.Open "select uniqueid,itemName,itemDesc,beginDate,
    ➥done,endDate,projectid from todo", db, adOpenStatic,
    adLockOptimistic
    Set adoPrimaryRS = DataEnvironment1.rscomToDo

    Dim oText As TextBox
```

4. Pull the bottom of the form downward to provide room for two command buttons.

5. Add two command buttons and name one cmdToDoOK and the other cmdToCancel (see Figure 12.7).

FIGURE 12.7

Two command buttons added to the ToDo entry form.

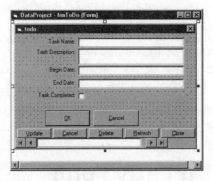

6. Set the Caption property of cmdToDoOK to &OK.

   Placing the ampersand in front of a letter in the Caption makes that letter the activation key for an Alt-key combination. You can see in the figure that the letter O is underlined.

7. Set the Default property of cmdToDoOK to True.

   This property will set the OK button to activate when the user hits the Enter key. Again, in this application try to make the user interface as similar to commercial applications as possible. Following the basic user interface customs will help the application become more successful.

8. Set the `Caption` property of cmdToDoCancel to `&Cancel`.

9. Set the `Cancel` property of cmdToDoCancel to `True`.

   Setting this property will make the Esc key activate the button.

10. Select the picButtons and picStatBox frames and set both the `Enabled` and `Visible` properties to `False`.

    These frames hold the controls for adding, updating, and navigation through the recordset. Because all navigation and setting will occur from the main form, these will just get in the way and confuse the user.

    By making the frames invisible and disabled, all the controls on these frames will also be disabled. This method is easier than deleting the controls, which can cause code that references a particular control to fault.

11. In the `Click` event of the cmdToDoOK button, insert the following code:

```
Private Sub cmdToDoOK_Click()
    DataEnvironment1.rscomToDo.Update
    Unload Me
End Sub
```

    This code is used to update a record for any edits that might occur and then unload and close the form. The `Me` referent is made to provide the pointer to the current form.

12. In the `Click` event of the cmdToDoOK button, insert the following code:

```
Private Sub cmdToDoCancel_Click()
    DataEnvironment1.rscomToDo.Cancel
    Unload Me
End Sub
```

    The ToDo entry form is now ready to go.

There is still no way to display the form. After you've added the code to the navigation buttons of the main form, you will be able to add, edit, and delete any of the tasks from the project. Because the data environment is available to all of the forms, the primary form will select the record to be edited. The ToDo form will then be displayed with the appropriate record (even if it is a newly added one).

Adding Access Buttons from the Main Form

The access buttons provide the navigation and the editing for the ToDo entries. Rather than using a Data Control–like interface, the entry is selected from the flexgrid for editing or deletion. Clicking either button displays a window to help the user complete that operation.

12

The Delete operation displays the name of the item to delete and confirms the user
choice before continuing. The Delete button is the only button that will not display the
frmToDo form.

1. Add the following code to the Click event of the cmdToDoAdd button:

```
Private Sub cmdToDoAdd_Click()
    With DataEnvironment1.rscomToDo
        .Close
        .Open "select * from todo", , adOpenDynamic
        .AddNew
        ' Set foriegn key to current project
        .Fields("ProjectID") = DataEnvironment1.rscomProjects.Fields
➥("ProjectID")
    End With
    frmToDo.Show 1
    ' Update the display
    DataEnvironment1.rscomProjects.Requery
    Set myRS = DataEnvironment1.rscomProjects.Fields("comTodoView").
➥Value
End Sub
```

You can see from the code that the recordset of the comToDo object in the data
environment is closed and then re-opened. The dynamic setting ensures that the
recordset can be edited.

2. Add the following code to the Click event of the cmdToDoDelete button:

```
Private Sub cmdToDoDelete_Click()
    ' Set evaluation to first column
    flxToDoItems.Col = 0
    tempval = "" & flxToDoItems.Text
    ' Reselect row
    flxToDoItems.ColSel = 4
    If IsNumeric(tempval) Then
        With DataEnvironment1.rscomToDo
            .Close
            .Open "select * from todo where uniqueid = " & tempval
            If .RecordCount > 0 Then
                result = MsgBox("Are you sure you want to delete the
➥item: " & DataEnvironment1.rscomToDo.Fields("itemName").Value,
➥vbOKCancel, "Delete")
                If result = 1 Then
                    DataEnvironment1.rscomToDo.Delete
                    ' Update the display
                    DataEnvironment1.rscomProjects.Requery
                    Set myRS = DataEnvironment1.rscomProjects.Fields
➥("comTodoView").Value
                End If
            End If
        End With
    End If
End Sub
```

3. Add the following code to the Click event of the cmdToDoAdd button:

```
Private Sub cmdToDoEdit_Click()
    ' Set evaluation to first column
    flxToDoItems.Col = 0
    tempval = "" & flxToDoItems.Text
    ' Reselect row
    flxToDoItems.ColSel = 4
    If IsNumeric(tempval) Then
        With DataEnvironment1.rscomToDo
            .Close
            .Open "select * from todo where uniqueid = " & tempval
            If .RecordCount > 0 Then
                frmToDo.Show 1
                'DataEnvironment1.rscomProjects.Requery
                'Set myRS = DataEnvironment1.rscomProjects.Fields
➡ ("comTodoView").Value
            End If
        End With
    End If
End Sub
```

4. Execute the application.

The application will now be able to add new task records. As you navigate through the projects, the flexgrid will automatically be updated to reflect the current project. Selecting one of the ToDo items in the flexgrid and clicking the Edit button (see Figure 12.8) will display the record for editing in the form.

FIGURE 12.8

Editing a current ToDo record entry.

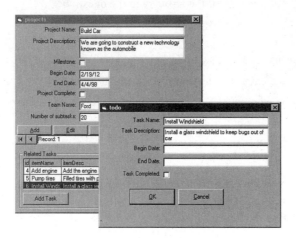

12

This complete application, particularly the modification code located in the Form Load events to access the data environment, can be used as a model for your applications.

Summary

This project has been the most complicated you have created so far. You enabled two forms to work interactively, created a hierarchical Command object relation, and connected wizard code to a data environment. Most database applications you will encounter will use variations of these concepts.

Q&A

Q Can a Data Control be used for multiple form solutions rather than the data environment?

A Providing access to a Data Control on another form is possible using public properties, but it is hardly worth the effort. Unless you need a project that is convertible to older versions of Visual Basic, use the data environment or the ADO objects directly for multi-form solutions.

Q Can controls on multiple forms be bound to the same Command object?

A Yes. The data environment provides a global way of accessing unified data sources.

Workshop

The quiz questions and exercises are provided for your further understanding. See Appendix C, "Answers," for the answers to the questions.

Quiz

1. True or False: The data environment doesn't require initialization.
2. Is the data environment the only way to share a recordset across multiple forms?
3. How do you create a Command object as a child of another Command object?
4. What does setting a relation for parent/child objects do?
5. What property is used to set ToolTip text for a control?

Exercises

1. Establish a data environment to the Northwind database. Create a form that displays all of the Order Details items in the flexgrid as the orders are displayed on the main form.
2. Add error detection code that allows the frmToDo window to be used as a non-modal window.

HOUR 13

Data Reporting

New in Visual Basic 6 is the ability to design complete reports from within the VB environment. Previously, only a special version of Crystal Reports was available for report generation. For a robust report design environment, Microsoft Access had to be used.

For the first time, a complete reporting environment has been integrated into VB that can take advantage of its data access capabilities. In the VB environment, a Data Report can be bound directly to objects in a data environment.

The highlights of this hour include:

- Overview of the data reporting system
- Exporting to HTML files
- Creating a Data Report from the Orders table
- Using multiple hierarchical tables in a report
- Coding the HTML export method calls

Data Report Overview

With most database applications, creating printed output of information is critical. A Data Report can be created in Visual Basic to print the output of queries in a professional format.

A Data Report is stored as a file similar to a VB form file. Like a form, global properties can be set for the report. These properties include BorderStyle, LeftMargin, RightMargin, and so on.

By default, when it is displayed, a report will show a preview window containing an image of the report that will be sent to the printer. The power of the Data Report is apparent in these features:

- Graphical VB report construction
- Automatic preview before printing
- Integration of VB code into the report processing
- Asynchronous operation for background processing
- HTML report export

Optional methods allow the report to be sent directly to the printer, a text file, or a formatted HTML file. These options provide the ability to easily publish a report to a file server or Web page.

The Data Report itself is created in a user-friendly form-like environment built into Visual Basic. In a Visual Basic project, Data Report files have the DSR extension like data environment files. The creation of the Data Report is accomplished by defining the various bands or sections that make up a report.

 A *band* is an area on a Data Report that is repeated as necessary, such as a Page Header or a Detail band.

Banded Hierarchical Reports

Each Data Report is made up of a series of bands or sections. Because the report can extend over a great number of pages, a band itself can flow over a page border.

There are only four primary types of bands: Report Header/Footer, Page Header/Footer, Group Header/Footer, and Detail bands. If you view the bands almost like peeling an onion, the Report Header/Footer is the outermost band, whereas the Details band is the innermost.

Report Header and Footer

The Report Header and Footer surround the report itself. These might contain the report title, the print date of the report, and other information relevant to the entire report.

Because the header only appears once on the report, it can be used to explain the general information concerning the report generation such as the query parameters. This section is also the place where an organization will typically place a logo or headline graphic.

The `ForcePageBreak` property can be set to `1 - rptPageBreakAfter` if you want the header or footer to appear alone on the page. This essentially creates a "title" page for the report.

Page Header and Footer

The Page Header and Footer bands will appear at the top and bottom of each page of the report. Page information is usually included in these bands in much the same way headers and footers are used for a word processing document.

The headers and footers are added to the page margins. Therefore, the margins should be set to determine where the headers and footers should begin.

 The margins for the header and footer of the page are set with properties for the `Data Report` object. These properties can be set either at design-time or runtime.

The Data Report also allows dynamic variable information to be included. This information might vary over the course of the report (such as the page number) or might be set before the report has been generated (such as the report title). On the Page Header or Footer band, you can include any of these dynamic variables:

Code	Function
%t	Short format Current Time
%d	Short format Current Date
%p	Page Number
%P	Total Page Numbers (for example, 2 of 45 pages)
%i	Report Title
%D	Current Date
%T	Current Time

These variables are added to the report by including them in labels with a Data Report code. These codes all begin with the percent (%) sign. To include a normal percent character in the label, use another sign directly following the first (%%).

13

Group Header and Footer

The Group bands are used to display the results of a hierarchical query. Hierarchical queries are essentially queries within queries. For example, a hierarchical query might return all the sales invoices in the last month as well as the individual sales for each invoice.

The Group section allows you to simply display summary invoice information, as well as itemize the sold items directly following each invoice number.

Related tables would use the Group Header and Footer to show the primary table information that would surround the more specific data presented in the Detail band.

Detail Bands

Although the other bands are used to present summary information for the report, the Detail section contains the controls for the actual data. The Detail band is the most critical section of the report. It provides the actual repeating part of the Data Report used to step through recordsets.

The Detail band is used to display the fields of a particular record using bound controls placed in the section. There are seven controls that can be used on any of the bands: RptLabel, RptTextbox, RptImage, RptLine, RptShape, RptPicture, and RptFunction. Only the RptLine control is not data-aware.

If all of the contacts in an address book needed to be displayed, the fields could be added to a Detail band to display them sequentially in the report.

Data Export Report

One of the most powerful features included with the Data Reporter is the ability to output the report as an HTML document. After the report is saved in HTML it can be easily:

- Posted to a Web page for easy intranet access
- Emailed to individuals who need to view it
- Downloaded to a handheld PC such as a Windows CE or Palm Pilot device for viewing
- Archived for later view and/or historical record

Because it requires only a little extra work to make this functionality available within your program, it is usually worth the effort. The extra coding involves invoking only one method, although the path and the filename where the report is to be stored will have to be determined.

Like a printed report, make sure the header or the footer of the report includes pertinent information such as the date the report was generated. Because a Web page might be left in place for a great while, providing the date context is critical. The more information you supply about the context in which the report was generated, the better understood the report will be when viewed apart from the time and place it was created.

The Data Report can also export its information in text file format. This includes both ASCII and Unicode output options.

Exporting the report is accomplished using the `ExportReport` method. Passing the method a report type constant (`rptKeyHTML`, `rptKeyUnicodeHTML_UTF8`, `rptKeyText`, or `rptKeyUnicodeText`) determines what type of output is generated.

If no parameter follows the report type, a file dialog box will be displayed to ask the user for the output filename. To create an HTML report, you would use the method like this:

```
DataReport1.ExportReport rptKeyHTML
```

To write to a specific filename and overwrite any existing file of the same name, this code could be used:

```
DataReport1.ExportReport rptKeyHTML, _
        "c:\myReport", True
```

The method will automatically add the .htm extension for a file of myReport.htm if no extension is specified.

Visual Basic can create ActiveX DLLs that can be used by either the Personal Web Server (PWS) or the Internet Information Server (IIS). You can use the HTML export capabilities to create a control that builds a custom HTML report when a particular Web page is activated.

13

Creating a Report from the Northwind Database

The Northwind database has a large amount of information already available, so it provides the perfect database to demonstrate the data report features. It also features related information that can be used to demonstrate hierarchical data sources.

You will quickly and easily create a report that displays order information, breaks down the orders into the various order details, and exports the report to HTML files.

The report you create will display the individual orders from the Orders table. You will then modify the report to show all the individual order items in the OrderDetails table. Finally, a button will be added to the project that will output the report as an HTML file.

After you've completed the construction of this sample report, you will understand how the report generator works and how it can be connected to multiple Command objects for robust information reporting.

Starting the Report

Although creating a report is straightforward, it is a good idea to begin by making a simple one. The report can then be enhanced to display more complex data. All the data access will occur through data sources you will create within the data environment.

Each report can be configured to point at a primary data source. In this project, the report will connect to the comOrders object in the DataEnvironment1, which will be configured to address the Northwind database.

To create the report, all the necessary technology is included with the standard Data Project. The controls you will find under the DataReports tab on the toolbox palette. You will start with a fresh VB project so you can see exactly what technology is used by the Data Report.

1. Create a new Data Project.

   The application, on the surface, will be much like the ones you've created in earlier projects. You will need a connection to the Northwind database so access to the tables is possible for use in the report.

2. Add a data source to connect to the Northwind database.

3. Configure the Connection object of the data environment to the point to NWind.mdb.

   Use the standard Microsoft Jet 3.51 OLE DB Provider and browse to select the database.

   The connection will provide an access method to connect to the Orders table that will be the primary dataset to be displayed in the report.

4. Create a Command object attached to the Orders table named comOrders.

5. Open the Data Report that is part of the project.

   In a Data Project, a report is automatically added to the project. Data Reports appear under the Designers folder, which you can see in the Project window. You'll use this default report to add the necessary bands.

Adding a new Data Report is just like adding a new form. You can select the Add Data Report option under the Project menu.

6. Set the Name property of the report to rptOrders.

Naming the report properly is important because the report is accessed like a form. Therefore, code must be used to call the report. If the name isn't clear, your code will be difficult to read.

7. Set the Caption property to Orders Report.

This caption will appear at the top of the report window when it is generated for a print preview.

For every report, there must be an associated data source that will be used to build the report and attach bound controls. In this report, you'll use the comOrders object in DataEnvironment1.

8. In the DataSource property, select DataEnvironment1.

9. Set the DataMember property to comOrders.

10. Right-click in the main band and select Retrieve Structure.

Make sure you have the Data Environment window open. It will be used to drag fields onto the report.

11. Drag the following fields into the Detail band:

OrderDate

ShippedDate

ShipName

OrderID

Just like dragging bound controls onto a form, drag the fields into the Detail band. Don't worry about the order of the fields at this time.

12. Drag the labels into the Header band.

The display will look like a standard column presentation of a dataset. By placing them in the header, the field names will not be reprinted with each record.

13. Position the fields below the appropriate headers and shrink both bands to the size of the fields (see Figure 13.1).

13

FIGURE **13.1**

FIGURE **13.1**

The fields and labels are correctly positioned and the bands resized.

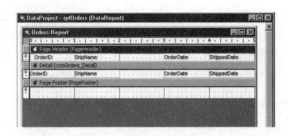

14. In the Page Footer band, right-click the mouse button.

    The context menu from this selection allows you to insert numerous controls directly into the report.

15. From the Insert Control submenu, select the Current Page Number option.

    You will see a Label control inserted into the footer that contains only the caption text %p. When the report is run, this text will be replaced by the current page number. By using a capital P in the same way, the total number of pages would be returned. Therefore, you can easily create a label to read *x* of *xx* pages.

16. Set the Caption property of the label to %p of %P pages.

17. Resize the footer to include just the label (see Figure 13.2).

FIGURE **13.2**

The page numbers label added to the footer.

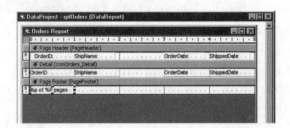

The report is now ready to be activated. You have to add some simple code to display the form. This can be easily accomplished by adding a command button to the default form.

The report is treated just like a form. In fact, it can even be set as the Startup object for the project. However, in this project, you will simply add a command button that will be used to activate the report through VB code.

18. Open the form frmDataEnv.

19. Add a command button and set the Name property to cmdReport.

20. To the Click event of the button, add the following code:

```
Private Sub cmdReport_Click()
    rptOrders.Show
End Sub
```

You will notice that the Show method is used just like a form. Likewise, you can load the report early in order to set various properties if this is needed for the report.

21. Execute the application.

    You should see a report like the one shown in Figure 13.3. If you scroll to the bottom of the report, you will even see the page footer notifying you that this page is 1 of 19 pages.

FIGURE 13.3

Finished report generated from the Orders table.

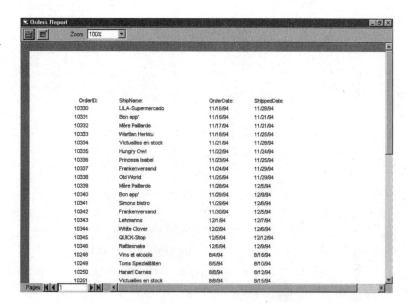

This report will be similar to most of the simple reports you will generate. With the addition of more attractive headers and footers, you have a professional report. However, there is data that requires more complex treatment for presentation.

Augmenting the Report

Because you now have a working report to show you all the most important summary information about the order, how about being able to report on the details of each order?

By adding a Command object under the Orders object that accesses the Order Details table and then relating the two, these can be used in the project to display a complete report.

13

After this new object is added to the data environment, it is a simple task to modify the report to display this additional level of information.

1. Open the data environment.

   You need to add the new Command object underneath the current one. That way it will be active hierarchically to display all of the details of each record in the parent recordset.

2. Right-click on the comOrders object and select the Add Child Command option.

   You can see that a Command object is added hierarchically underneath the current Command object (see Figure 13.4).

3. Open the Properties window of the second Command object.

4. Set the Name of the object to comOrderDetails.

5. Select the Database object as Table and the Object Name to Order Details.

6. Select the Relation tab.

   When you look at the Relation tab, you can see Visual Basic automatically checked the Relate to a Parent Command Object check box and selected the comOrders parent in the combo box. Also, the OrderID field is selected in both the Parent Fields and Child Fields combo boxes.

7. Click the Add button in the Relation Definition frame.

   By adding the link, the Command object will now have a relation between the two tables (see Figure 13.5).

8. Click the OK button to accept the Command object properties.

   Leave the Data Environment window open because in a moment you will need to drag the fields onto the report.

FIGURE 13.5

Relating the two
Command *objects*
through the OrderID
field.

9. Open the Data Report.

10. Right-click in the Detail band and select Retrieve Structure.

This option will cause all the fields you placed in the data report before to be eliminated. This destruction is necessary because the structure of the data source has
been fundamentally altered.

11. Click the Yes button to continue.

Visual Basic will retrieve the new data structure and reformat the report to reflect it
(see Figure 13.6).

FIGURE 13.6

The reformatted Data
Report reflects the new
child Command *object.*

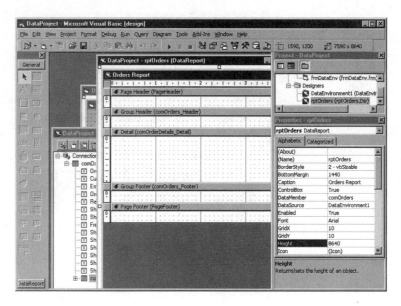

13

The Group Header band now has the object it will display in parentheses as comOrders while the Detail band specifies comOrderDetails. You'll need to start the reconstruction by adding the Orders fields to the Group Header.

12. Drag these fields onto the Group Header band:

    OrderDate

    ShippedDate

    ShipName

    OrderID

    Again, move the labels into the Page Header. If you want a little change this time, you can set the Font properties of these labels to bold to make them stand out.

    After you have formatted all these fields, you can begin to add the information from the child Command object.

13. Drag the following fields onto the Detail band:

    ProductID

    ShippedDate

    ShipName

    OrderID

14. Drag the labels into the Group Header (see Figure 13.7).

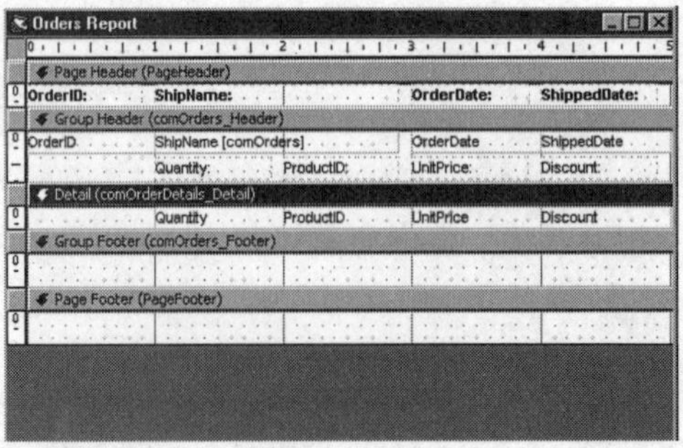

FIGURE 13.7

Completed Detail band with the new fields.

15. Insert the Current Page Number control into the Page Footer band and set the
    `Caption` property to `%p of %P Pages`.

16. Execute the application and click on the command button.

    The Data Report now generated (see Figure 13.8) contains both levels of data inte-
    grated into a single report.

FIGURE 13.8

*Executing the new
report reveals all the
details of each order.*

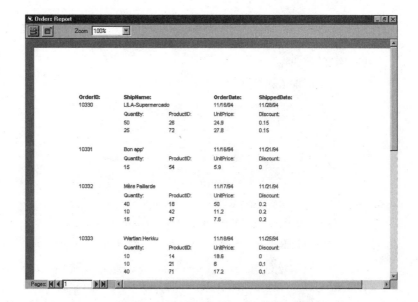

The report can actually take more than two levels of grouping by adding additional
`Command` objects. Remember, the more levels of complexity you add to the report, the
slower the processing of the report will be.

Although the Data Report can display one `Command` object child, it cannot
display more than one child from the same `Command` object. From the Data
Report you will only be able to access the first child object. Therefore, for
tables to be used in a Data Report, make sure all of your hierarchical
`Command` objects have only one child that needs to be displayed.

13

You can see how powerful this technology can be. Recognize that generating a hierarchical report requires far more processing than a simple report because for each record, all
of the connected child records must be located and displayed.

After the report has been created, the simplest option is to print it. However, the Data Report is far more powerful. It can easily be exported in a number of formats.

Exporting the Report to HTML

Instead of simply displaying or printing the report, it could instead be output as a text or HTML file (in either ASCII or Unicode format).

Because the report is functioning properly, you can now add a few lines of code to make the report export into HTML format. By using the ExportReport method, you can save the report to disk.

1. Open the form frmDataEnv.

2. Add a command button and set the Name property to cmdExport.

3. Add the following code to the Click event of the button:
   ```
   Private Sub cmdExport_Click()
       rptOrders.ExportReport rptKeyHTML, _
           "C:\Temp\OrderReport", True, _
           , rptRangeAllPages
   End Sub
   ```

4. Execute the application and click the command button.

   An OrderReport.htm file will be created in the Temp folder of the C: drive.

The ability to output the report provides substantial extra capability. In this example, the file was simply written to the Temp directory. By writing it with a common filename into an active Web directory, it could be immediately available to a Web browser.

Toolbox Controls

A Data Report is much like a form, but it cannot use standard ActiveX controls embedded within it. Instead, VB ships with a number of custom ActiveX controls available under the special DataReports tab of the toolbox palette that can be used on any report.

When a Data Report window is open, the toolbox palette (see Figure 13.9) allows selection of the specialized controls that are made to be used within a Data Report. Each of the controls is the parallel control of an OCX available for use on a standard form.

The six controls included with Visual Basic are

- TextBox control—format text or assign a DataFormat
- Label control—label fields and sections
- Image control—although it can be an image it cannot be bound

- Line control—draws simple lines on the report
- Shape control—draws rectangles, ovals, and triangles
- Function control—a text box that calculates a value when the report is generated

FIGURE 13.9

The Data Report tab in the toolbox palette reveals six Data Report controls.

All these controls can be used by placing them with particular bands of the final report. The data environment allows drag-and-drop support onto a band and will insert the proper TextBox and Label controls to represent the desired field.

Summary

The Data Report allows you to easily add a complete reporting mechanism to your Visual Basic applications. In addition to supporting standard report capabilities, the Data Reporter is able to export reports to text or HTML formatted files.

By creating a multiple level Data Report from two hierarchical Command objects, you were able to represent most of the crucial order information stored in the database in a single report.

Q&A

Q Can reports from one project be imported into another?

A Yes. The files are stored as DSR files, so importing works the same as exchanging a form with another project. If you have the report bound to a data environment, be sure to transfer this file to the new project as well.

13

Q Is there a way to send the report directly to the printer without a preview?

A Yes, and it takes up less memory when the report is generated. Simply use the command:

```
DataReport1.PrintReport True
```

in which the `True` parameter will display the printing dialog box. Sending `False` will simply print the report without any display.

Workshop

The quiz questions and exercises are provided for your further understanding. See Appendix C, "Answers," for the answers to the questions.

Quiz

1. Can an HTML report be generated by the Data Reporter?
2. True or False: Images can be display on the report from linked fields in the database.
3. How can multiple tables be used in a report?
4. What report control can be used to display a calculated field?
5. Can code be executed within a report?

Exercises

1. Create a Data Report of children objects for the hr5.mdb. List all of the projects and the ToDo items that are related to each project.
2. Using the Timer control, set up the Data Report to automatically publish an HTML report to a specified directory every hour. If you have a Web server on the machine, publish the directory to see it automatically updated by the application.

Hour 14

Graphing Data

Graphical representation of certain types of data can be extremely useful. The old saying "A picture is worth a thousand words" is especially true when analyzing quantities of data. Although overall trends are often difficult to discern in a table format, graphs make these same trends immediately apparent.

Toward this end, Microsoft has included the Microsoft Graph control that can display data in a variety of graphical formats. The Graph control is also data-aware, making database interaction a simple proposition.

The highlights of this hour include

- Overview of the MS Graph control
- Binding data from the Data Environment
- Binding data using a dynamic ADO connection
- Adding data to the control manually
- Using constants to specify the graph type

Overview of the Graph Control

Included with Visual Basic is the powerful Microsoft Graph control that can display numerous chart types. Most of these graphs are available in both 2D and 3D renderings.

The data from the graphs can have three primary sources: random data, a Data Grid object, or a ADO data source. The Graph control can be bound directly to a Data control or Data Environment.

The chart types supported by the control include

- Pie charts
- Bar/Pictograph charts or histograms
- Line/Log charts
- Area charts
- XY or Scatter charts
- Step charts
- High/Low/Close charts

Because the only primary difference between these chart types is the number of data sets that they graph (that is, pie charts are only one-dimensional, whereas bar charts are two-dimensional), the graph type can even be reset at runtime without reinitializing the data display.

> The Graph control will add approximately 700KB to your project. Before implementing a project that uses the Graph control, realize that it will require a larger install image and memory to execute.

The Microsoft Chart control is like any other OCX component. You can add it to the project in the Components option under the Project menu as Microsoft Chart control. In Figure 14.1, you'll see an example of some of the basic chart types possible with the control.

Setting the type of chart is as simple as specifying a single property. The ChartType property indicates the graph type to display. By default, random data is used to display the chart. For this reason, the charts will appear populated even at design-time.

If you don't want the random data to appear, the RandomFill property can be set to false. During testing, it is usually a good idea to leave it active so the chart, legend, and axes can be examined more realistically.

FIGURE 14.1

Sample form with graph types.

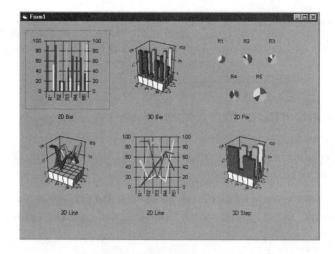

FIGURE 14.1

Sample form with graph types.

 If the graphing capabilities of the Microsoft Graph control are too limited, you can use the Excel Object Model to control Excel. That way all the graphing technology of Excel can be utilized.

To fill the chart with information, the easiest method is binding it directly to a Command object in the Data Environment that has been explicitly created to return only the data needed for display.

Binding the Graph Control

The Graph control has the capability to be bound to a data source in much the same way as a text box or list box control. Unlike other controls, selecting the fields to appear within the control is not as convenient. Other bound controls enable you to select the field to bind to the control. Because multiple data sets are used in a graph, the standard interface isn't possible.

Instead, the Graph control expects the data to already be culled from the table data for the numeric values that are to be graphed. Although an entire table can be sent to the control, this will cause the control to attempt graphing all the fields (numeric and non-numeric) in the chart.

For this reason, both in code and within the Data Environment, you can use the SQL language to select just the fields to be displayed. Don't worry if you don't understand SQL yet because Visual Basic has tools included to graphically construct the language commands.

14

> The data-aware capabilities of the Graph control are new to the control available with Visual Basic 6 through the ADO technology. If you're creating a project with an older version of VB, you will need to load all data manually.

Binding in Design-Time

Using the Data Environment to bind to the Chart control is not much more difficult than the general table connections that you are familiar with creating. After the data source has been added, binding it to the control is possible by setting only two properties.

In this section, you will construct a complete Chart that graphs the unit price of some of the products that are present in the Northwind database. You can start this project from scratch and quickly generate the entire application.

1. Start a new Data Project.

   The Data Project type, which you have used many times by now, includes all the data aware controls that you'll need except the Graph control itself. You'll have to add the component later. First, you can configure the data environment to return the data that will be graphed.

2. Open the Data Environment.

   The Data Project wizard will automatically add a Data Environment with a single Connection object. This connection will be used to access the NWind.mdb file.

3. Configure it to point to the Northwind database.

   Using the Properties window of the Connection1 object you will find the traditional connection configuration settings. Under the Provider tab set the OLE DB Provider to the Microsoft Jet 3.51 OLE DB Provider. Under the Connection tab, select the Northwind database (NWind.mdb).

4. Add a new Command object to the connection.

5. In the Properties window, set the Name of the Command object to comProducts.

   With the Command object named, now you need to configure it to properly point at the data to be returned. In this case, you need to create a SQL language query to return specific product information.

6. Click on the SQL Statement radio button.

   SQL, the query language that will be described in detail in Hour 18, "Using SQL," is used to specify the fields that you want to retrieve from the database. After all, not all the information contained in a table will need to be graphed. By creating a SQL statement to retrieve only the data you need, the Graph control can simply graph this data.

Don't worry that you don't understand the SQL language yet. Microsoft has included a wizard known as the SQL Builder that will create these statements for you with a simple user interface.

When you select the radio button, you will see that the SQL statement box becomes enabled, as does the SQL Builder command button (see Figure 14.2).

FIGURE 14.2

The Command *object with the SQL statement text box activated.*

7. Click on the SQL Builder button to display the wizard.

You will see the Data View window and a window labeled Design: comProducts (see Figure 14.3). The Data View window enables you to drag data sources onto the SQL Builder window for use within queries.

FIGURE 14.3

The SQL Builder and Data View windows.

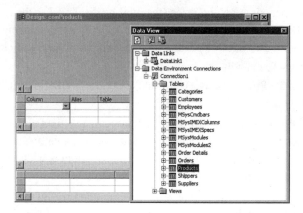

If you expand the Connection1 item and the Tables folder within it, you will see all the tables available in the Northwind database. From this list, you can drag table references into the wizard so they can be used within a query.

14

8. Click on the Products table and drag it into the SQL Builder table area.

When you release the table over the table area, a small window will be added that displays all the fields or columns of the table (see Figure 14.4).

FIGURE 14.4

The Products table after it has been added to the SQL Builder table area.

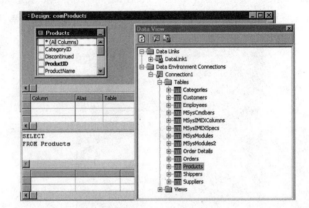

You can close the Data View window now if it is in your way because you have already added the only table you'll need for this example. To display the Data View window again, you can use the View menu or the icon on the main VB toolbar.

With the table in the wizard, the fields that are going to be used by the graph must be selected. For the graph, you will need the product name (to display as labels along the axis), the unit price (that will be displayed as the numeric value to be graphed), and the supplier ID number (to reduce the number of items to be graphed). The wizard provides a simple way to select the fields that will be returned by the query.

9. Check the ProductName, UnitPrice, and SupplierID fields in the Products table window.

Checking these fields will add them to the list of field data that will be returned by the query. The ProductName field contains the name of each product whereas the UnitPrice is the item's price. The SupplierID field is what you will use to limit the amount of data returned.

There are a great number of products contained within the Products table of the Northwind database. For this example, displaying all the product makes the graph cluttered and unreadable.

By setting an arbitrary criterion, such as numerically limiting the items displayed using the supplier ID, the chart will be more easily readable.

10. In the Criteria column of the SupplierID row, enter the text <5 (see Figure 14.5).

FIGURE 14.5

The SQL Builder with criteria adds to the SupplierID field.

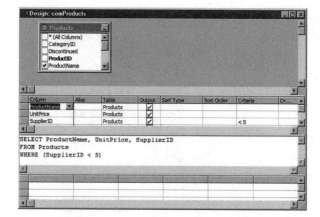

The number 5 limit was chosen because this provided a reasonable amount of display information given the default data that exists in the Northwind database. As a test, you might later remove this criteria and view the chart with every product contained in the table displayed.

11. Close the SQL Builder window and click the OK button to update the Command object.

    You might have noticed that at the bottom of the SQL Builder window a statement was being constructed (it began with Select ...). This is the actual SQL code that is entered into the Command object and used to execute the query.

12. Open the frmDataEnv form.

    The Data Project Wizard automatically creates a single form that you will use to add the Chart control.

13. Add the Microsoft Chart Control 6.0 (OLEDB) using the Components option under the project menu.

    The Microsoft Chart control should then appear as an icon on the VB tool palette.

14. Expand the form and draw the Graph control on the form as shown in Figure 14.6.

    The size of the form should cover a large portion of the screen.

If the control is not large enough on the form, the axis labels will not be drawn. Therefore, if your graph isn't showing the axis labels, try enlarging the size of the control on the form.

14

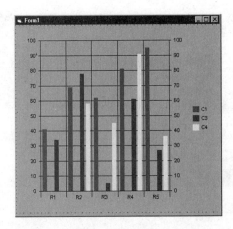

15. Set the Data Source property to DataEnvironment1.

16. Set the Data Member property to comProducts.

17. Set the ShowLegend property to True.

18. Execute the application.

   You will see the chart shown in Figure 14.7. The data displayed was retrieved from
   the Products table of the bound Data Environment.

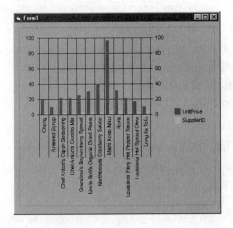

Hiding the SupplierID Field

The SupplierID field is the field used to limit the amount of data returned by setting the criteria and is included in the returned data set for this reason. Although it is necessary in the query, there is no reason to include it in the graphed data.

You could return to the SQL code and modify the code by hand to not include this field in the returned data set. However, the Chart control itself enables configuration of how the data is displayed. By modifying a property on the control itself, you can exclude data that should not appear.

1. Stop the application by closing the window or clicking on the Visual Basic Stop toolbar icon.

   If you left it executing in the previous section, you need to halt execution so you can make changes to some of the properties.

2. Open the Custom properties window by right-clicking the chart and selecting the Properties option.

   Although most properties are available in the standard Properties window, the Chart control has a custom property wizard so modification of certain features specific to a chart can be made easily.

3. Select the Series tab.

   Each set of data is known as a series. In the bar chart that you created, there are two series included in the data set. The first series is the UnitPrice that should be graphed. The second, the SupplierID, should be ignored.

4. Use the series combo box to select the series C2.

5. Click on the Exclude series check box (see Figure 14.8).

   Selecting the Exclude option means that the Chart control will entirely ignore data received in this column.

FIGURE 14.8

Excluding the SupplierID series from the Graph.

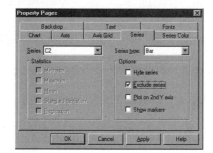

14

6. Click the OK button to accept the property changes.

7. Execute the application.

Your Chart should now be perfect (see Figure 14.9). The final chart will display only the UnitPrice data, as well as the horizontal axis labeled with the names of each product.

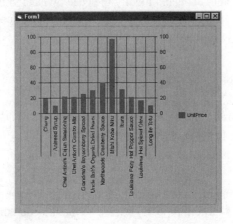

Binding with Code

Although binding the control at design-time is extremely convenient, there are often times when the data set will have to be created at runtime. This is especially the case when provided drill-down support for data analysis.

By using the ADO data connections, you can bind the Chart by setting the proper reference for the DataSource property. To construct this example, you can simply modify the existing application that has its data source in the Data Environment.

1. Clear the Data Member and Data Source properties.

   In the Properties window, select the text in these properties and press the backspace or delete keys to leave them blank. This will clear the references to the current data environment. It will be easier to see the data populate the chart if the initial presentation is simply the random data.

2. Add a command button and set the Name property to cmdLoadData.

   You'll now add code to the command button that will select the data to be displayed in the graph. It will use the ADO connection (described in Hour 17, "Understanding ActiveX Data Objects (ADO),") to create a new connection. First you will need to define Connection and Recordset objects that will be used to hold the graph data.

3. Enter the following code into the General Declarations section of the form:

```
Dim myRS As New ADODB.Recordset
Dim myConnect As New ADODB.Connection
```

The data loading code will open a connection to the Northwind database. Using a custom SQL string not unlike the one created by the SQL Builder, the data will be selected into a recordset. Then the recordset will be connected to the graph control using the DataSource property.

4. Enter the following code into the Click event of the command button:

```
Private Sub cmdLoadData_Click()
    Dim myStr As String

    ' Create new connection to the Northwind database_
    myConnect.ConnectionString = _
    "Provider=Microsoft.Jet.OLEDB.3.51;Data Source=" & _
    "C:\Program Files\Microsoft Visual Studio\VB98\nwind.mdb"
    ' Open the connection
    myConnect.Open

    ' Set up SQL query string
    myStr = "Select ProductName, UnitPrice, " & _
    " FROM Products WHERE SupplierID < 5"

    myRS.Open myStr, myConnect, adOpenKeyset
    MSChart1.ShowLegend = True
    Set MSChart1.DataSource = myRS
End Sub
```

5. Execute the application and click the Command button.

You might notice that the code in the SQL query string line differs slightly from the SQL code generated by the SQL Builder. In the first part of the SQL statement (after the Select and before the From), the SupplierID has not been included.

Do you remember when you excluded this field from the final graph? With this SQL code, the SupplierID field isn't even included in the returned recordset.

Because this query is opened dynamically at runtime, any database query can be used to supply data to the graph at runtime. This enables the program to enable the user to select parameters that will be used in the query and displayed in the chart.

Adding Data Manually

Although binding data sources is quick and simple, there are often situations where the requirements are more complicated. Data might need to be totaled or massaged before it is appropriate for display.

14

The Chart control enables the data displayed to be added manually. All the data can be stored within the Data Object that is contained within the control. By adding another button to the existing project, these features can be demonstrated.

1. Add a command button and set the Name property to cmdManualGraph.

   The code you add will set up the graph to display 10 columns of data added by a For...Next loop. After the code sets the number of columns (ColumnCount property) and the number of rows (RowCount property), the legend is added. Each row contains the actual numeric data value to be displayed, just like the row in a table.

2. Enter the following code into the Click event:

```
Private Sub cmdManualGraph_Click()
    With Form1.MSChart1
        .ChartType = VtChChartType3dBar
        .ColumnCount = 10
        .RowCount = 10
        For column = 1 To 10
            For row = 1 To 10
                .Column = column
                .Row = row
                .Data = row * 10
            Next row
        Next column
        .SelectPart VtChPartTypePlot, index1, index2, _
index3, index4
        .EditCopy
        .SelectPart VtChPartTypeLegend, index1, _
index2, index3, index4
        .EditPaste
    End With
End Sub
```

3. Execute the application and click on the new button.

The chart will now be modified to show the data that was created dynamically within the code.

Recordset

In Hour 17, you'll learn about using the ActiveX Data Objects (ADO). One of the methods included with the ADO model is the GetRows method. This method will load specified rows into an array that is passed back to the calling routine.

You can use the GetRows method to get the data need to populate the Chart control. Simply add the data to the chart using a method such as the one shown in the previous section and you can determine exactly what data will be presented and how it will appear.

Chart Type Constants

In Table 14.1, you can see the list of constants that can be used to define the type of chart. The chartType property can accept any one of these values and can be adjusted either at design-time or runtime.

TABLE 14.1 TYPES OF CHARTS

Constant Name	Description
VtChChartType3dBar	3D Bar chart
VtChChartType2dBar	2D Bar chart
VtChChartType3dLine	3D Line chart
VtChChartType2dLine	2D Line chart
VtChChartType3dArea	3D Area chart
VtChChartType2dArea	2D Area chart
VtChChartType3dStep	3D Step chart
VtChChartType2dStep	2D Step chart
VtChChartType3dCombination	3D Combination chart
VtChChartType2dCombination	2D Combination chart
VtChChartType2dPie	2D Pie chart
VtChChartType2dXY	2D XY chart

You can use any of these constants to set the display appearance of the Chart.

Summary

The Microsoft Chart control makes displaying data in a graphical format extremely simple. Because a Data Environment, recordset, or Data Control can be directly bound to the Chart control, information can be charted instantly.

Most of the characteristics of the control can be set either at design-time or runtime. Although the control itself has a fairly large footprint, the flexibility that it provides will fulfill most of the needs of a program that needs charting capability.

14

Q&A

Q Can I access the data shown in the Chart?

A Yes. Through the Data Object, all the displayed values can be addressed. If the information comes from a bound data source, it would probably be easier to address the fields directly.

Q Is it possible to use multiple Command objects on the same chart?

A No, only one data source can be bound at a time. Using advanced hierarchical Command objects, information could be retrieved from multiple places, but this requires a complex implementation.

Q Can I set the colors shown in the Chart?

A Yes. In the Custom properties dialog, the color values of each series can be set. The color properties can also be addressed at runtime for dynamic modification.

Workshop

The quiz questions and exercises are provided for your further understanding. See Appendix C, "Answers," for the answers to the questions.

Quiz

1. True or False: The Microsoft Graph control is data-aware.

2. What two properties must be set to bind the graph to a data source?

3. Can the graph be bound to a data source at runtime?

4. Is a SQL statement required to use the Chart control?

5. What could the problem be if the labels for one of the chart axes don't appear?

6. How do you make a series invisible?

7. What is a Data Grid object?

Exercises

1. Add radio buttons to the current form and enable the user at runtime to determine the type of chart used to display the data.

2. Create a table Command object in the Data Environment. Connect the table to the Chart control and observe the results of many fields and non-numeric data as the chart attempts to graph them.

Hour 15

Multi-User Database Design

Often database applications are constructed for use in a networked environment. The database file is placed on a file server and shared by a number of people. Sharing the database in this method provides a simple way to centralize data collection and querying.

Supporting multiple users who have simultaneous access to a single data file requires special considerations, including potential simultaneous access problems. Visual Basic includes several options to aid you in choosing how the database engine will handle conflicts.

The highlights of this hour include:

- Sharing a database on a file server
- Configuring a `Connection` object
- Understanding locking types

Sharing with a File Server

Most applications used by more than one person eventually need to be shared. The Jet engine and the MDB format files that it accesses are made for just that sort of environment. Special features are included in the database engine to allow simultaneous access by multiple machines.

To actually use the database file in a shared environment, you only need to

- Place the file in a shared directory.
- Make sure the file server is configured so each user has read/write access to the directory that contains the database.
- Configure the data sources contained in your application to point to the file in the shared directory.

Having the file on the centralized directory will allow all the client applications to read, write, and update records to a central place. This prevents the fragmentation that occurs if the various data files are kept separately.

> The maximum number of concurrent users to a Microsoft Access database is 255. However, if you have more than 15 simultaneous users, you should consider moving your database to a more robust system such as Microsoft SQL Server.

As soon as users are simultaneously addressing a single data source, problems can arise, such as two users trying to update the same record at the same time. The Jet engine included with Visual Basic has a substantial amount of technology included to ease such problems.

Database Locking

When more than a single user needs simultaneous access, preventing users from colliding during operations such as updates is critical to providing an effective system. To this end, the Jet engine provides a complete set of locking mechanisms.

If access collisions occur, especially when they concern an operation that requires several interconnected updates, the transaction technology is used (complete information on transactions is included in Hour 21, "Sharing the Database"). By placing database operations within a transaction, errors that might cause data consistency problems can be avoided. Although the transaction technology can be used to handle problems after they

15

occur, it is more effective to prevent them in the first place. To avoid failed operations, record locking is the most common and powerful solution. When users simultaneously access a single record, a number of potential problems can occur:

- Both users attempt to update the same record, causing a data collision
- One user updates a record in the background while another user has the record visible, making the visible data out-of-date
- Both users attempt to update the same record, one after another, making the second changes write over the first
- One user deletes a record while another user is editing it

Any of these situations can cause problems with keeping your data clean. To solve this problem, databases use certain methods of locking to prevent multiple-users conflict. No method is perfect and each one has trade-offs.

> The more advanced the database system, the more precise the locking control. In Microsoft Access files (MDB), locking might occur only down to the record level. For an advanced system such as SQL Server, locking down to the field level is possible.

The locks are set up when you are configuring the connection. In Figure 15.1, you can see that the Advanced tab allows a variety of lock settings for the connection.

FIGURE 15.1

The Advanced tab of the connection properties allows configuration of locks.

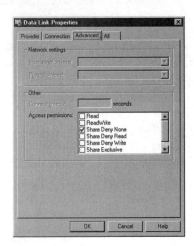

When the connection is actually made between the program and the database at runtime, the MDB file logs the user on the database as a unique user (even if no password is required). The Jet engine then uses the locking specifications made in the connection to limit the access rights of the user.

> The locks for a database are actually stored in a dynamically created file with the .LDB extension. This file is created when the first user accesses the database and holds the locking settings. The LDB file is created with the same root name as the database and is automatically deleted when the last user logs off the database.

File Locking

The simplest, safest, and most user-unfriendly method is locking the file itself while one user accesses it. Reading or writing access can be blocked. For example, a primary user is allowed to open the file with read/write access. Other users can then only read from the file.

This is known as Exclusive mode because it allows reading, but only one user can make changes. These changes include modifications to the database structure itself including changing or deleting tables.

> When you open a database in Microsoft Access that someone else already has open in Exclusive mode, a dialog warns you that you cannot make any changes to the structure.
>
> Visual Basic allows you to explicitly specify the opening method. If you request read/write access and it is not granted for the database, an error is generated with the information returned in the Error object.

By allowing only a single user to address the database at a time, you create a database that is limited in aspects of multi-user use although shared on a file server. The other locking mechanisms built into the Jet engine are far more practical for Visual Basic applications.

Pages

Before you actually begin to understand how record locking with the Jet engine works, you must understand the underlying technology of pages. Pages are used to organize a database in the background. Although you will never directly access database pages, their operation will affect your use of record locking.

15

The Jet engine uses a page organization to allow fast access to parts of a database file. A page is a section of the database file generally about 1,024 bytes (1KB) long. For managing record additions, insertions, and deletions, the file is organized into pages internally by the Jet engine to allow for faster performance.

It is normal to assume that any locking or access restrictions would occur on an individual record, but that is not the way it works. Actually, locks occur on individual pages that contain the records.

NEW TERM A *page* is a block of disk space used internally by the Jet engine to quickly manage changes to a database. Locks perform their functions on page units within the database.

Figure 15.2 shows that several small records can actually exist within a single page. Therefore, when a lock occurs, records before and after the intended record might be placed off-limits. You can see in Figure 15.2 that if record #5 were locked, the entire page #2 would be locked. This means that records #4 and #6 would be inaccessible as well.

FIGURE 15.2

Multiple records can occur within a single page.

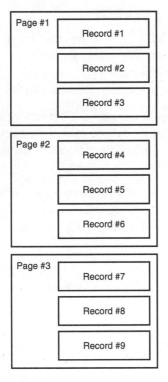

Although the figure shows each record occurring on a single page, this is not necessarily the case. If a record is large or occurs on the edge of a page, it can actually spread across two or more pages. When locking occurs, all the pages that the record even partially inhabits are locked.

This locking occurs behind the scenes. From the programmer's standpoint, the lock is placed on a single record. The database locates the page that contains the record and locks that page.

Although large database servers (such as Oracle and Informix) feature row-level locking, the Jet engine must use page-level locking for speed and performance reasons. Therefore, if you encounter an error writing to a record that isn't locked, you might be attempting a write onto a locked page.

Page locking also occurs within the index definition. Indexes are managed on pages as well. Most often when a lock is encountered and the user knows that the current record isn't being edited by anyone, the lock occurs because the index page is locked for an update.

Shared and Exclusive Locking

Because locking occurs on individual pages, it is important to select the right locking method for your application. Choosing the proper lock minimizes the number of errors potentially generated by data collision situations. The simplest locks to manage are those placed on the entire database, such as Shared or Exclusive locks.

An Exclusive lock allows only a single user for whatever lock type is set (that is, deny-read and so on). If the entire database is opened in Exclusive mode, other users are denied access to it. To make changes in the structure of the database requires you to open it with exclusive privileges.

The database engine itself will momentarily switch resources within a database into Exclusive mode. For example, when updating an index used in a referential integrity relation, for the duration of the update the index pages being modified are placed in Exclusive mode.

A Shared lock explicitly places the database in Shared mode. Shared mode means numerous users can log on to the database and read or write to it. After a resource within a database is set to Shared mode, Exclusive mode cannot be set on that resource until all sharing users have relinquished control.

User Locking

Not only does the Jet engine provide usage locking, it also asserts locking to avoid potential access problems.

For example, user locking is included in the Access database to prevent more than one user of the same name from logging into the database. If active, user locking prevents a single account from accessing the same database simultaneously. However, it does not prevent multiple connections from the same machine at the same time.

Write Locks

If the whole database file is not secured from simultaneous access, the first level of security is to set the proper write-level access. Avoiding problems writing data should be addressed as you define the connections and access for your project.

Write locks are the most common form of locks used in a multi-user implementation. Because multiple users can access the same records at the same time, some type of limits must be set to prevent data collision.

The Jet engine supports two primary types of write locking: optimistic and pessimistic. Optimistic is the default setting and it presumes there will be few instances of two users simultaneously editing the same record at the same time. Therefore, the record is locked only during the time the update is actually occurring.

NEW TERM *Optimistic locking* exists only in the instant that the record is actually being updated as a lock placed upon it. Because of the short period of time for a lock, conflicts seldom occur.

Optimistic locking is the default method used by the Jet engine. Optimistic locking presumes that, during a majority of the time, no two users will be modifying the same record. The larger the number of records in the table, the more likely that conflicts will not occur. However, if you have only a small table with many users, you might consider pessimistic locking.

Pessimistic locking locks the record as soon as the editing mode is activated. This ensures that after a person has activated editing on the record, all other requests for editing will be rejected. Keep in mind that because of page locking, as soon as the edit mode is activated, the page or pages that contain the record will be locked. Any records that co-exist on one of these pages will be locked as well.

NEW TERM *Pessimistic locking* occurs when a user accesses a record; none of the other users may access it in write mode.

Write locking is the opposite of read locking. When a record is being updated by a user, other users are denied access to the record.

Read Locking

Read locks specify that if more than one user is reading the record, users are denied the ability to write to it. When no other users are reading the particular record, it may be updated or deleted.

Table Read and Write Locking

Rather than locking individual records, the settings on an entire table might determine which locking is used. The Command object in a data environment allows setting of record-locking type.

In Figure 15.3, you can see a Command object's properties being configured for pessimistic record locking. The locking settings of the Command object supercede those set by the connection.

FIGURE 15.3

Setting the locking configuration of a Command *object.*

When you choose a locking mode, try to keep it consistent across the entire application. Because your error handling routines must react to errors that occur, the task is greatly simplified if you can reliably know what type of errors might be expected.

If a user is disconnected in some way during a write to the MDB file, the lock for that user remains on. When the user attempts to reconnect, he will be told the database is corrupted. The Repair Database option, available in the Visual Data Manager and through Access, will repair the damage.

Summary

Sharing a Jet database is simple to accomplish if you have a network and a file server. By placing the file in a centralized directory and pointing the various data sources at the file, numerous client applications can read and write into a single file.

15

When you share a database, special concerns must be addressed. Primary among them is the type of locking that will be used on record editing. By realizing the limits to the locking settings, you can configure the database to function as required by your objectives.

Q&A

Q Will setting up a locking configuration allow more exact handling of errors that might be generated?

A Certain locking settings might increase the number of errors that occur while writing to a database. Optimistic locking results in the fewest possible errors generated because more than one update must occur at the precise moment a different update is being written to the database. More errors might be caused by more strict locking settings such as pessimistic locking, but the likelihood of serious data collision (after multiple users update the same record) is reduced.

Q Will the Jet engine eventually eliminate page locking in favor of record locking?

A It is unlikely because Microsoft's complete database server, SQL Server, now features row-level locking. If the exacting level of row locking is needed, you probably have an application that would be more appropriate to a more advanced data source.

Workshop

The quiz questions and exercises are provided for your further understanding. See Appendix C, "Answers," for the answers to the questions.

Quiz

1. Why is locking necessary?
2. What is the maximum number of users that can access an MDB file at the same time?
3. True or False: The LDB file holds the current locks for an open database.
4. What is a page?
5. Can a record be locked even though no one explicitly requested a lock on it?
6. True or False: An Exclusive lock can be placed on a resource that is already being shared.
7. What type of lock is used to prevent more than one machine from logging on to the same account?
8. Is optimistic locking the default method of locking for MDB files?

Exercises

1. Create two simple programs that open connections to a data source. Have the first program access a record with pessimistic locking. Run the second program and attempt to write to the same record.

2. Look at the Northwind database with all of its relations. With enforced referential integrity, how many tables would be unable to accept new records if the Customers table were locked?

HOUR 16

Object Diagrams

If you are unfamiliar with object model diagrams, this hour will introduce you to a new skill that can be incredibly useful. By learning how to read an object model diagram and using it in conjunction with the Object Browser window, you will open a whole world of object development.

Many programs and numerous other technologies (such as the Access database engine) are constructed of objects that can be called from a Visual Basic program. By knowing how to examine an object diagram, you can use these models, often with very little additional documentation.

Learning this methodology is important to a database programmer because most of the real database programming addresses the ActiveX Data Objects (ADO) object model. By learning how to interpret this model, you can design nearly any solution that you might need.

The highlights of this hour include

- Reviewing general object technology
- Reading an object diagram
- Activating the Object Browser
- Using the Excel object model to control the application

How Do Objects Work?

Let's quickly review how objects work in general. An object is a self-contained unit that contains programming code and variables that are related to that code.

The functions or procedures of an object, known as *methods*, are typically called to execute changes on the variables (properties) of an object. A form is an example of an object that uses methods such as the Show method (that displays the form) to manipulate the object and change properties such as the Visible property.

NEW TERM   A *method* is a function or procedure contained within an object. A method typically makes modifications to the object itself.

There are two important concepts you must know to use objects effectively:

- Classes
- Instances

For each object to be created in memory, that object must have a blueprint. The object's blueprint is known as an *object class*. Using a class, you can create many different objects of a particular type. To use a common example, if you were planning to build a housing development, you would need a house class. From this house class (or blueprint), you can create numerous instances (or actual houses).

When an object is created from a class, that object is created in memory as an *instance*. As many instances as are required can be created from a single class. The act of creating an instance is known as *instantiation*.

NEW TERM   An *instance* is the creation of an object in memory from a class definition. More than one instance can be created from a class.

When there are two forms displayed in an application, it means there are two instances of the form created from the form class.

To create an object in code, you might use the following command:

```
Dim myObject As New myClass
```

The `myClass` could be any object class such as a form, controls, or class defined on the Windows system.

You can also create an object using the generic object definition (without the `New` keyword) and a subsequent `CreateObject()` method call.

```
Dim myObject As Object

Set myObject = CreateObject("myClass")
```

The object models you will be using are actually object classes. From the classes (for example, the Excel class) you can instantiate objects (such as the Excel application) in memory.

Object models also have a method of storing multiple objects of the same type. Multiple objects that are stored together are known as a *collection*. Like an array for objects, individual items within a collection can either be referenced using their index number (like an array) or directly using the item's name.

You might have noticed that within a database, fields are accessed in a collection. To retrieve the value from the Field object containing a last name, you might use code like this:

```
a = myRS.Fields("LastName").Value
```

As shown in the code preceding, a `Collection` is typically named as the plural of the individual object name. Be sure to check your documentation if you get an error, though, because there are exceptions.

Reading an Object Diagram

An object diagram is traditionally in the format of an inverted tree diagram like those used for genealogy trees. In Figure 16.1, you can see a simplified diagram of the PowerPoint object model. The complete diagram would span several pages, so this diagram shows only the primary objects.

From the organization of the object tree, you can see the `Application` object that represents the PowerPoint application itself appears at the top of the tree.

Each of the objects on the tree are known as *nodes*. A node can represent either an object or a collection within the object hierarchy.

FIGURE 16.1

A simplified object model diagram of the PowerPoint application.

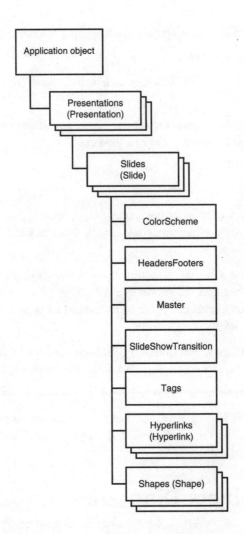

NEW TERM Nodes are objects or collections that appear within an object diagram like leaves on a tree.

The primary object at the top is called the *root node* of the tree. From the root node, navigation down the tree is accomplished within the programming code using the dot (.) command.

NEW TERM The *root node* is the primary node on the tree. From the root, all other nodes descend.

When objects occur together, it is known as a *collection* of objects. A collection is essentially an array of objects where each object can be referenced either with an index or the name of the object. Collections traditionally include the method Count() that will return the number of objects in the collection.

NEW TERM A *collection* is essentially an array of objects.

16

By using an object model diagram, you can understand the relations between objects and their collections. Note that not all models (such as the ADO model) are directly hierarchical. In a hierarchical model, nodes that are lower in the hierarchy require the creation of higher nodes before they exist. As in genealogy, a child cannot exist without a parent already existing. In nonhierarchical models, objects can be created independently.

Most of the object diagrams can be found either in the online documentation or through the Microsoft site. For all the Office model diagrams, you can check at the Web address:

http://www.microsoft.com/officedev

Using the Object Browser

Visual Basic also has a general method of examining an object model. The Object Browser will display all the objects, collections, methods, and properties of any object model currently available to the open project (see Figure 16.2). The object Browser is available in VB and any of the VBA applications.

FIGURE 16.2

The Object Browser displayed from within Visual Basic.

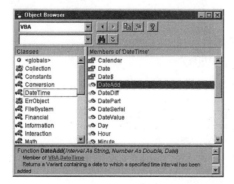

The Object Browser is used in conjunction with each object model diagram. After the diagram is consulted and the object hierarchy is determined, the Object Browser is used to determine exactly which methods and properties are available. Use either the Object Browser menu option under the View menu or hit the F2 function key to display the window.

In order to view an object model, you will need to set a reference for the model within the project. The References dialog enables this to be done.

As you can see within the browser window, there are two combo boxes. The top combo box is used to select the model that will be displayed in the Classes and Members frames of the window. The default setting displays all the object models available to the project.

> Most of the time when you're using the Object Browser, it is a good idea to select exactly the object model you want from the combo box. Otherwise, it is easy to become confused about what objects are included in the desire model.

To find a particular item within the models, the second combo box enables you to enter a term that will be used to search the current objects.

Controlling Excel from VB

A powerful example of using an object model is the ability to control other programs from VB. Because most VB users have the Microsoft Excel application already installed, it is quite easy to control the application using its object model (see Figure 16.3).

Although database technology is still new to you, you are most likely already familiar with basic spreadsheet concepts. Therefore, a simple example of controlling Excel and placing some simple information in a workbook will go a long way toward demonstrating how the object diagram is used.

1. Create a new project.
2. Insert a command button on the form.
3. Set the name property to cmdExcel.
4. Enter the following code in the button Click event:

```
Private Sub cmdExcel_Click()
    Dim appExcel As Object, wbMyBook As Object
    Dim wsMySheet

    Set appExcel = CreateObject("Excel.Application")
    appExcel.Visible = True
```

```
        Set wbMyBook = appExcel.Workbooks.Add
        Set wsMySheet = appExcel.Worksheets.Add
        wsMySheet.Name = "Hello"
        wsMySheet.Cells(1, 1) = "MyCell"
    End Sub
```

5. Execute the application and click the button.

FIGURE 16.3

Simplified Excel object model.

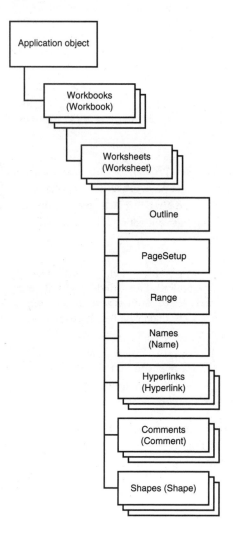

16

If you examine the object diagram, starting at the Application object level, you'll realize that you need to create an Excel application object. This is done in the button code using the CreateObject() function.

After the Excel application is created, the New() method is used to create a new workbook. The object diagram clearly shows that the workbooks occur under the Application object. Therefore, you would use the Object Browser to determine whether there is a method used to create a workbook.

> Always check the Object Browser to see if there is a creation or initialization method for an object that occurs on the next level down in the hierarchy. Usually this method will activate specific initialization code not activated by simply creating the object using the New keyword in a DIMension statement.

From using Excel in the past, you probably realize there are default worksheets created within a new workbook. From the object diagram, you can see that the sheets are stored in a collection. Because there are already sheets present, they can be referenced either by name or index number through the collection.

> In an unfamiliar new object model, default objects (such as worksheets) might not automatically be created. Almost all collections support the Count() method which returns the number of objects in a collection. Use this method to determine whether there are any objects already created.

In the button code, the index value of the first sheet is used to select it. Then the code follows to execute the Cells() method that returns a Range object. The actual values are then modified for the Range object through the Value property.

You should be able to see the relation between the object model diagram and actual implementation code. Now that these basics are clear, you can see how the ADO object model can be interpreted to program database access.

Summary

Understanding the interpretation of object models is critical to creating useful programs. Many of the abilities of Visual Basic are available not through its foundation commands, but through the various object models included with it. Primary among these object models is the database access object model known as ADO.

Q&A

Q Where can I get the diagrams of typical object models?

A The Microsoft site is often the best place to look, particularly the Office Development page (www.microsoft.com/officedev). Also, the online help for most VBA applications includes an interactive object diagram. The Microsoft Office applications with examples on how to use them are included in *Visual Basic Programmer's Reference* (ISBN 0-07-882458-3), which I wrote.

Q Do I always have to include a reference to the root node?

A Not if you are working in the host application. For example, when coding in VBA within Excel, any references without a prefix will implicitly reference the parent application object. Therefore, to set the Visible property from within the application, the code

```
Visible = True
```

can be used instead of

```
Application.Visible = True
```

Q Can the Object Browser examine an object model not installed on the current system?

A No, the model must be installed and registered on the system for it to be browsed. Additionally, within a programming environment such as Visual Basic, the object model must be added in the References dialog to be available for viewing.

Q Are the names of Collections the same as the single object with an added letter s?

A Usually, but not always. In the PowerPoint object model, all the collections are plural forms (for example, the Slide object is stored in the Slides collection). However, the Excel model has a few exceptions (for example, SeriesCollection whereas the single object is named Series). Make sure to check the diagrams before use.

Workshop

The quiz questions and exercises are provided for your further understanding. See Appendix C, "Answers," for the answers to the questions.

16

Quiz

1. True or False: Many instances of an object can be created from a class.

2. What is the difference between an object and a collection?

Exercises

1. In the References dialog box, add a reference to the Microsoft Word objects. Examine the object model in the Object Browser.

2. Find the object model diagram on the Microsoft Web site. Use the object model to close the current window in Excel.

HOUR 17

Understanding ActiveX Data Objects (ADO)

Most of your experience up to this point has been focused on using the Data Control to link a data source to the controls on a form. Although the Data Control is easy to use and quick to set up, it is limited in its power. Directly programming the data objects is a far more robust method of adding database access to an application.

As you become a more advanced database developer, you will use the ActiveX Data Objects (ADO) extensively. You will continue to use the Data Control for prototyping, but most of the code in your final application will use the data objects.

The highlights of this hour include

- Examining the structure of ADO
- Learning how to use ADO in your programs
- Using the Connection, Command, and Recordset objects
- Reviewing the objects that make up ADO

What Can ADO Do?

So far, you have been exposed to accessing a database through controls only. As a matter of fact, the Data Control itself merely provides a user-friendly interface for actual ADO objects. Through the Recordset property, you can actually directly access the ADO objects represented by the Data Control.

ADO simplifies and provides a single-object structure for a number of technologies such as:

- Jet engine—The standard Microsoft Access database engine used to manipulate Access, dBASE, FoxPro, and other database files
- ODBC—The industry standard data connection standard for interfacing to almost any type of database (including Oracle, Sybase, DB2, and so on)
- OLE DB—A new database connectivity standard from Microsoft that enables access to heterogeneous data sources

To make it more explicit, ADO acts as an interface between Visual Basic almost any type of data source available for Windows. ADO acts as a piece of middleware, or bridge software, that provides a generalized interface for Visual Basic programs to access data (see Figure 17.1).

FIGURE 17.1

The relation of ADO to other middleware technology.

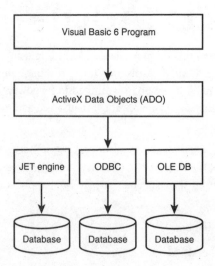

NEW TERM　*Middleware* is software that provides a bridge between two normally incompatible types of software interfaces. Middleware traditionally has no visible user interface but works as a translator between the two interfaces.

Using ADO, an OLE DB or ODBC driver can be plugged into the data environment to enable access to a specific type of data without requiring any reprogramming. After a program has been built to access a data source through ADO, the program can generally be switched to point to a different data source type without any recoding, as long as the structure of the tables being accessed remains the same.

What Does ADO Look Like?

Before you continue learning about the theory of ADO, it might be a good idea to create an ADO access program to see it in use firsthand. Then as the details of ADO are covered, you'll have a least a little framework through which to understand the specifics.

This ADO sample you will create will be a form with a single button on it. When clicked, the button will display the names of the first five customers in the Northwind database.

17

1. Execute Visual Basic and begin a new project.

   This project can be a Standard EXE project because you will add the ADO object model to it.

2. Add the Reference to the Microsoft ActiveX Data Objects 2.0 library.

   In the References section of the Project properties is the list of all the object models available in the current project environment. You need to add the ADO object model so that object types such as the Command and Connection objects are understood by VB.

   After the object model has been activated in the References window, it can be accessed from the Object Browser. In the Visual Basic environment, hit the F2 key to display the Object Browser to examine all the objects, methods, and properties available to ADO. In the Object Browser, the ADO object set will be listed as ADODB (see Figure 17.2) in the Project/Library combo box.

3. Create a command button on the form and name it *cmdShow5*.

   This button will be used to activate the code to retrieve data from the Northwind database. Because all the initialization of ADO is completed in the code itself, the procedure doesn't require any form initialization before it can execute. Therefore, this code could even be placed in the Form Load event.

FIGURE 17.2

The ADODB objects shown in the Object Browser.

4. Make sure that you alter the line that specifies the path to find the NWind.mdb to match the path on your system. If VB 6 has not been installed in the standard place on the C drive, the path will be different.

Enter the following code into the Click event:

```
Private Sub cmdShow5_Click()
    Dim myRS As New ADODB.Recordset

    ' Set up connection string
    Const ConnectStr = "PROVIDER=Microsoft.Jet.OLEDB.3.51;Data
    ➥Source=C:\ProgramFiles\Microsoft Visual Studio\VB98\Nwind.mdb;"

    ' Create new record set
    Set myRS = New ADODB.Recordset

    ' Set property to automatically create a connection
    myRS.ActiveConnection = ConnectStr

    ' Open recordset with query for all customer records
    myRS.Open "Select * from customers"
    ' Check if recordset is empty
    If myRS.BOF And myRS.EOF Then
        MsgBox "Recordset is empty!", 16, "Empty recordset"
    Else
        ' Make sure that you're on the first record
        myRS.MoveFirst
        ' Loop through 5 records to display company name
        For i = 1 To 5
            MsgBox myRS.Fields("companyName"), _
                vbInformation, "Company #" & i
```

```
            ' Move to next record
            myRS.MoveNext
        Next
        ' Close recordset
        myRS.Close
    End If
    ' Set to nothing to eliminate object
    Set myRS = Nothing
End Sub
```

In the code, there are a number of comments included to provide a brief explanation of what each line is doing. As a Visual Basic programmer, most of the programming language should be already familiar. Even using the data objects should be fairly clear because they are used in a way that seems almost common sense.

5. Execute the application and click the command button.

   You should see the message box shown in Figure 17.3. In the title of each message box is the number of the record that is being displayed.

6. Click the OK button to step through the records.

17

FIGURE 17.3

The message box displaying the company name data retrieved from NWind.mdb.

You've now made your first use of ADO! By simply creating a Connection object, attaching a Recordset object, and performing a query, the data has been returned. With some basic hands-on experience, it is now a good idea to step back and address some of the larger issues that concern an ADO programmer.

ADO Object Model

The ADO object model, because of its nonhierarchical nature, is best diagramed as shown in Figure 17.4. Unlike most other object diagrams that look mostly like an inverted tree or complex organizational chart, the nature of ADO lends itself more to a flow diagram. You can see that the Connection, Command, and Recordset objects are connected on the left at the same level to indicate they might be used separately but might be connected.

FIGURE 17.4

The ActiveX Data Object model.

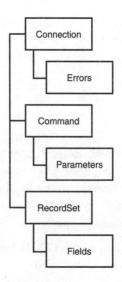

> If you read magazines or other books on Visual Basic, you will see a good deal of information on Data Access Objects (DAO) or Remote Data Objects (RDO). Until VB 6, DAO and RDO were the object technologies used for all database access. Now ADO supercedes all the previous data object implementations. However, DAO and RDO are still included in VB 6 for backwards compatibility.
>
> ADO and DAO still resemble each other in a number of ways, so converting code to ADO is not too complicated. In Hour 23, "Older VB," the previous data access models are covered so you can understand legacy Visual Basic code.

All the primary objects in the ADO can be instantiated using the New keyword. For example, to create a Connection object, you could use this code:

```
Dim myConnect As New ADODB.connection
```

Although this would create the object, it will not initialize it. The initialization of each ADO object is different, but will be detailed in this hour.

ADO Object Overview

ADO consists of only seven objects, four of which occur in collections. Unlike most other object models, the ADO model is not strictly hierarchical. Most of the objects can be created independently. For example, the Recordset object can be created separately from any Connection and attached when the actual data source needs to be addressed.

Table 17.1 describes each of the objects available in the object model. Because the model is not strictly hierarchical, it might be difficult for you to understand how they relate to each other. For this reason, this hour provides examples of using all three of the major objects: the Connection object, the Command object, and the Recordset object.

TABLE 17.1 ADO OBJECTS LIST

Object Type	Description
Command	Holds a command to be executed against the data source. Most often an SQL command or stored procedure.
Connection	Object that actually provides the link to a data source including path, password, and connection options.
Error	Contains error information about any errors that occur during data access.
Parameter	Stores individual parameters for use by the Command object.
Field	Collection of all the fields contained in the recordset.
Property	Properties of the data source returned by the Data Provider driver.
Recordset	Holds the records that fulfill the query parameters in a recordset as well as a cursor to navigate the records.

All the ADO objects are held in the object library known as ADODB. Because these objects are registered with the OLE Automation registry, you can use ADO from any program that supports OLE Automation.

> You might have noticed that the Command object can represent a construct known as a *stored procedure*. A stored procedure is a procedure that exists within the database itself and can be executed as if it was a small program. Stored procedures are mostly used in larger database systems (such as Oracle or SQL Server) and are beyond the scope of this book.

Programs that can use ADO include Active Server Pages, all the Office applications (through VBA), Visio, AutoCAD, and many other programs. The ADO objects are available either natively (in ASP) or through the object model References. In the object model References, you might have noticed the listing for ADORS. ADORS is a subset of the complete ADODB library and is used for only very specific client-side applications.

The ADO model uses the Data Provider drivers stored on the system to provide the data access. Therefore, when creating an install for a client machine, makes sure the appropriate drivers are included.

17

In the newer ADO terminology, because data sources are accessed through the data objects, they are known as Data Providers.

Connection Object

Through the Connection object, data is read into other objects such as a Recordset. The Connection object creates and maintains an open connection to the data source. Setting the parameters of the Connection object occurs through the three properties: Mode, ConnectionTimeout, and ConnectionString. These properties determine how the connection will react to both the connection established and for other users of the data source.

 One of the easiest ways to generate the connection string is to use the Data Control. If you place the Data Control on a form, the ConnectionString property is available in the Properties window. Use the wizard for this property to generate the string you need. Simply copy it and paste it into your program code, and then delete the Data Control.

Using the Connection object requires only that you specify a connection string. Setting additional properties allows you to refine the behavior of the connection. In the project you created earlier, you can follow these instructions to see an isolated code example of the use of the Connection object.

1. Make sure that the references to the ADO objects are available.

2. Place a command button on the form and name it cmdConnect.

3. Enter the following code in the Click event of the button:

```
Private Sub cmdConnect_Click()
    Const ConnectionString = "uid=myname;pwd=mypw;driver={SQL Server};
    ➥server=myserver;database=pubs;dsn=,,connection=adConnectAsync"

    Dim myConnect As New ADODB.connection

    myConnect.ConnectionString = ConnectString
    myConnect.ConnectionTimeout = 10
    myConnect.Open
End Sub
```

Although this code will create a connection to the data source, that connection won't do anything just yet! You will need to use the Command or Recordset objects to actually access data through the connection.

Objects that have been created are made to be destroyed automatically when they go out of scope. In the preceding code, this means that because the object was created within the procedure, the end of the procedure execution will delete the object.

It is still good programming practice to set the object to Nothing to eliminate it from memory. When you begin creating global objects, following this practice will ensure that objects do not remain in memory after their use is complete.

Command Object

The Command object is used to execute commands against a connection. Most often, the commands available will be SQL execution statements. However, as Universal Data Access becomes more popular and various types of new data sources become available, commands will probably become more varied based on the types of information to which access is desired.

The Command object is made to execute an operation against the data source. That operation might be the creation of a Recordset object, execution of a bulk operation, or changing the structure of the data source itself.

The Command object is used primarily for executing stored code on a full database server. However, here the Command object is used simply to execute a query to return some record information.

This small code sample shows how a stored procedure named incrementCounter might be called. You can ignore this sample if you won't be using a large database server, but it demonstrates essentially how a Command object can be used in a different way from a table or SQL statement:

```
Const ConnectStr = "uid=myname;pwd=mypw;driver={SQL Server};
server=myserver;database=pubs;dsn=,,connection=adConnectAsync"
Dim myCommand As New ADODB.Command

' Point command at SQL Server data source
myCommand.ConnectionString = ConnectStr
' Set the name of the stored procedure
myCommand.CommandText = "incrementCounter"
' Execute the command
myCommand.CommandType = adCmdStoredProc
Set myCommand = Nothing
```

As soon as the CommandType property is set at runtime, the ADO will attempt to execute the current command settings.

17

Recordset Object

The Recordset object is perhaps the most important object within the ADO framework and is certainly the one that you will manipulate the most. Within a recordset, access to all data, fields, and results from a query exists.

The Recordset object actually holds the records retrieved from the query. Using the methods included in the Recordset object, you can move within the available records, update data, insert new records, and set a filter to view only specific records within a data set.

Now with ADO 2.0, recordsets can even be remotely executed; for example, allowing a client-side recordset for a Web-based application. Most of the same methods and calls can be used on the client-side recordsets.

> When the Recordset object is initialized with the Open() method, the query for the set is executed. If the set is empty (no rows are returns), both the BOF and EOF properties will be set to False. Checking these two properties will determine whether any records are contained in the recordset.

When a recordset is initially opened, the parameters that define the connection, the type of recordset, and the access parameters are sent to it. The Recordset object is very flexible and multiple recordsets can be created from a single session.

The Recordset object supports transaction processing. This means that a series of database changes either will all occur or none will occur. This prevents the possibility of data corruption. The classic example is a database system that handles money.

If a bank wants to transfer $2,000 from Account A to Account B, two operations must be performed: The money must be removed from Account A and credited to Account B. What happens if some error occurs after the money has been removed from Account A but before it is placed in Account B? Or if a server failure occurs at this time?

Calling the Open method will perform the initial query used to fill the recordset with information. After the recordset has been created, the Field collection can be used to access all the information returned by the query.

To demonstrate the Recordset object, you can make a variation on the original ADO example. Add a command button to a form and name it cmdRS. In the click event, enter the following code:

```vb
Private Sub cmdRS_Click()
    ' Set up connection string
    Const ConnectStr = "PROVIDER=Microsoft.Jet.OLEDB.3.51;Data Source=C:\
    ➡Program Files\Microsoft Visual Studio\VB98\Nwind.mdb;"

    Dim myConnect As New ADODB.connection
    Dim myRS As New ADODB.Recordset

  With myConnect
     .ConnectionString = ConnectStr
     .ConnectionTimeout = 10
     .Open
  End With

    ' Create new record set
    Set myRS = New ADODB.Recordset

    ' Set property to automatically create a connection
    myRS.ActiveConnection = myConnect

    ' Open recordset with query for all customer records
    myRS.Open "Select * from customers"
    If myRS.BOF And myRS.EOF Then
        MsgBox "Recordset is empty!", 16, "Empty recordset"
    Else
        ' Make sure that you're on the first record
        myRS.MoveFirst
        ' Loop through 5 records to display company name
        For i = 1 To 5
            ' Clear temporary string
            temp$ = ""
            ' Loop through all of the record fields
            For j = 1 To myRS.Fields.Count - 1
                temp$ = temp$ & myRS.Fields(j) & ","
            Next
            ' Display list of field values
            MsgBox temp$, _
                vbInformation, "Company #" & i
            ' Move to next record
            myRS.MoveNext
        Next
        ' Close recordset
        myRS.Close
    End If
    ' Set to nothing to eliminate object
    Set myRS = Nothing
End Sub
```

17

The simplest example of accessing a recordset is to simply create a new Recordset object and execute the Open method. A Connection object will automatically be created for the recordset and the connection will be made. However, because the initial ADO example already did this, you made a change.

In the new example, the Connection object is created and used as the connection link for the Recordset. The Connection object functions such that it can be used for multiple recordsets.

The Recordset example uses the Field object collection with an index number to step through all the fields available and display the values held for that record. In Figure 17.5, you can see all the values for the first record.

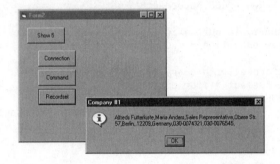

FIGURE 17.5

The Recordset object displays of all the Field values for the current record.

The code uses the implicate Value property of the Field object. If you want to display the names of all the fields instead of the values contained within them, you can simply add the Name property reference. The code would look like this:

```
temp$ = temp$ & myRS.Fields(j).Name & ","
```

Recordset Cursors

Cursors are memory constructs used by a database to select a record within a multirecord dataset and are used extensively by ADO. Because the ADO model supports both client-side and server-side cursors, you will have to choose the location of the processing that will occur when a query is executed.

There are four different types of cursors available to a recordset:

- Dynamic cursor—General cursor type that supports all capabilities including insertion, modification, and deletions.

- Keyset cursor—Like the dynamic cursor, but prevents the user from seeing records others have added or access to records others have deleted.

- Static cursor—Like a snapshot of the data, creates a read-only recordset that does not update when changes are made by other users. The only cursor available for client-side recordsets.

- Forward-only cursor—Acts just like the dynamic cursor but can only move forward through a recordset, thereby increasing performance.

Setting the type of cursor is done either by setting the CursorType property before the Open method is called or passing the cursor type as one of the parameters to the Open method. ADO uses the forward-only cursor as the default.

17

Recordset Object Details

In Table 17.2 you can see all the most important methods of the Recordset object. For the complete list of methods, see the Visual Basic manual. The methods available for completing transactions are particularly important to research.

TABLE 17.2 THE METHODS AVAILABLE TO THE Recordset OBJECT

Method	Description
Open	Opens the recordset.
ActiveConnection	Either a string to provide the creation of a new connection or a reference to an existing Connection object.
UpdateBatch	Stores all the changes of the batch to the database.
NextRecordset	If the recordset is based on a compound Command object, the next query is executed for the recordset.
GetRows	Copies the information from a recordset into an array.

Transactions encapsulate multiple operations within a single transaction. The BeginTrans method is used to open a transaction. When all the operations have been entered, the CommitTrans method can be called to commit the changes to the data source. If an error were to occur, the RollbackTrans method can be invoked to roll back and eliminate all the transactions at once.

To update any changes made to the current record, the Update method can be used. To cancel these changes, you can use the CancelUpdate method. The Update method will send the OLE DB driver the signal to attempt an update, which might include a SQL Update command.

In many cases, it is necessary to update a number of records in a given data source. Loading each record and subsequently submitting an update to the data source can be a processor and time-intensive process. However, if all the updates could be cached at the recordset until an update was requested, all the record modifications could be sent to the data source at once. Batch updates should only be performed with keyset or static cursors.

Other ADO Objects

These other objects supported by ADO primarily work as objects created under the primary three objects. You can look at the earlier "Using" examples to see samples of the use of some of these objects.

Error Object

The Error object is used to return err code information about the attempted operations including updates, queries, and inserts. The collection of the Error objects is stored in the Connection object.

All the Error objects are contained within an Errors collection. They can be referenced by individual item number. They can also be accessed by their particular error type.

Parameter Object

The Parameter object is used when a variable is selected to be passed in a query when the recordset is created. A Command object to the Data Environment that requires a value to be passed to it uses a Parameter to accept the value. That value can then be used in the query.

For example, a complex query might be constructed to do numerous comparisons to the Customers table. A Parameter could be used to specify the city of the customers to be returned in the query. When the recordset is activated, the desired city name is passed to it and the query executes using the passed value.

The Parameter object supports the following properties:

- Direction
- Type
- Value

Field Object

The `Field` object is primarily used within the `Recordset` object to hold the fields as well as access the values available through those fields. Each field object has the following values:

- Value
- UnderlyingValue
- OriginalValue

The `Fields` collection provides a variety of ways that the data stored within a field for a row can be accessed. Because a collection is a group of objects that can be referenced either using a index value or the name of the individual object itself, you can use either of these methods on the field link.

To access the `LastName` field value in `Recordset`, you can use this:

```
myRS.Fields("LastName").Value
```

You could also use the `Fields` index number to access a field value:

```
myRS.Fields(2).Value
```

Beware that a value stored in a field might contain a `Null` value. This can cause problems if you manipulate the field without determining its status. For example, if the `LastName` field is a `Null` in the current record, the following statement will generate an error:

```
myRS.Fields("LastName").Value + ", " + myRS.Fields("FirstName").Value
```

> You can use the ampersand (&) command in order to avoid the `Null` problem. Instead of using the + command for concatenation, use the ampersand like this:
>
> `a& = "" & myRS!LastName`

Property Object

A `Property` object can be created in the collection of many different objects including the `Recordset` object, `Command` object, `Collection` object, and others. It contains a property set by the Data Provider.

Property objects are one of two types: built-in properties or dynamic properties. The built-in properties are accessed like standard VB properties using the dot (.) commands. Dynamic properties are not native to ADO.

A dynamic object can be created by a vendor of a specific database. If that vendor, Oracle for example, wanted to provide specific capabilities or information that wasn't supported by the general ADO object, they could be added through Property objects added to other objects.

Summary

The ActiveX Data Objects (ADO) are a set of objects that provide complete access to database technologies from the Jet engine to ODBC to OLE DB. Through ADO, you can entirely program data access for multiple diverse connections to any data source that has a Data Provider available. Using the Connection, Recordset, and Command objects, an infinite variety of data solutions can be created.

Q&A

Q Where is ADO used?

A Most professional programmers use ADO for all their application programming. The Data Control is very limited in the flexibility that it offers. With the VB Data Form Wizard providing the option of generating ADO code, ADO can be used for even the simplest solutions.

Q Is ADO a hierarchical object model?

A No. Because the Command, Connection, and Recordset objects can all be constructed individually, it is not treated like a hierarchy. However, you can use it much like other hierarchical models (such as DAO) simply by attaching the objects in the proper order.

Q Is there an easy way to construct a form that uses ADO code?

A Yes. The VB Data Form Wizard will construct the same form as displayed with the straight Data Control, but will generate the ADO programming code instead. Simply select the ADO code option in the dialog where the form type must be chosen.

Q Is ADO compatible with older DAO code?

A No, but the conversion is not prohibitively difficult. The code used to program ADO is fairly similar to DAO and very similar to RDO code. The online manuals included with Visual Basic include an entire section with examples that demonstrates how to make the conversion from older Visual Basic code to the new ADO model.

Workshop

The quiz questions and exercises are provided for your further understanding. See Appendix C, "Answers," for the answers to the questions.

Quiz

17

1. How does using ADO differ from the data control?

2. What is the Command object used for?

3. What keyword is used to create the ADO objects?

4. What other programs support ADO?

5. True or False: A snapshot can be used to modify and update information.

6. What method is used to refresh the data contained within the recordset?

Exercises

1. Create a connection to access the Biblio database and return the names of all the tables that it contains. You will need to use the Connection object as well as the OpenSchema method.

2. Create an ODBC connection to the Northwind database and alter the code that was used to access the Recordset object in this hour to access the data through the ODBC data source instead of directly.

HOUR 18

Using SQL

You have now been using the capabilities included with the Visual Basic data access components for some time. So far, all the connections made to a data source have been created by individually setting the properties such as the ConnectionString and RecordSource.

However, to truly tap the power of the database capabilities available through both ADO and ODBC, you will need to learn how to program the language made specifically for database access: SQL. SQL is a language that was created specifically to address the needs of selecting and returning only specific data from within a large database.

The highlights of this hour include

- Learning the basics of the SQL language
- Understanding how SQL relates to Visual Basic
- Using the Visual Data Manager to test SQL queries
- Examining SQL comparison operators

What Is SQL?

SQL is the standard language used in making queries to return specific data. It can be used to select certain criteria for matching within a table. SQL can be used through ADO or ODBC.

In this hour, you'll use the Northwind database to test SQL queries that return data. Before you start executing SQL statements, let's take a look at a simple SQL query.

Remember when you set the query in Hour 3, to a statement like this:

```
lastname = 'Smith'
```

This command returned all the records with the value stored in the lastName field equal to the value of Smith. This statement was really a SQL statement with the other pieces of the statement implicitly added by Visual Basic. The entire SQL statement would look like this:

```
select * from customers where lastName = 'Smith'
```

The statement begins with a Select command that is the cornerstone of any SQL query. The asterisk (*) that follows the Select command is a wildcard that specifies that all the fields for the query should be returned with the resultant data.

The next command in this line is the From command. The From command determines which table or tables within the database will be selected for query. In this example, the customers table will be accessed.

Finally, the Where command specifies the actual conditions to be checked to return the proper records. You can see that following the Where command is the same text that was entered in the simple query.

There is a great deal more power in constructing complete SQL commands than the abbreviated form initially introduced. You can very specifically determine exactly what type of information should be returned in the recordset and what table is used. Multiple tables can even be searched at the same time!

Understanding SQL only takes learning a handful of commands. You've already seen most of them in this simple example. Like an erector set where complex structures can be created from a few simple pieces, it is the same with the SQL query commands. The language can easily locate, collate, and organize information requested from a data source with a minimum of text.

History of SQL

SQL is an acronym for Structured Query Language. Originally created by IBM, SQL has become a nonproprietary public standard and is the most widely used method of retrieving information from databases. In fact, SQL has become the *de facto* standard for relational database access.

NEW TERM *SQL* or *Structured Query Language* is a results-oriented query language used to access data sources for querying, insertion, updating, and structural modification.

Although the SQL language is most powerful in its capability to provide queries, it has much more powerful uses than simple data retrieval. It can be used to

- Perform simple or complex queries
- Create databases
- Create and modify the structure of tables
- Insert new records
- Modify existing records
- Create multi-table relations

18

The standards committee ANSI adopted SQL as the standard relational database system language initially in 1986. Since then, the most significant revision occurred in 1992 for the standard labeled SQL-92.

Before SQL, most databases required stored data to be manipulated one record at a time. SQL allowed handling sets of records. Even when you are using the Data Control, you are actually implicitly using a SQL query.

Although the basic commands of SQL have been standardized, most vendors of SQL solutions (including Microsoft) have made extensions to the language. Therefore, if you need to study SQL in depth, be sure to read books and other resources that apply to the particular system that you will be using.

SQL as a Results Language

SQL is a results language rather than a procedural language like Visual Basic. Visual Basic executes one statement after another in sequence. Your program in Visual Basic tells the computer exactly what operations to perform.

SQL, on the other hand, is a language that was created to tell the database WHAT you want to do, not HOW you want it done.

A query simply passes a request for records that match certain criteria. The database server that understands SQL determines the most effective means of fulfilling the data request.

> Although you cannot tell SQL exactly how to perform a query, there are ways to optimize a query by determining how the query is actually performed. Although it is beyond the scope of this book to describe its operation, Visual Basic Enterprise Edition includes a SQL debugger called Transact-SQL Debugger. It enables examination of a query when it is executing on a Microsoft SQL Server. See the VB books online documentation in the *Guide to Building Client/Server Applications with Visual Basic*.

The SQL language is primarily constructed to enable robust querying. Here are some examples of simple tasks that can be accomplished from SQL when querying the Northwind database:

- Finding all customers within a particular state
- Looking for orders made between two dates
- Locating a customer with a particular last name by ZIP code
- Totaling the average order for last month
- Creating a list of all the customers who haven't ordered in more than 60 days

Although many of these tasks could be accomplished using Visual Basic code, a query is much more efficient. Because the SQL engine in any database system you use (such as the Jet engine) is optimized for data access, all the actual database processing in the engine is optimized for exactly these types of results.

The SQL language does have its limitations. The general SQL language is missing conditional execution operators. In Visual Basic you're familiar with using the If...Then structure to change the flow of the program execution.

The SQL language, made to describe the returned results and not the exact method of execution, does not include these conditional operators. Learning how to have SQL return complex results requires a way of thinking different from traditional VB programming that can only be acquired with experience and practice. However, you probably won't need to create complex queries for some time.

If you see conditional operators in some SQL code, you are probably looking at one of the vendor-specific additions to the SQL language. Companies such as Oracle and Microsoft have extended the SQL language to add requested features.

A general SQL statement has basically four forms:

- `select`—Generates a query
- `update`—Modifies the data stored in one or more records
- `insert`—Inserts a new record into the specified table
- `create`—Constructs a new table, view, or other database structure

Through ADO, Visual Basic automatically handles most of the other aspects of table manipulation so you will probably never have to use commands other than `Select`.

Covering the nonquery aspects of SQL are beyond the scope of this book. You probably won't need to use them unless you progress to the use of a complete database server such as Microsoft SQL Server. At that point, there will be many advanced books that will address exactly the system you will use.

18

What Does a Query Do?

The foundation of SQL excels in its abilities to query a database. A query can do much more than simply return records that match particular criteria. In fact, queries can:

- Sort records
- Choose fields
- Choose records
- Cross tabulate multiple tables
- Perform calculations
- Provide a source of data for forms, reports, or other queries
- Make changes to data

Because queries can do all these things, doesn't it seem important to learn the SQL language to take advantage of the features already built into Visual Basic? In fact, learning SQL is neither difficult nor particularly time-consuming. One of the most difficult challenges of using SQL is finding examples for the type of query that you're trying to create.

> Also in the Sams Teach Yourself series is the excellent *Teach Yourself SQL in 14 Days*. You might consider getting it if you will be doing more SQL work.

This chapter will provide numerous examples of actual queries that can be executed against the Northwind sample database. You can then adapt these queries to your own use to solve many of the problems you will face when creating a SQL query for your own application.

Visual Basic 6 provides perhaps the best SQL environment on the market. Just added to VB 6 is the Query Builder that simplifies both the creation and optimization of your SQL queries. This means that you can run sample queries against the data source that you will be using and refine your SQL statement before you even need to place them within your program or data environment.

Experimenting with the Visual Data Manager

The Visual Data Manager that is accessible from the VB Add-Ins menu enables direct entry of SQL statements. When a SQL statement is entered, you can execute it against the currently open data source.

You can enter any of the following code into the SQL Statement window of the Visual Data Manager. Likewise, this code can be entered into the `RecordSource` property of a Data Control to specify what data will be available to bound controls.

Selecting a Table: The `From` Clause

In a `Select` statement, the `From` clause determines what table(s) the data is retrieved from. The order in which the tables are listed in the `From` clause has no significance to the operation of the command.

```
select * from customers
```

Let's use this simple query from the Visual Data Manager.

1. Execute the Visual Data Manager.
2. Open the Nwind.mdb database.
3. Enter this code into the SQL Statement window:

   ```
   select * from customers
   ```
4. Click the Execute button. When asked if this is a SQL Pass-Through statement, click the No button.

You should now be presented with the query window as shown in Figure 18.1. As you can see at the bottom of the browsing window, the query selected 91 records to display.

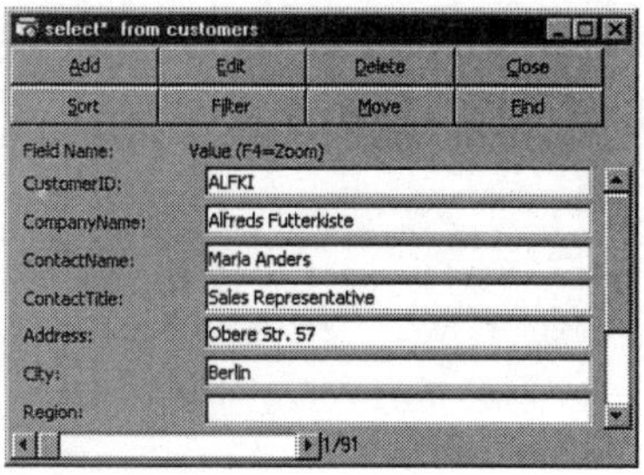

FIGURE 18.1

Executing a SQL state-ment in the Visual Data Manager.

This query returns the information from a single table. To retrieve information from multiple tables, just add additional table names separated by a comma (,). If you execute the following query, all records from both tables will be concatenated and returned as a single read-only set:

```
select * from customers,orders
```

The data set that is returned is not organized. All records are simply dumped into the returned data set. You can specify a relation between the two tables to show the orders as related to the individual customers. This is accomplished by using the CustomerID key field.

By telling the query to return only records that contain matching CustomerID fields, you can use a query like this:

```
select * from customers,orders where customers.CustomerID =
orders.CustomerID
```

Execute this query in the Data Manager and notice that far fewer records are returned. You can see in the SQL query code that the dot(.) command is used to specify the field name in a query that has multiple tables. If many field accesses are required, this would mean a great deal of typing.

Instead, in the From clause, an alias to the name of the table can be specified. Setting an alias merely determines how the table will be referenced in the rest of the SQL state-ment. Using an alias can often make reading code more easily understandable. A simple alias might appear like this:

```
select * from customers as c
```

18

This statement will enable all references in the Where clause (used to define conditions of the returned dataset) to address the customer table as c. This capability is really most useful when there are multiple tables addressed such as your recent query:

```
select * from customers as c,orders as o where c.CustomerID = o.CustomerID
```

The alias can also be used on the field names that are to be returned by the query.

Specifying Fields

You know how to do a simple query now to select all the records of a specified table. However, up until now you've used the wildcard(*) operator to return all the fields of a table.

Returning all the field data can be unnecessary and time-consuming when only a few fields are needed from the data returned. In the example, maybe you only need the contact name and phone number returned from the data set.

Simply placing explicit field names after the Select command will return the desired fields.

```
select contactName,phone from customers
```

If you execute this query from the Visual Data Manager, you will see that only the two fields from the table are returned (see Figure 18.2).

FIGURE 18.2

Selectively returning the fields of a table.

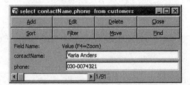

The Where Command and Comparison Operators

Making the selections of the table and fields are the primary decisions, but filtering what data will be returned is the primary use of the SQL language commands. The Where command in a SQL statement determines what data will be returned. In order to use the Where command, you must also use a comparison operator in the query to specify the criteria.

In the SQL language, there are a number of special operators used to do comparisons with fields that are different from normal Visual Basic commands. Because the SQL standard evolved as a platform-independent standard, it uses some operators that are more common in the general programming community.

Table 18.1 shows the operators for standard comparisons. The not equal to, not greater than, and not less than operators use the exclamation point notation like that used in the C++ language.

TABLE 18.1 COMPARISON OPERATORS AND THEIR DESCRIPTIONS

Operator	Meaning
like	String Comparison Operator
=	Equal To
>	Greater Than
<	Less Than
>=	Greater Than Or Equal To
<=	Less Than Or Equal To
!=	Not Equal To
!>	Not Greater Than
!<	Not Less Than

The first comparison operator listed in the table is the Like operator. The Like command is a special command for case-insensitive string comparisons. The Equal (=) command, when used for strings, searches for exact equivalents.

To use the comparison operator, simply insert the desired field comparison after the Where command:

```
select * from customers where city = 'Portland'
```

On the Northwind database, this query should return two records. You can easily use the other comparison operators when querying fields such as number and date fields. For example:

```
select * from orders where orderdate > #12/1/95#
```

For the Jet engine, dates must be surrounded by the pound sign. However, other SQL implementations can use different date notation. For example, SQL Server requires a date to be surrounded by apostrophes ('). Check the appropriate documentation for the system you will be addressing.

18

Wildcards

You can use wildcards to find partial matches.

You might already be familiar with wildcards such as the asterisk (*) character for searching for files on your hard drive. To find all the files with the .doc extension, you can use the *.doc search criteria. Wildcards in SQL work in the same manner.

For example, to find all the last names that begin with the letters SM, your query could look like this:

```
select * from customers where customerName like 'sm*'
```

Boolean Operators

The Where clause can also use the full spectrum of Boolean operators. Those supported in SQL include:

And

Not

Or

If you needed to find all the Smiths that live in California, you could use a statement such as:

```
select * from customers where customerName like 'smith'
➥and state like 'California'
```

Parentheses are also supported when using Boolean operators to specify precedence.

Labeling Returned Columns

So far, all the queries that you've executed have returned all the columns (or fields) labeled by their field names.

You do not have to receive data back only in columns labeled with the field names.

```
select contactName as cName from customer
```

After the columns are labeled, you reference them from ADO as if the labels that you attached were field names. For example, this code would display the value in the newly labeled cName field:

```
myLastName = myRS!cName
```

When you need to return summary fields, it is a good idea to label them properly for easy access from your program.

Sorting Records Using the Order By Clause

A SQL statement can also use the Order By command to determine the sort order that the returned recordset will use.

```
select * from customers order by contactName
```

This example will return the fields of all the records from this table sorted by the contact name values.

Remember that the Order By statement uses an index for a field if it is available. Fields that are not indexed can be very slow to sort in a large database. Therefore, try to ensure that the most commonly sorted fields have an index.

SQL Keywords

As stated earlier, there are very few keywords that actually make up the SQL language. Most of the keywords are actually modifiers to the Select statement.

Table 18.2 shows most of the keywords available in the SQL language. These keywords all involve querying and modifying records within a table.

TABLE 18.2 SQL KEYWORDS

Keyword	Description
SELECT...FROM	Returns a recordset from one or more tables
WHERE	Defines the conditions used to evaluate the returned records
WHERE...LIKE	Defines the pattern used to evaluate the returned records
WHERE...IN	Defines a group of values used to evaluate the returned records
ORDER BY	Defines the sort order that the records in the returned recordset will take
GROUP BY	Groups the records of the returned recordset by certain criteria
SELECT...INTO	Stores the records that meet defined criteria into another table
INSERT	Inserts a new record and specified values into the table
UNION	Returns a recordset that contains the combined sets of two or more queries

continues

TABLE 18.2 CONTINUED

Keyword	Description
UPDATE	Updates one or more records to specified values
CREATE TABLE	Defines a new table in the current database
ALTER TABLE	Defines new fields within the table
DROP TABLE	Deletes the table from the database
CREATE INDEX	Creates an index for the table given a specified field or column
DROP INDEX	Deletes the index for a particular column

Although you need not understand all these keywords, you can see how few commands actually comprise the SQL language. By learning to use the Select command effectively, you will most likely be able to solve all the query problems that you encounter.

Summary

The SQL language is a powerful query language that can be used from Visual Basic. By learning the fundamentals of SQL and using the tools included with VB, even the beginning SQL programmer has access to powerful specific querying capabilities.

Q&A

Q Is it necessary to learn SQL?

A No, the Data Control and the wizards will handle most simple database tasks. However, if you intend to program database access through ADO, you will need to learn the fundamentals of SQL described in this hour.

Q Can Visual Basic treat the data returned by a SQL query as if it is an actual table?

A Yes; in fact, there is a term for this structure. It's called a *view*. A view can even be embedded in the database itself (in Access it's called a query) and treat the data like a table.

Q When I've created SQL code, will it execute on any SQL system that contains tables in the same format?

A No, like any standard that is not rigorously enforced, there are many deviations. Although the fundamentals of the query should work on any SQL system, each SQL-compatible product has created its own unique aspects. For example, the wildcard for the Jet engine is the asterisk (*); whereas Microsoft SQL Server has adopted the percentage (%) character as the wildcard.

Workshop

The quiz questions and exercises are provided for your further understanding. See Appendix C, "Answers," for the answers to the questions.

Quiz

1. What does SQL stand for?

2. Are all versions of the SQL standard compatible?

3. Which clause is used to determine which records are or aren't included in the final data set?

4. True or False: SQL is a procedural language.

Exercises

1. Establish a Data Environment that includes Command objects to three of the tables within the Northwind database. When the objects are created, make a single form that displays some of the field record information from each of these four tables simultaneously.

2. Create a connection within the Data View window. Use the drag-and-drop interface to move the connection to a Data Environment.

18

HOUR 19

Database Application Deployment

Numerous factors are involved in creating a successful database application. By now, you understand all the critical aspects of making an application work. Some of the refinements you can make are important to consider even for an application that will be used by only a few people.

Areas that most deserve focus include optimizing the performance of both the application itself and the database, refining the end-user experience, and creating an installation program. By paying attention to these details, your application's effectiveness will be improved.

The highlights of this hour include:

- Optimizing database applications
- Using multi-field indexes
- End-user tuning
- The Application Setup Wizard
- Connection issues

Optimizing Database Applications

After you have your program running, you will want to optimize it for the best performance and efficiency. A well-designed program not only runs better, but also will be easier to understand and maintain when you need to make changes to it in the future.

While you're optimizing your application, consider the two types of optimization you can provide:

- Real speed
- Perceived speed

Although this section will address real speed issues, understand that perceived speed is equally, and perhaps more, important. Perceived speed means the user feels that the application is fast.

Simple additions can often dramatically affect the perception that an application is fast:

- Progress bars—If a user is forced to watch an hourglass cursor for more than 20 seconds, a process can seem slow. Adding a simple progress bar showing how much of the process is left can make a huge difference in perceived speed.
- Splash screens—Like progress bars, a splash screen provides something to look at and indicates that something is occurring, particularly when a program is first loading and initializing.
- Pre-loading—Common forms and data files can be loaded when the application is launched, when the user expects to be waiting. When the desired function is activated, the display is almost instantaneous.
- Hidden forms—Rather than loading and unloading forms, hide forms that are dismissed if the program is small or memory is not a problem. Rather than unloading forms, setting the `Visible` property to `False` will keep them ready to display in the future.

These items will aid you in increasing the perceived speed of your application. To increase the real speed of the program, you will have to make changes in the implementation.

Using Multiple Indexes

The best way to optimize database performance is to make the indexes used by the application more effective. Often a query is performed on multiple fields at the same time (for example, finding all customers with a city of San Diego and a state of CA). Customizing the indexes can make these queries much faster.

When you create an index, you can actually create a multiple-field index that coordinates multiple fields. The Jet engine uses an advanced technology known as bitmapped indexing that makes multi-field searches very fast.

Therefore, for queries that commonly use two or more fields, define an index that contains all of these fields. These types of indexes are very simple to create using the Visual Data Manager.

For the Projects table, you might want to create an index that contains both the beginDate and endDate fields (see Figure 19.1). Because most of your project queries concerning dates will determine within a range of begin and end dates, this dual-field index will speed the searches.

FIGURE 19.1

Creating a single index for two fields (beginDate and endDate).

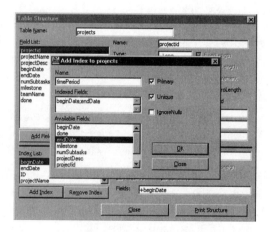

19

To use multi-field indexes effectively, study the most common queries used by your application. After you understand which queries are the most time-consuming, consider implementing multi-field indexes to increase the speed at which results to a query are returned.

Remember that each additional index will slow down record modification and new record insertion. Therefore, make sure that the multi-field query is actually used in instances where speed is important.

Performance Monitor

Performance Monitor is included with Visual Basic. The monitor can examine the executing portions of a VB program to determine the amount of time and processing resources used by individual parts of the application.

Using Performance Monitor can also allow you to understand how your program operates. By doing tests on the most commonly used features, you can determine which parts of the code are the best to spend resources targeting for optimization.

> Although Performance Monitor can be used to optimize very slow routines and particular bottlenecks, database applications are not typically processor intensive except when interfacing to the database. Therefore, for most database applications, use the Profiler sparingly. Instead, focus on optimizing your indexes and queries.

Compiled Versus Interpreted Code

Visual Basic allows two types of applications to be created: interpreted and compiled. Interpreted code is usually more compact and easier for the Visual Basic environment to produce and execute. Compiled code is generally larger but faster.

An interpreted application uses a large library of functions known as the Visual Basic runtime. An interpreted program is compiled into a string of bytes known as pseudo code (p-code). p-code is programming instructions that have been compiled into a number of references that call routines in a runtime library. Unlike true compilation, which generates actual machine code, p-code doesn't actually execute on the microprocessor. Instead, p-code calls routines in the runtime that execute.

NEW TERM   *p-code* is a list of references to routines in a runtime library. To execute a p-code program, a p-code interpreter reads each instruction in sequence and calls the appropriate routine in the library that actually executes on the microprocessor.

Compiled code, in contrast to p-code, is actual machine language instructions that execute on the microprocessor (the Pentium instruction set) rather than calling a runtime library. Because the processor is used directly, compiled code is generally faster than p-code.

You should consider making your application compiled if the program

- Is mathematically intensive, such as a financial number-crunching program or a fractal display
- Requires a substantial amount of bit manipulation
- Predominantly functions as a parsing program that manipulates and concatenates large numbers of strings in batches

If none of these items really apply (and most don't to the majority of database programs), leave the compilation option set to the default VB setting of p-code generation. Most database programs you write will use the majority of processing power when querying a database. With the substantial performance of today's Intel PCs, you don't have to worry as much about normal execution.

Because interpreted p-code is smaller in the compile than native compilation, most database programs benefit from having a smaller memory footprint and install image. Unless your application needs every execution speed advantage, choosing the p-code option might be the best choice.

End-User Considerations

In Hour 11, "Creating a User Interface," you examined some aspects of user interface implementation and design. To create an interface, you learned how to create a design plan for implementing an application. To go one step further, there are two common methods of design: creating an exacting specification and favoring a user-chosen design method.

Specifications

A specification can be used to great effect when trying to mold the uses of the application to the needs of the end user. A detailed specification can outline the functions of a program and how they might be implemented.

The specification can become the central document used for development. It can enable you to budget your time and recognize how development is progressing toward completion.

Specifications typically generally outline

- The purpose of the program and its central features
- Hardware and software requirements for the program, as well as any support technology (such as servers, input devices, and so on)

19

- Scheduling for begin, milestone, and completion dates
- The testing methodology that will be used to ensure the quality of the software
- Special dependencies such as where the data will come from or technology (such as an Excel interface) that is needed

When using a specification, the wants and needs of the user must always be considered. However, when writing a specification, the intended functionality of the program is the key guiding criteria to implementation. Another method can be used when the needs of the user are not very explicit.

User-Selected Design

There will be times when you have to design a program in which the functionality is not exactly known when the project begins. This circumstance is common when the application is being created to fulfill a need that isn't already served by another system (such as a paper-based system or an outsource supplier).

In this design process, a rough prototype is created that will, by all estimates, look nothing like the final application. This is primarily because the users don't know what they need, only that they need a new system.

1. Create a simple "window-dressing" version.

   When you are attempting to fulfill unrefined wants, it is not a good idea to spend much time on your first prototype. In the best circumstances, make a judgement call on how a number of the tasks requested might be presented to the user.

   At this point in the design, it is not even important to have the program actually reading data, although the simplicity of the Data Control allows for quick prototypes.

2. Use a database definition with many miscellaneous fields so data can be added easily.

   In your initial database creation, include many generalized fields such as miscdate1, miscdate2, and so on that can easily be added to a form without requiring alteration to the database structure.

3. Modify it quickly and provide a new version right away.

   If you act on the feedback you receive quickly, people will continue giving you ideas. Turning it around right away will also ensure that if you misunderstood any suggestions, problems will be quickly resolved.

4. Have scheduled revision updates.

   Try to produce a new version update on a schedule, such as on Tuesday. In this way, you will be able to schedule time for feedback with the users.

5. Document why some changes have not been made.

   For your own development reasons, be sure to document features that are not implemented. This will prevent you from having to re-discuss operations that proved unsuitable or difficult to develop.

This type of open-ended development works best on small projects or pieces of larger projects. Because the goal is to get the project into production as quickly as possible, this type of development makes it unlikely that development will simply drag on forever.

Application Setup Wizard

When the database application is complete, you will need to create a set of installer setup disks. The Application Setup Wizard included with Visual Basic 6 has been expanded to cover the new features added to this version.

The application Setup Wizard now contains support for all three object models:

- ActiveX Data Objects (ADO)
- Data Access Objects (DAO)
- Remote Data Objects (RDO)

That means the necessary data source and registration files will be included in your installer if you use these data access technologies.

The actual images created by the Application Setup Wizard will contain compressed files for all of the individual controls, drivers, and other data required by your application. The files created by the wizard are shown in Table 19.1.

TABLE 19.1 PRIMARY FILES CREATED BY THE APPLICATION SETUP WIZARD

Setup.exe	This program expands the files contained within the CAB files to a temporary directory on the target install volume.
Setup1.exe	The actual installer program executed after the files have been expanded with Setup.exe.
LST file	The LST file contains all the destination directories and registration entries of the application.
CAB files	Compressed images of all the files from your application.

19

The images the Application Setup Wizard creates will contain all the pieces necessary for your program to execute on the install machine. Remember that help and database files are not automatically detected by the wizard and must be added as additional files to the file list.

> The LST file contains all of the installation instructions (file installs, folders, OLE registration, and so on) for the installer. This file is stored in text file format. You can edit the file manually. See the "Distributing Your Applications" section of the Visual Basic Programmer's Guide included with VB for complete instructions.

CAB Files

A Cabinet (.CAB) file is a compressed file that can hold a number of individual files, much like the familiar ZIP compressed file. CAB files have several advantages over standard ZIP files, such as

- Code signing prevents unauthorized installation
- Better file compression
- Automatic file splitting
- Internet support

A CAB file can be used to hold all the various install files within either a single file or multiple split files. If all the split files are contained within a single directory, the installer will automatically find and use the subsequent files.

> Even if you're going to do a network install, consider making the images the size of floppy disks. Because the install will be transparent anyway, it won't make any difference to the user.

Registry Entries

Any ActiveX controls used by your projects need to be registered with the destination system. The wizard automatically takes care of these registrations for you.

If the OCX files ever need to be moved to a different directory, you can use the command-line utility regsvr32 to unregister them from their current location and re-register at the new directory. Executing the regsvr32 application from the command line without any switches will provide simple instructions. Registering a file requires a simple command such as:

```
regsvr32 -r myControl.OCX
```

User Login

Allowing the user to log in to the database is an important aspect of the opening interaction with the user. Because most of the security for an application is determined by the user login, appropriate presentation of a user login screen is important to the final application.

Several options can be used to log the user on to the system. You can either provide a custom login form or use the default forms supplied through the ODBC interface.

Login Dialog Form

Visual Basic includes a wizard that will automatically create a login form for you. From the Add Form dialog box, select the Login dialog from the list and it will create a standard login form such as the one shown in Figure 19.2.

FIGURE 19.2

The Login form created by the Add Form Wizard.

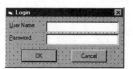

After the user has entered her username and password, you can store them in variables to be passed to the database connection routines. Leave the ConnectionString property setting for username and password blank in the Connection definition. When you open the connection initially, you can use the information retrieved from the txtUserName and txtPassword text controls to log in the user to the database.

ODBC Data Sources

If you don't want to construct your own login form, the Open Database Connectivity (ODBC) connection will provide a login window by default. ODBC is an industry standard; drivers are available for nearly any data source type including the Jet/MDB database.

ODBC is an industry standard driver architecture used to provide data access to heterogeneous data sources.

If you prefer to use the ODBC driver to access the MDB file, the user login screen is already supplied. Simply not including a username and password will automatically prompt a window that provides the information sent to the database.

Using an ODBC connection is also useful if you want to share the connection with other resources such as Personal Web Server and ASP. Because a data source for ODBC can be given a common name, all of your programs that need access to this data can use a connection.

Using a common connection allows multiple programs to access it by name. The program doesn't have to know the name of the database at compile time. As long as the data source remains constant, the database file can be located anywhere or named anything as long as the ODBC entry correctly points to it.

Most ODBC connections are kept in each desktop machine's ODBC source directory. If you will be installing your application on many different machines, you can avoid adding an ODBC data source to each machine by using a file data source.

A file data source is created as shown in Figure 19.3. These files have .DSN extensions and need only be pointed to from within the program. Using a file data source, you can avoid individual machine ODBC configuration.

FIGURE 19.3

File data sources saved as a DSN file.

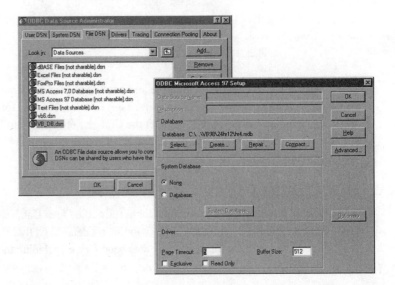

Asynchronous Processing

The ability to process a query in the background without halting the execution of the program can be very powerful. Although using this technology is slightly complicated and beyond the scope of this book, you should consider it in your final solutions.

Asynchronous processing can return control to the querying application before the database engine has completed the requested action. Therefore, if a user needs to continue work within the same application while an advanced query takes place, this implementation can add quite a bit of polish to your program. Check your Visual Basic manual for complete implementation details.

> Programs that use asynchronous processing must be very well-designed to avoid problems. For example, if a query is occurring in the background, it is usually a bad idea to allow updates to be made to the table being queried.
>
> Making changes to the queried table will slow down the return of the results and can also give the user inaccurate information if the query results do not reflect the newest changes, but the user believes that it does.

Summary

Developing and deploying a database application requires an understanding of many disciplines. Using some of the techniques and performance hints in this chapter, you should be able to refine your database applications.

Installation of an application on a foreign machine can be complicated. Be sure to generate a few test installs using the Application Setup Wizard well in advance of actual deployment. Sometimes the number of unexpected problems can be large.

19

Q&A

Q What is the best way to implement a progress bar?

A Included in the Windows Common Controls (available through the Components menu option) is a progress bar control that is built into the Windows 95/98/NT system. You're probably already familiar with it because it is used during file copies.

Q If the compiled code option is selected, can I generate a single-file EXE?

A No. Visual Basic cannot create a single-file EXE. Even the compiled version of an application needs some of the routines included in the VB6 runtime.

Workshop

The quiz questions and exercises are provided for your further understanding. See Appendix C, "Answers," for the answers to the questions.

Quiz

1. True or False: A multi-field index can be defined in a table.

2. What is p-code?

3. Besides a specification, what is another method that can be used from database application design?

4. What is a CAB file?

Exercise

1. Use the Application Setup Wizard to create an installable standalone application of one of the database applications you've created.

2. Create an ODBC data source that points to the hr4.mdb file. Use the VB Data Form Wizard to create a form that connects to the data source through the ODBC connection.

Hour 20

Accessing Outlook

Microsoft Outlook is becoming one of the most popular organizing and scheduling packages in use by individuals and organizations. In Hour 16, "Object Diagrams," you learned about reading an object model diagram. In this hour, you can use this knowledge to access the information stored in the Outlook database.

Because many database projects require an address book and email integration, why not use the features already included in Outlook? By accessing Outlook through its object model, you will be able to use code to manipulate it to do everything that can be done by a user.

The highlights of this hour include

- Accessing the Outlook object model
- Adding an Outlook appointment from VB
- Creating a Contact item
- Retrieving field information from a contact
- Searching Outlook information
- Referencing unique Outlook items

Accessing Outlook

The object model of Outlook (see Figure 20.1) is based on the metaphor of folders. If you've used Outlook before, you know that all contacts, appointments, notes, and other entries are stored within their individual folders.

FIGURE 20.1

The simplified Outlook object model.

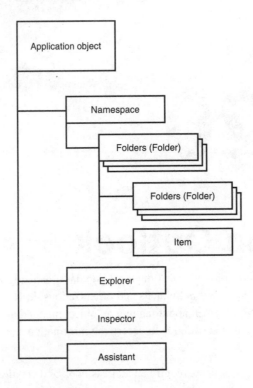

Each contact, appointment, and so on, is stored as an *item* object. If you add the Microsoft Outlook Library to the references of a Visual Basic object and use the Object Browser, you can see all the objects supported by Outlook (see Figure 20.2).

From the Object Browser, you can see that there are seven different item object types: `AppointmentItem`, `ContactItem`, `JournalItem`, `MailItem`, `NoteItem`, `PostItem`, and `TaskItem`.

Each of the item object types contains its own properties specific to its function. For example, the `ContactItem` has the `FullName` property to access the full name contained in the referenced item.

Using the object model diagram in conjunction with the Object Browser will allow you to manipulate the Outlook application.

FIGURE 20.2

The Object Browser displays Outlook item-type constants.

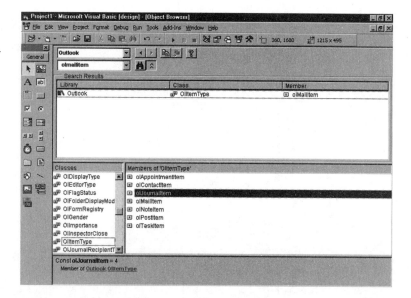

Adding an Appointment from VB

To begin your adventure manipulating Outlook, you'll start with a simple addition of an appointment item to the Outlook scheduler.

1. Begin a new project with a blank form.

2. In the References dialog under the Project menu, place a check beside the Microsoft Outlook Object Library.

   By adding this object model to your Visual Basic project, all the available Outlook object types can be used from within your program.

3. Add a button and set the Name property to cmdAddAppt.

4. Enter the following code into the Click event of the command button:

```
Private Sub cmdAddAppt_Click()
    ' Define an object to contain the Outlook app
    Dim objOutlook As Object
    Dim objItem As AppointmentItem

    ' Create an instance of the Outlook application
    Set objOutlook = CreateObject("Outlook.Application")

    ' Create a new Appointment item
    Set objItem = objOutlook.CreateItem(olAppointmentItem)

    ' Modify the new item
```

20

```
With objItem
    .Subject = "My first VB appointment"
    ' Set when the appointment is to begin as
    ' the current time
    .Start = Now
    ' Set when it is to end as the current time
    ' plus one tenth of a day
    .End = Now + 0.1
    ' Save the appointment
    .Save
End With

    ' Eliminate the object references
    Set objItem = Nothing
    Set objOutlook = Nothing
End Sub
```

5. Execute the application and click on the button.

When the application is executed and the event code activated, Outlook creates a new appointment in the current default appointment folder. The settings for the subject, start, and end times of the appointment are set, and the new appointment is saved.

The code creates an instance of the Outlook application to access and creates a reference to it in the objOutlook variable. After it is created, a new item of type olAppointmentItem is created. The Subject, Start, and End properties are set before the new appointment is saved into the Outlook folder.

In Figure 20.3, you can see how the appointment looks on the schedule. In this example, the number for a tenth of a day was added, but explicit dates can easily be set.

FIGURE 20.3

Outlook displaying the newly created appointment.

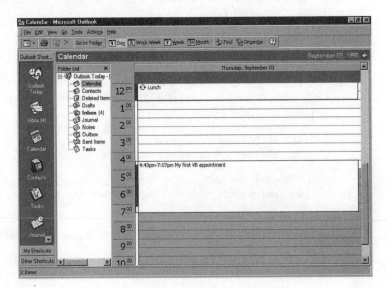

You might begin to recognize the power of Outlook for just about any automated task related to the functional areas it supports: contact lists, task lists, meetings, and email.

Because your Visual Basic program can access any common data source, data can be easily pulled from a database and entered directly into Outlook. Even a simple application such as using a database containing the common holidays to set reminders for each date in Outlook can be readily accomplished.

> You might notice that the CreateObject method is used to create an instance of the Outlook application for use. If Outlook is already open, you can manipulate the one in memory already.
>
> Simply replace the CreateObject code with the GetObject method, so the reference line looks like this:
>
> Set objOutlook = GetObject(, "Outlook.Application")

Creating a New Contact from VB

You've created one item type, the Appointment item. It is just as simple to create any of the other items with nearly identical code.

By simply changing the item type (in both the dimension code and the CreateItem method) and altering what properties are accessed, a VB program can create any type of item.

Add another command button to the form and set the Name property to cmdAddContact. Then enter the following code into the Click event:

```
Private Sub cmdAddContact_Click()
    ' Define an object to contain the Outlook app
    Dim objOutlook As Object
    Dim objItem As ContactItem

    ' Create an instance of the Outlook application
    Set objOutlook = GetObject(, "Outlook.Application")

    ' Create a new Appointment item
    Set objItem = objOutlook.CreateItem(olContactItem)

    ' Modify the new item
    With objItem
        ' Enter the name
        .FirstName = "Thomas"
        .LastName = "Rommell"
        ' Set the telephone #
        .HomeTelephoneNumber = "213-555-1212"
```

20

```
            ' Save the appointment
            .Save
      End With

            ' Eliminate the object references
            Set objItem = Nothing
            Set objOutlook = Nothing
      End Sub
```

When you execute this code, a new contact will be created with the primary information entered that should look like the contact shown in Figure 20.4. The three fields (first name, last name, and home telephone) are entered in their appropriate fields.

FIGURE 20.4

Outlook displaying the newly created contact.

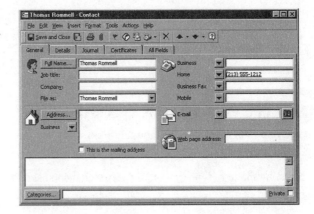

The capability of adding new contacts this way can be incredibly useful. If you have a database, text file, or list of contacts in an odd data format, or you need to selectively add contacts, a small Visual Basic program can provide the ultimate importing flexibility.

Accessing Contact Information

More often than adding contact information, there arises the need to access the information that is already stored in Outlook. If you're writing a database program that needs to store and retrieve contacts, Outlook can be used almost invisibly to provide this functionality.

As you'll see in this section, your program can easily search Outlook data either record-by-record or by using the Find routines included in the Outlook object model. After an entry has been found, your program can recover the unique number that identifies each item. This number can even be stored in your own custom database for a link to an Outlook item.

All the techniques in this section, although applied to Contact items, can be equally applied to other item types. Therefore, you can step through the appointment items or search the available tasks using the same methods.

Record-by-Record Access

The easiest way to address individual contacts in the Outlook model is to reference them through their default folders. Every item is stored in an object called a MAPIFolder. There can be folders within folders, so by obtaining the default folder, this becomes the easiest method available to search.

Add another command button to the form and set the Name property to cmdShowContacts. Enter the following code in the Click event:

```
Private Sub cmdShowContacts_Click()
    ' Define an object to contain the Outlook app
    Dim objOutlook As Object
    Dim objItem As ContactItem
    Dim nms As Object, folderRef As Object

    ' Create an instance of the Outlook application
    Set objOutlook = GetObject(, "Outlook.Application")

    ' Create a reference to the folder namespace
    Set nms = objOutlook.GetNamespace("MAPI")
    ' From the namespace, retrieve the default Contacts folder
    Set folderRef = nms.GetDefaultFolder(olFolderContacts)

    ' Display the total num of contact found
    MsgBox "Number of contacts:" & folderRef.Items.Count

    ' Step through each contact and display the full name
    For Each objItem In folderRef.Items
        MsgBox objItem.FullName
    Next

    Set objItem = Nothing
    Set objOutlook = Nothing

End Sub
```

When this code is executed, the FullName of each contact listed in the folder will be displayed in a message box. This information could just as easily be written into an external data source or stored to a text file.

20

> This code will display the names of every contact in the Outlook database. If you have a great number of contacts, this could take quite a while. You could instead substitute the For...Each loop with a For...Next loop and use the item indexes. The loop could then be limited to display the first 10 contact names.
>
> If the For...Next loop used the variable i, the individual object reference would appear like this:
>
> MsgBox folderRef.Items(i).FullName

Searching Outlook Data

Locating data using the method of single record stepping is very inefficient compared with using a native Outlook searching method. Therefore, the Find method was included for all item collections. A filter or query is defined to locate the first record that meets the specified criteria.

After the first record to match the filter is located, the FindNext method can be used to find subsequent appropriate records.

Add another command button to the form and set the Name property to cmdFindJohns. Enter the following code in the Click event:

```
Private Sub cmdFindJohns_Click()
    ' Define an object to contain the Outlook app
    Dim objOutlook As Object
    Dim objItem As ContactItem, found As ContactItem

    Set objOutlook = GetObject(, "Outlook.Application")
    Set nms = objOutlook.GetNamespace("MAPI")
    Set folderRef = nms.GetDefaultFolder(olFolderContacts)

    ' Find first contact with a first name of John
    Set found = folderRef.Items.Find("[FirstName] = ""john"" ")

    ' If none were found, notify user
    If TypeName(found) = "Nothing" Then
        MsgBox "No contacts found to match filter"
    End If

    ' Display full names of all the Johns found
    Do While TypeName(found) <> "Nothing"
        MsgBox found.FullName
        ' Move to next record that meets criteria
        Set found = folderRef.Items.FindNext
    Loop
```

```
    ' Eliminate the object references
    Set objItem = Nothing
    Set objOutlook = Nothing
End Sub
```

You might notice a few odd things about this code. The filter string is defined with the desired field in brackets [ ]. For filters, any fields must appear within brackets to be recognized. The brackets enable Outlook fieldnames to have spaces in them, unlike a Visual Basic variable name that cannot have any spaces.

For the desired criteria value, you will note that the value is enclosed within four sets of double quotes. Within VB code, placing two double quotes consecutively (" ") adds a quote character to the string that is being defined rather than closing the string definition. String matches within the filter string must be enclosed within quotes to be recognized.

The code locates the first instance of the matching contact and then advances through each to display the FullName field of the contact. The TypeName function will return the string Nothing when there is no object in an object reference.

> You can create a filter like the one available in Outlook to make the data
> set appear as if it only contains those data items that match the necessary
> criteria. To create this filter, use the Restrict method.

Relating to Outlook Data

Because you know how to access and search the database in Outlook, you can use the information in your own programs. As an added bonus, each Outlook item has a unique identifier or primary key. This key can be used to uniquely identify any of the items in Outlook.

The unique identifier allows you to relate one of your own external databases with an Outlook item. That means that rather than duplicating information from Outlook into your database, you can simply store a reference to a record in a field of one of your tables.

The id number for each item is stored in the EntryID field or property. If you examine the EntryID for an Outlook item, it will look something like this:

000000002B28534A8A2BD111A1CF0080C88394C304582100

20

This number is unique for each item stored in the Outlook database. The EntryID is stored as a String data type in the Outlook database. If you create a String data type in your database, you could record the EntryID with a simple command like this:

```
myRS!OutlookID = objItem.EntryID
```

To look up the record later, simply use the Find method to create a match between the stored value and the EntryID field of an Outlook item.

Summary

Accessing data within the Outlook application can add an entirely new dimension to your database programs. Data can be easily imported and exported from Outlook with precision using the object model to reference individual items and fields.

By storing the EntryID values of particular items in an external database also allows a manual relation to be created between individual Outlook items and external programs.

Q&A

Q Can I create only Outlook application objects in the General Declarations of a form and use it with many routines?

A Yes. Be aware that an instance of the Outlook application object takes up the memory of an entire copy of Outlook. Therefore, keeping it loaded will lock a large amount of memory away from general application use.

Q Can I reference other folders beside the default folder?

A Yes. The NameSpace object contains the complete collection of all the folders available from Outlook. You can even create a new folder through Visual Basic code.

Q If I store the EntryID reference in my database, what problems can occur?

A The EntryID is unique for each item, so confusion among items is not possible. However, items can only be searched within a particular folder, meaning that you either have to rely on the default folder remaining the same or record the folder id as well.

Additionally, if the item that is referenced is deleted or archived, the reference will no longer be valid.

Workshop

The quiz questions and exercises are provided for your further understanding. See Appendix C, "Answers," for the answers to the questions.

Quiz

1. What type of object are most pieces of information stored as?
2. Do all item types have the same properties?
3. True or False: The Outlook Object Model only provides access to a limited number of fields.
4. Which method can be used in place of `CreateObject` to acquire an application object reference?
5. How are items organized within the Outlook object model?
6. Can items be referenced by an index value?
7. What method is after the initial `Find` method to advance through the filtered list of items?
8. Which data type is used to store the `EntryID` value?
9. What are the two consecutive double quotes ("") used for?

Exercises

1. Use the sample code as the basis of a program to add a task to Outlook. Look in the Object Browser of the `TaskItem` object to determine what properties are available for setting.
2. With the `Find` method for the folder object, query the Outlook database for a number of contacts and add the full names of the located contacts to a combo box control.

20

Hour 21

Sharing the Database

In Hour 15, "Multi-User Database Design," you learned about the various aspects of database locking when creating a multi-user system. Although locking provides a technical solution to concurrent access, what happens if a record update fails? With the potential of a locked record, a single failed update in a series of important operations can corrupt your database.

To solve these problems, the Jet engine includes the capability of transactions. Using transaction technology can prevent data corruption and ensure database integrity.

The highlights of this hour include:

- Basics of transaction methods
- Ensuring data consistency, durability, and scalability
- Using transactions in Visual Basic

Data Integrity

If the data contained in the database is not accurate or consistent, it becomes much less useful and potentially damaging. In the end, a database application will be judged on the integrity of the data it stores and reports on.

Through the use of transaction technology, you can make sure that complex update operations, if they fail, do not threaten the integrity of the database.

Transactions

A transaction is a method of encapsulating several database operations within a single all-or-nothing execution command. When a single operation performed in a transaction fails, the program can eliminate all the previous steps in the transaction, returning the database to the condition it held before any of the operations were attempted.

The easiest way to describe a transaction and emphasize its importance to accurate data storage is to use an example of a banking system.

Imagine a database system that needs to be constructed for a bank. This system can perform electronic transfers of funds between accounts. To accomplish a transfer, a certain amount must be withdrawn from one account and that same amount added to another account.

This transfer process actually occurs in a series of discrete steps (see Figure 21.1). In the figure, $500 is subtracted from Account A and $500 is added to Account B.

FIGURE 21.1

The data flow of an electronic funds transfer.

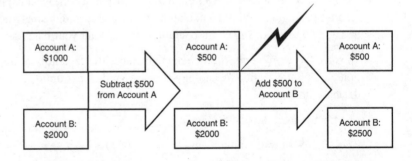

If the database system fails between when the money is withdrawn from Account A and the amount is added to Account B, $500 would disappear from of the system! Obviously this type of problem could cause widespread data corruption.

In a multi-user system, problems of this type can be particularly acute. If many records have to be updated within a single transaction, the chances of data collision are much higher than a single-record update.

Transactions were created to solve this problem. A transaction will either record all of the changes it encapsulates or record nothing. In the bank example, the failure of the database system will cause the initial withdrawal to never occur.

A transaction encapsulates the two different operations and treats them as a single operation. If anything occurs to cause an error for either of the modifications, neither will be written into the database.

NEW TERM A *transaction* encapsulates a number of database operations and treats the operations as a single unit. A transaction will either record all of the changes within it or record nothing.

To begin a transaction, you simply need to use the `BeginTrans` method on a `Connection` object. Afterward, any operations that modify any data sources linked to the connection are contained within the transaction.

The updates aren't actually written into the database until the `CommitTrans` (commit transaction) method is executed. This can actually speed data modification over a large number of records because the changes are cached. When the commit actually occurs, the changes can all be made simultaneously.

NEW TERM The *commit* is the final action in a transaction. The commit actually writes all of the changes within the transaction to the database.

Many problems can occur within a transaction, however. Perhaps one of the key fields is locked and cannot be written into. The values for a field might exceed the maximum acceptable value for the field type (that is, a very large number is greater than the 32KB limit of an Integer field). Whatever occurs that prevents the success of all the operations, the transaction will need to be aborted.

The `RollbackTrans` method is used to revoke the operations that have been completed up to this point. The transaction itself is nullified and all changes to any of the data sources since the `BeginTrans` method are returned to their initial state.

NEW TERM A transaction can be aborted by activating a *rollback*, which revokes all of the operations within it. You can activate a rollback at any time during a transaction.

You might notice how simple the transaction technology is to implement. The Jet engine takes care of all the advanced capabilities and allows you to focus on when to begin a transaction and when to commit it.

It makes little sense to include every database operation within a transaction because of the overhead associated with opening the transaction. It is also a bad idea to include a vast array of unconnected updates within a transaction.

21

Try to group the operations within a transaction to a unified objective. In the previous example, the objective was to transfer funds from one account to another. An operation to update the name on the client's account doesn't belong within the transaction.

> Transactions might seem like technology that is mostly useful for large systems, and large systems are where the greatest benefit is achieved. However, because of the ease of implementation, you should try to implement transactions in all but the smallest solution. They can help ensure that your data remains valid.

Consistency

When you begin using transactions, you will recognize that encapsulation helps solve other problems with keeping effective data consistency.

A database is consistent if all the rules embedded within the system are satisfied. Most consistency restraints are supported by referential integrity or business rules.

For example, an inventory and sales system must keep constant track of removals and additions to inventory. If the balances of all of the inventory quantity accounts don't match the number being sold, the sale might need to be suspended until the discrepancy can be discovered.

At the end of a transaction, but before it is committed, a function can be used to verify the consistency of the database. If the database is not consistent, the operations might need to be aborted.

Consistency will temporarily go out of balance during a transaction. However, as soon as all operations are complete, the system should become consistent again.

Durability

Durability for a database system is essential. Durability means that despite hardware or storage failures, the data remains consistent. This is the key area in which transactions are useful.

Two aspects of the Jet engine provide for durability: transactions and reparability. Transactions ensure that during a failure, incomplete updates are not made. The Jet engine also provides a repair function that will examine the database and resolve any problems or discrepancies.

Scalability

Transaction capabilities you create in your MDB application are scalable if you ever need to move your application to a more robust database solution. Most of your shared applications place a central database file on a file server so it can be accessed across the network.

This method uses the file server as a way to provide concurrent access. Large systems feature a different type of server known as a database server. With a file server–based system, all the query processing actually occurs on the individual desktop machines.

A database server, however, accepts a query and returns a dataset. All the processing actually occurs on the central server. This allows specialized optimization and dramatically reduces the bandwidth required to send the information back and forth.

NEW TERM A *database server* is a server dedicated to receiving and processing database queries, updates, and insertions. The specialized nature of a database server allows it to handle large numbers of users.

Through the Visual Basic data environment and ADO, all the code for transactions that you create can be scaled to a full database server if you need more power for processing. In fact, Microsoft Access provides a tool known as the Upsizing Wizard that can move your MDB file onto the Microsoft SQL Server. After the program is redirected to the database server, the Jet transactions will be operational without any new coding.

Transactions in Visual Basic

Visual Basic implements the transactions through the ADO object model. All `Connection` objects support the `BeginTrans`, `CommitTrans`, and `RollbackTrans` methods.

To begin a transaction, the `Connection` object, as well as the `Command` objects to which the operations are to be committed, must be instantiated . After the transaction has been opened, your database code will be now different from traditional update code.

> The OLE DB drivers for both the Jet engine and Microsoft SQL Server support transactions. However, if you are using an alternative data source, be sure to check the proper documentation. Not all data sources support transactions and some sources are limited in their transaction abilities (such as being unable to maintain transactions across multiple tables).

21

To demonstrate the transaction, you can write a simple program to make modifications to every record in the todo table of the hr5.mdb project.

This example will make modifications to all the records contained in the todo table if the OK button is clicked, so be certain you don't have any data you want to preserve if you OK the changes.

1. Start a new data project in Visual Basic.

2. Open the data environment.

3. Configure the Connection to point to the hr5.mdb.

   Use the Jet OLE DB driver and browse to select the hr5.mdb file as you have in the past.

4. Add a Command object to the connection, name it comtodo, and point it at the todo table.

5. In the Advanced tab of the Properties window, set the Command object to optimistic locking.

   By default, new Command objects are set to be read-only. Because you are going to be doing updates against the fields, your program will need write access.

6. Click OK to accept these changes to the Command object.

7. Open the frmDataEnv form.

   On the form, you will place a command button that will activate a transaction to occur to the database file.

8. Add a command button to the form and name it cmdTransUpdate.

   The code for the command button uses the connection created in the data environment to access the recordset for that table. It then modifies all of the records, but encapsulates these changes within a transaction.

   Before the changes are committed to the database, the user is prompted to determine whether the changes should be saved. Following the user's response, the changes are either written into the database or the Rollback method is called.

9. In the Click event of the button, enter the following code:

```
Private Sub cmdTransUpdate_Click()
    Dim myConnect As Connection
    Dim myRS As Recordset

    ' Initialize command object
    DataEnvironment1.comToDo

    ' Create a reference to the Connection object
    Set myConnect = DataEnvironment1.Connection1
```

```
' Create a reference to the recordset of the
' conToDo Command object
Set myRS = DataEnvironment1.rsconToDo

' Move to the first record
myRS.MoveFirst

' --- Begin the transaction ---
myConnect.BeginTrans
i = 1
Do Until myRS.EOF
    ' Change description field
    myRS!itemDesc = "Trans Desc #" & i
    ' Increment variable and record count
    i = i + 1
    myRS.MoveNext
Loop

' Ask if changes should be saved
result = MsgBox("Save the changes to the records?", vbYesNo _
    , "Save Changes?")

If result = 6 Then
    ' --- Commit all operations ---
    myConnect.CommitTrans
Else
    ' --- Revoke changes ---
    myConnect.RollbackTrans
End If
End Sub
```

10. Execute the application and click the button to begin the transaction.

The code will progress through each record of the database and set the itemDesc field to hold the value of Trans Desc # plus the record update number. All these changes are contained within the transaction and are not actually written into the database until the user clicks the OK button.

The code shows you that implementing transactions does not require a large amount of extra work. Recognize that because the changes for a transaction are not written into the database until all of the operations complete successfully, an error occurring before the update is complete could result in a loss of the data stored so far.

> Transactions can actually be encapsulated within transactions. Like having nested If...Then structures, each deeper BeginTrans statement will produce another level of depth. There should be a matching number of commit or rollback statements to complete each transaction level.

21

Summary

The transaction capability supported in the Jet engine and available through Visual Basic is a major tool you can use to keep your databases consistent and uncorrupted. Although transactions add a little overhead for initial establishment of the transaction environment, they can actually speed batch updates.

By encapsulating all the actions specific to a certain type of operation within the BeginTrans, CommitTrans, and RollbackTrans methods, the ability to simply add all-or-nothing updates to your database can be implemented. Because transactions can be nested, you are not prevented from having substantial control over the grouping of related operations.

Q&A

Q Is transaction encapsulation necessary for single-field/single-record updates?

A No, in fact, to update a single field in a single record is much slower than without transaction encapsulation and has no advantages. However, if a batch of records has a field that needs to be updated, making the updates within a transaction can speed the process.

Q Why aren't transactions available for every database type?

A Implementing transactions from a database vendor's perspective is not an easy task. Like an Undo command, the actual changes must be recorded so they can be undone. Some simpler databases simply don't include the technology for transactions.

Workshop

The quiz questions and exercises are provided for your further understanding. See Appendix C, "Answers," for the answers to the questions.

Quiz

1. What is a transaction?
2. If a CommitTrans method is used to accept a transaction, what is used to abort a transaction?
3. Do transactions make the MDB database system more durable?
4. True or False: Transactions can be nested.

Exercises

1. Set up two programs that access a common database. Set pessimistic locking on one of the connections and open a record for updating. Use the other application to attempt an update for this same record within a transaction.

2. Use the Timer method to test updates that use transaction encapsulation. Are numerous individual updates faster inside or outside of a single large transaction?

21

HOUR **22**

Database Security

After you begin sharing data among multiple users, security considerations become paramount. The database can be set up to allow only users with permission to read data, modify data, or even change the database structure.

Before you begin installing a shared type of database, consider the ways you can implement security. By providing basic security on your database, you can make sure your Visual Basic 6 application is not compromised through vicious intent or accidents.

The highlights of this hour include:

- The need for database security
- How to plan security frameworks
- Setting security on individual objects
- Placing security on the hr4.mdb database

Why Should I Worry About Database Security?

You might think the information in your database is not very secret and therefore doesn't require implementation of security. The database might not contain confidential information such as salary levels or passwords, so protection is just an extra task. Confidentiality is only the most obvious reason for establishing security for your database.

Three primary reasons to add security to a database are

- To protect confidential information
- To prevent information misinterpretation
- To guard data from accidental corruption or loss

Many people recognize the need to stop unauthorized access, but think this is the limit of their concern for database security. When considering security, you should give more thought to the other two dangers (misinterpretation and accidental loss), which can potentially create more problems in a small-use system than malicious intent.

Misinterpretation of information is very problematic even with a small number of users. Data stored in a database is often meant to be viewed using certain procedures with an understanding of assumptions that might or might not be correct. Someone trained in examining the data will be able to make a judgement call on the validity of the results. An inexperienced user can easily misinterpret data and that misconception can create unspoken resentment.

An example of this problem can occur with something as small as a label. Imagine that you run a database to track your home business. You create a table to track people's training on the application Microsoft Excel. Their level of training is specified with a number from one to nine and the table used for tracking is named Trained.

Someone examining the numbers stored in this table (perhaps even your spouse) might be insulted by the low number used to rate workers, not understanding that this relates only to a specific type of training. Although this is a simplistic example, it is very easy to see context plays a large part in understanding information. Data not meant to be viewed by untrained people can have an extremely negative effect without the injured party saying a word.

Untrained users can also affect another area: data validity. When a user accesses data he does not understand, it is often done through a part of the application he does not understand how to use. Data corruption and data loss are two of the potential results from an unfamiliar user.

22

It is extremely common for a personal database application to provide easy methods to accomplish a powerful task such as the deletion of all selected records. Such features make it easy for the few people who know how to use the program to accomplish an otherwise complicated task. To a new or untrained user, though, these features can be as dangerous to your data as a loaded gun can be to a child.

For all of these reasons, you should take some time implementing a security system within any shared database.

 Adding security to a database does little good if it is not updated and maintained. Security will become one more constraint to people getting their jobs done. Therefore, make sure whoever has administrative privileges maintains the proper security system.

To implement an effective security system, you must pay attention to how the security will be structured. This requires good advanced planning.

Planning Database Security

Planning is perhaps the most essential step in security implementation. Actually adding security will take very little time if the issues involved are considered in advance. Database security planning can be complicated mostly because it relates to decisions regarding user access needs.

As a place to begin, make a quick sketch of all the objects contained in the database including:

- Tables
- Queries
- Fields

Which of these objects needs to be protected from unintended or unauthorized viewing or modification? For a particular process (such as recording an order), what objects are needed to complete the operation?

After you have an idea of how these objects relate, examine the possible extensions to the database that will be required in the future. If the system is expanded, the security should likewise be revised. In the next section, you will see how security can be organized around the concept of groups of users. As additional people need access, they must be added to the appropriate security groups.

Recognize that security is important for nearly any database project beyond a single-person operation. Because of the potential for even unintentional data corruption, serious considerations should be given to how security will be handled.

> If you have Microsoft Access, it is a good idea to use it to print a security report after the security is constructed. In the User and Group Accounts window (accessed from the User and Group Accounts option under the Security submenu), the Print Users and Groups button will generate this report. The Access security report will list all users and groups, and their various permission levels. The report can either be printed or exported to Microsoft Excel or Microsoft Word.

Placing security on a database during development is usually difficult because so many pieces of the project are in flux, including the database structure itself. Therefore, it is usually unnecessary to place security on the database immediately after it is created.

However, security should be added before the first test deployment. The inability to access certain secure objects can be extremely frustrating to users new to the system, especially if they should have permissions. Ironing out the problems with security early in the deployment cycle is a good idea.

Users and Groups

After you have an accurate idea of what objects will be available for security protection, you need to determine the key groups that will need to have access to these objects.

The primary rule when creating a secure system is

Define groups and provide those groups with permissions before giving permissions to any individual users.

Adding permissions to individual users is a bad practice unless necessary in a special exception. If permissions are added individually, it is very easy to overlook providing a user with needed groups or granting permission to unauthorized tables.

Keeping permissions at the group level also makes it more likely security will be maintained because upkeep is simplified. Rather than adding or removing a permission from ten users, simply changing the group that holds them will instantly modify permission of all users involved.

Groups are usually created around various user types, such as Guests (often only given read-only access), Users (such as data-entry operators), PowerUsers (provided with full access but no structural modification privileges), and Administration (complete control). If your system is simple, you might only have two groups: Users and Administration.

After the groups are created, you need to decide which users belong in which groups. Any user can be stored in more than a single group, so try to break down the groups by functional area. If access to both inventory and sales data is necessary, simply place the user in both groups.

You can follow the security flowchart shown in Figure 22.1. This flowchart shows the recommended steps for properly setting up a security system. Note that this addresses initial setup and not necessarily the maintenance routine.

FIGURE 22.1

The steps to create an effective users and groups implementation.

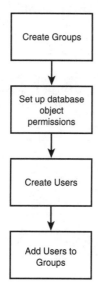

Types of Permissions

A variety of controls can be placed on a user who is accessing the data source. As shown in Table 22.1, a number of potential areas can be managed using the security permissions.

TABLE 22.1 PERMISSION TYPES FOR AN MDB DATABASE

Type	Description
Read Data	Permission to read data from the database
Read Design	Permission to read the structure of tables, queries, forms, and so on contained within the database
Modify Data	Ability to modify existing data
Modify Design	Permission to alter design structure of objects within the database
Enter New Data	Allows insertion of new data, but cannot modify or delete existing data
Delete Data	Delete information in the database

These settings can be modified down to the table level in an MDB file. All the settings can be assigned to a group or user for specific privileges.

Every database security system has different capabilities. All the information presented here involves the Jet/Access database type capabilities. If you are accessing another database system, consult the appropriate documentation for the security settings supported.

Visual Basic Security

Visual Basic uses the same security as Microsoft Access, so the security settings created in one application can be accessed and are supported in the other.

The security to protect an MDB file is actually located in two different places. The user-names, groups, and passwords are stored in a centralized file known as System.MDB. Individual database object permissions are stored in the database itself.

System.MDW File

For MDB files, all the security is centralized in a single file for each system. This file, the System.MDW file, is addressed by all Access and Visual Basic applications that use MDB files.

The System.MDW file holds the following:

- Users
- Groups
- Passwords

22

This security file is the central point of login for an MDB file. However, all individual object permissions (such as tables, fields, and so on) are stored within the database file itself.

NEW TERM   A *System Identification code* (SID) is a unique identification number stored in the security file System.MDW. A SID identifies a user or group by that user login.

Permissions to objects store each SID that has permission to access that resource. The structure of the objects stored in the System.MDW file is shown in Figure 22.2. Understanding the basic structure of the file is not as important as recognizing that the key information for all the database security is held in this file. If the file is lost, so is the login access to all of the databases it secures.

FIGURE 22.2

The structure of the System.MDW file.

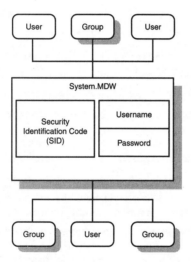

Locking Database Objects

After users and groups are defined within the security file, security must be set for specific structures within the MDB file. Two types of security are directly available from a Visual Basic database: password security and individual object security.

Password security requires a password to enter the database at all. This option is rarely used in Visual Basic solutions and is primarily available for Access solutions. Because Access stores its forms and code within the MDB file itself, this barrier can be used for development security as well.

If the database is replicated (a procedure in which mirrors of the database are made that can be synchronized), don't set a database password. If a password is on the database, synchronization is impossible.

Individual object security allows you to set security for objects within the database, such as tables and fields. Individual object security, also called user-level security, requires the administrator to define users and groups. The users and groups are set to have certain privileges.

The level of control for the security settings is known as the granularity. In Microsoft Access, the granularity is limited to database tables. In larger systems such as Microsoft SQL Server, locking can occur down to the level of individual fields.

NEW TERM *Granularity* is the precision that is possible when placing security settings for individual users and groups.

Individual objects (such as tables) are subject to permissions for all of the levels listed in an earlier section (such as data reading, data modification, structure reading, and so on).

If you made a sketch of all the objects you wanted to protect in the planning stage, you will have a much easier time deciding and setting permissions.

In a typical database, it is very easy to miss one of the myriad of objects available for security authorization. As permissions are set, note that the changes have been made on your plan.

There is such a thing as too much security. Every time a more complex layer of security is added (such as field protection), the amount of time required for upkeep increases. Try to be sure the security on that level is really necessary.

Often there are alternatives. If salary information is to be kept private, consider placing it in a related table rather than in each employee record. That way the salary table can be secured without placing locks on individual fields within the employees table.

After security is set, the Administration account should be password protected. If the default Admin account is left with the blank password, the entire security system can be breached by a knowledgeable user.

Controlling security for various tables also helps limit the record-locking problems that occur with multi-user access. If a certain group of users is limited to read access on a table, there is no chance a record might be accidentally placed in edit mode, suspending use for other users.

When more than 100 users are accessing the same database at a time, an error might be generated that doesn't allow additional users to log on. You might have to edit the line in the client system's AUTOEXEC.BAT to provide more locks. If you experience this bug, check the Microsoft site for the tech note on how it can be resolved.

Implementing Security on hr5.mdb

All the database security you've learned about so far is really simple to implement using either the Visual Data Manager within VB 6 or the Microsoft Access application. These programs allow groups and users to be added simply and permissions granted or removed.

Because both of these environments use the Jet engine, the settings placed on the database object will appear in both applications.

Using Visual Data Manager for System.MDW

The Visual Data Manager requires that you select the System.MDW file in order to provide the security for the MDB databases. Typically, this file is located in the directory C:\Windows\System.

Under the Utility menu in the Visual Data Manager, you'll find the option System.MD?... that you can use to select the MDW security file for the system. The Data Manager will use this file to retrieve user and group identifications for database access.

If you have never accessed security on the system before, an error might be generated when you attempt to access the Visual Data Manager. You can use Microsoft Access to add the first security group. Afterward, the Data Manager can be used for all MDB security needs.

From the Visual Data Manager, you have complete access to the security settings (see Figure 22.3) from the Groups/Users/Permissions window. Accessing this option requires you to have an MDB file open and can be selected as the Groups/Users option found on the Utility menu.

FIGURE 22.3

*The security settings
window in the Visual
Data Manager.*

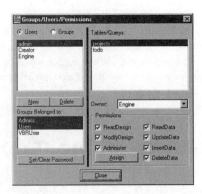

Adding a New Group and User

To provide a demonstration, you can create a new group, give the group explicit
permissions for tables within the hr5.mdb file, and add a user to the group. Anytime that
database is accessed after these permissions have been recorded, you can log on to the
database system using the new user account and access capabilities will be restricted to
those of the group.

Use the Visual Data Manager to

1. Open the hr5.mdb file.
2. Select the Groups/Users option under the Utility menu.
3. Set the option button to Groups.

   The option button is used to select whether the new item will be created as a user
   or a group.
4. Click the New button under the Groups list box.
5. Type Hour4User in both the Name and PID fields (see Figure 22.4) and click the
   OK button.

FIGURE 22.4

*The security settings
window in the Visual
Data Manager.*

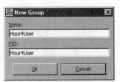

6. Click the Hour4User group in the Group list box.

7. Select the Projects table in the Tables/Queries list box.

8. Click on the ReadData check box (see Figure 22.5).

   Notice that the ReadDesign box is automatically checked when this occurs. Data cannot be effectively read without the table structure being known. However, the opposite is not true, so ReadDesign can be checked without permission to access data.

FIGURE 22.5

Setting the ReadData option on the Hour4User group.

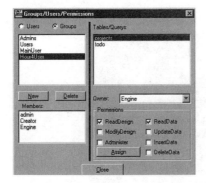

9. In the Permissions frame, click the Assign button.

   The table is now set to read-only permission to the Projects table.

10. Perform the same operations to give ReadData permissions to the ToDo table.

    Because security is assigned to the Hour4User group, there is still no way to log in to the system. You must define a user who is a part of the group.

11. Set the option buttons to Users.

12. Click the New button under the Users list box.

13. Type SimpleUser in both the User Name and PID fields and click the OK button.

14. Select the SimpleUser item in the user list and then select the Hour4User group to add the user.

The security settings are now included in this database. In a deployable implementation, make sure both the Admin account and the new account don't have a blank for a password.

Adding Security to a Connection Object

After the security is defined, you can access the database using this new user through a Connection object in the data environment, the Data Control, or directly through ADO database access code.

For your projects, you can modify your data environment connection like this:

1. Open the Connection object properties.

2. Click on the Connection tab and enter the SimpleUser username.

In the configuration window for the Connection object, you can set the connection to access the data source through this user account (see Figure 22.6). Now any access to the hr5.mdb file will occur through the SimpleUser account.

FIGURE 22.6

Using the SimpleUser user account for connection login.

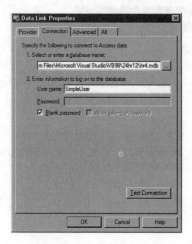

Summary

Establishing and maintaining security is important for any database that has more than a single user. The two most important aspects of security planning are deciding what objects need security and what groups should be able to access individual objects.

Security permissions for objects should then be added to a group. Individual users are then added to the groups that meet their requirements. For MDB security, all the groups, users, and passwords are stored in the System.MDW file.

Q&A

Q Does a group placed within another group inherit the permissions of the parent group?

A Yes, unless you intentionally override the settings of that group.

Q Should a secure database keep an Admin group?

A There is no choice because the Admin group cannot be deleted. However, make sure you change the Admin password from the default blank password to make the database secure.

Q What is the best way to maintain the security of the database?

A Microsoft Access has the best user interface for maintaining security on MDB files, but all of the basic functionality is available in the Visual Data Manager.

Workshop

The quiz questions and exercises are provided for your further understanding. See Appendix C, "Answers," for the answers to the questions.

Quiz

1. What are the three primary reasons for adding security to a database?
2. Where can you print a list of all security levels, users, and groups for an MDB file?
3. When is the best time to add security?
4. True or False: The proper way of adding security is to place the permissions on groups and then add users to the appropriate group.
5. What is the System.MDW file?
6. True or False: It is possible to allow a user to add new information, but make the user unable to see any existing information in a table.
7. What folder is the System.MDW file usually located in?

Exercises

1. Establish a data environment that contains a connection using the SimpleUser user and attempt to modify some record information.
2. Create a new group that has permission to modify data, but not read it. Bind some controls to a Data Control pointed to the source. Execute the application and try the navigation keys.

Hour **23**

Older VB

As you become a more experienced programmer, you will probably encounter projects created with older Visual Basic versions. You might also need to interface with a network database system using a previous VB revision. If you are developing projects for different people, or if you work on a Visual Basic project that someone else created, you might need to interpret a legacy Visual Basic project.

NEW TERM *Legacy* software is an old system or program that is being actively used. Although useful, legacy software usually uses out-of-date formats or protocols.

Interfacing or upgrading legacy systems requires special skills. You must understand the current standards as well as past limitations. For Visual Basic, this means that knowing how both VB and the included data access functionality has changed is critical to working with older systems.

Additionally, a great deal of sample code online or in magazines you encounter will be not be written for Visual Basic 6. There is some basic information that will greatly aid you in understanding and adapting these old projects.

The highlights of this hour include:

- Learning the various data object models
- Studying differences between DAO, RDO, and ADO
- Upgrading projects from earlier VB versions
- Sharing a database between 16- and 32-bit systems

Data Object Models

The portion of Visual Basic that has evolved most dramatically over the years as new versions of VB has been released is the method used to access databases through programming. Microsoft has refined and made database access more powerful over the years.

You learned about ActiveX Data Objects (ADO), the current access method, in Hour 17, "Understanding ActiveX Data Objects (ADO)." There were two primary precursors to the ADO: DAO and RDO. Both DAO and RDO are still included with Visual Basic 6, but will be progressively phased out in future versions.

Data Access Objects (DAO)

The Data Access Objects (DAO) were the initial object model used in Visual Basic 3 when database access was added. DAO has been updated with every version of VB and is included in Visual Basic 6. Because ADO has evolved from the DAO foundation, both implementations are fairly similar.

Rather than separating connections and recordsets as ADO does, an active connection in DAO is required before a recordset can be created. Therefore, DAO cannot instantiate a recordset before a connection object is created as is possible in ADO.

> The primary difference between the two object models is the hierarchical structure. DAO is strictly hierarchical and requires the parent objects (such as a Database object) to be instantiated before the children objects can be created.
>
> ADO doesn't have this limitation. All the objects (such as the Recordset and Connection objects) can be created independently.

Converting DAO code to ADO code is fairly simple, however. For example, here is the code necessary to open a recordset and generate a message box with the first contact name using DAO:

```
Dim myDB As Database, myRS As Recordset

Set myDB = OpenDatabase("nwind.mdb")
Set myRS = myDB.OpenRecordset("Select * from customers")
MsgBox myRS!ContactName
```

The same task is accomplished with ADO like this:

```
Dim myRS As New ADODB.Recordset

Const ConnectStr = "PROVIDER=Microsoft.Jet.OLEDB.3.51;Data
Source=nwind.mdb;"
Set myRS = New ADODB.Recordset
myRS.ActiveConnection = ConnectStr
myRS.Open "Select * from customers"
Set myDB = OpenDatabase("nwind.mdb")
Set myRS = myDB.OpenRecordset("Select * from customers")
MsgBox myRS!ContactName
```

You can see how similar the two code samples actually appear. Most of the differences between the two models are comprised of the new Connection objects available to ADO, but not included with DAO. Most of the functions of the Connection object are available through a variety of objects such as TableDefs, QueryDefs, and other Database object children in DAO.

If the code you need to convert is a simple use of the database, the preceding code might provide enough guidance to complete a conversion. For more complex adaptations, you will need to consult the Visual Basic manual. In the VB 6 manual, there is a section included on converting DAO and RDO code to the new ADO model. See this manual section for more information.

Remote Data Objects (RDO)

Remote Data Objects (RDO) were first included with Visual Basic 4 and provided a simple user interface to the robust connectivity drivers available through Open Database Connectivity (ODBC). RDO created a fast interface to the low-level programming interfaces previously available only to system-level programming languages such as C++.

ODBC is a generic method of interfacing to numerous database types (such as Oracle, Sybase, Informix, SQL Server, and so on). In the Windows system, an application is written to print to the Windows printer system—any printer can be used as long as a compatible driver is available. ODBC works the same way, except it supports drivers for database access. By writing a program to interface to the ODBC driver system, a compatible ODBC driver can be used to access any data source that has the proper tables and fields.

For example, a program could be written to read and write to certain tables through the ODBC system. As long as the appropriate driver for the desired data source (such as an Oracle or Sybase database server) is installed on the machine, the program can access it with no programmatic alterations.

NEW TERM *Open Database Connectivity (ODBC)* is an industry standard for providing generic database access. ODBC drivers are available for nearly any current database system.

With DAO, accessing an ODBC data source requires that all requests are processed through the Jet engine. This can slow access considerably. RDO provides an interface that is programmed much like DAO, but eliminates the Jet engine layer.

In the current ADO model, rather than having two separate object models, the requested data source type is specified by the ADO driver. Therefore, a single data object model can be used without the performance penalties previously associated with DAO.

Converting RDO code to use ADO is nearly identical to the methods used for converting DAO code. Because DAO and RDO are almost identical in their implementation, consult the DAO information for guidelines.

ActiveX Data Objects (ADO)

The ADO model was first included with Microsoft's Web server known as Internet Information Server (IIS). Although DAO was primarily used by Visual Basic as a database access model, Microsoft has positioned ADO to be the standard access method regardless of the technology used.

ADO can be used in IIS, VBA, VB, VBScript, Visual C++, Visual J++, and nearly any programming environment. Because a single data model is used by all these environments, only ADO needs to be installed on the client system instead of numerous technologies. It also means that the procedures for addressing data is standard regardless of the development system used.

ADO is a significant improvement over DAO in its ability to pool database connections. For multiuser systems, particularly through a Web server, the solution provided by ADO is vastly superior.

ADO is also much simpler than earlier models. ADO really only consists of three primary object types, whereas other models have more extensive object collections.

Data Environment—New to VB 6

The Data Environment covered in Hour 7, "Data Environment," is not included in any version previous to VB 6. Only a rudimentary add-in known as a UserConnection was included in version 5. The UserConnection, however, could not be bound to data-aware controls and therefore its use was not widespread.

When examining legacy projects, you won't encounter any projects that use the Data Environment. However, when converting up to VB 6, it might be effective to re-evaluate the implementation of the project and consider whether using a Data Environment would be more effective than the choices made in the present code. Because the Data Environment provides the perfect implementation for project-wide common data source access, it might provide a better solution than the one implemented by the project.

Also be aware that projects that use the Data Environment will not be in any way backward-compatible if, for any reason, you have to convert to an older version of Visual Basic.

> Although the Data Environment is not backward-compatible, you can use ADO in older versions of VB. Because ADO is simply another object model, you can use the References dialog to add its objects to a project.

Upgrading Legacy Projects

Because Visual Basic has been so popular for so long (there are currently more than 1 million users), it is very likely that you will encounter a project created on an older version of VB. Whether inheriting a project from another programmer or downloading a sample project from the Internet, you will probably need to adapt the project to the newest VB version.

The basic conversions are fairly straightforward. The language itself is completely backward-compatible, so you won't encounter any problem with that. However, upgrades that involve conversion from 16-bit operating systems to 32-bit operating systems include more challenges.

General Project Upgrades

Upgrading a project is typically an automatic process. If the project that you are adapting was created in VB 4 (32-bit) or VB 5, the Visual Basic 6 system will recognize the older project version and verify that you want to upgrade it before loading the project.

When the upgrade occurs, if any problems are encountered, a log file is automatically created that explains each error. The log file that related to a particular problem file (such as a form conversion) will have the same name as the initial file with the addition of a .log extension.

If the source files are saved in text file format (as opposed to binary format), you can load them into any text editor. This includes any form or class files in addition to module files. Occasionally, you will run into a problem with the automatic conversion that causes the form to not load properly.

Because a log file is automatically created listing the error, you might be able to correct it by hand. First make a backup of your original source code file. Then load it into the text editor and make the desired alteration. Then try loading it into Visual Basic.

Windows 3.1 and 16-Bit Systems

There might be times when you will have to create a project that runs on an older system or upgrade one on an older system. Windows 95 was the first major operating system upgrade that made 32-bit programs standard.

Previous Windows operating systems, primarily Windows 3.1 and Windows for Workgroups, were 16-bit operating systems. Up until mid-1997, these older versions of Windows were still installed on a majority of desktop systems.

The exploding popularity of Visual Basic at the time of the 16-bit Windows dominance caused huge numbers of 16-bit programs to be constructed, primarily with Visual Basic 3. Visual Basic 4 was released about the same time as Windows 95 and provided the primary bridge between the two worlds.

Transition to VB 4

Visual Basic 4 contains substantial capabilities to allow for simultaneous maintenance of both 16- and 32-bit versions of the same project. It also includes the most robust capabilities necessary to move a 16-bit project into the 32-bit environment.

Up until Visual Basic 3, the file extension of .mak denoted a Visual Basic project. This created confusion, however, because Visual C++ used the same extension for its projects. With Visual Basic 4, the standard extension for a VB project changed to .vbp.

When converting from a VB 3 to a version 4 project, it is a good idea to leave the extension as .mak until conversion is complete. After the Visual Basic system has loaded and effectively converted the proper forms and code modules, save the project and quit VB. Now alter the extension to .vbp so Visual Basic will not have any future problems identifying the project type.

If your final destination for a 16-bit project is 32-bit, it is often a good idea to begin by simply converting it from a VB 3 or earlier project to VB 4 16-bit. This will allow you to ensure that it executes properly under VB 4. After this is complete, then convert from VB 4 16-bit to VB 4 32-bit.

> If your local software vendor does not have a copy the older version of Visual Basic that you need, try taking out a classified ad in a local paper or computer magazine. There are numerous older versions gathering dust that someone would be happy to sell you for a small fee.

23

VBX Controls

Before OLE Controls, also known as OCX or ActiveX controls, there were Visual Basic eXtension (VBX) controls. VBX controls are 16-bit components that can be used in Visual Basic 3 and the 16-bit version of VB 4.

When you move a project from a 16-bit to a 32-bit system, you need access to OCX components that are compatible with the original VBX controls. Most vendors sell compatible controls for upgrades. All the Microsoft controls available on the earlier VB systems have compatible OCX controls available.

> There are times when a custom 16-bit DLL or VBX used in a legacy system is not available in a new 32-bit version. If the control or DLL is absolutely necessary (such as when it accesses a custom piece of hardware), there is an option.
>
> Although a 16-bit control cannot be used in a 32-bit program, a program known as a wrapper that provides the interfaces in 32-bit format and interfaces to the 16-bit code can be written as a 32-bit DLL. Unfortunately, the wrapper program must be written in C++. If the application is critical to your needs, hiring a C++ programmer to create the wrapper might be an option.

VBX controls were far less robust than current ActiveX/OCX controls. They could only be used within the VB environment, unlike OCXs that can be used even in word processing applications! Not surprisingly, there are a far greater number of OCX controls available.

If the vendor of the original VBX is no longer in business or does not offer an OCX upgrade, you can probably find an alternative control that fulfills your needs. Check the online catalog of VBXtras, a vendor that specializes in ActiveX controls (www.VBXtras.com).

Sharing Data with a 16-Bit System

If you need to write an application where the database is shared by many different machines, you might encounter a situation where an existing application has been created on a 16-bit version of VB or Access. Newer versions of the Jet engine can address older data files, but not vice versa.

Databases stored in Access 2.0 format can be easily accessed on 32-bit systems such as Windows 95/98 and Windows NT. Therefore, if you need a program to share data with a 16-bit system, leave the file in its original format.

> If you decide to upgrade the entire Access 2.0 database file to a newer version, BE SURE TO MAKE A BACKUP before conversion. After the file is converted to a newer version, it cannot be returned to its original state.

Another alternative is to use the Attached or Linked table functionality included in Access. Access can have a table attached to it that is not in the current Access database format. However, to programs addressing the database, they treat the attached table as if the data was actually stored in the current database.

Summary

Converting older Visual Basic projects can require a fair amount of time. Most of the basic conversion of the project files is handled automatically by Visual Basic. Because the language itself is backward-compatible, you probably won't run into many syntax problems. Examining the older data models and issues with the 16-bit to 32-bit conversions, you will be able to effectively translate a legacy solution into a current application.

> This chapter provides only an overview of the problems you will encounter during a translation to a newer version. If you have a large project to convert, be sure to attend a local Visual Basic user's group. Almost all user's groups have one or more users who have used older versions and can give you recommendations on how best to accomplish your upgrade.

Q&A

Q Can a 16-bit VB project be converted into a 32-bit project?

A Yes. Visual Basic 4 was the last version to support both 16- and 32-bit systems. For conversion, it is probably a good idea to acquire a copy of this version to simplify the upgrade. Also, any VBX controls used within the original program must be installed and available as OCXs on the system for the conversion to work properly.

Q Can a 16-bit application and a 32-bit application read and write from the same data source?

A Yes, but the data source must be stored in 16-bit format. The ODBC and Jet drivers included with the Visual Basic system are backward-compatible with older versions of the Access file format. However, you will sacrifice the newer database features included with the 32-bit versions.

23

Workshop

The quiz questions and exercises are provided for your further understanding. See Appendix C, "Answers," for the answers to the questions.

Quiz

1. True or False: DAO is not included in Visual Basic 6.
2. What is a VBX?
3. Does Visual Basic 6 support both 16-bit and 32-bit projects?
4. Should I convert my 16-bit database to 32-bit format?

Exercises

1. Search for conversion information on the Microsoft Web site. There are several white papers explaining how upgrades are done with various sample projects.
2. Examine the What's New section of your Visual Basic 6 manual. Skim through the current changes to the system so when loading older code, you will recognize the new technologies that can be used in place of earlier code.

Hour 24

Raw Data Conversion and Migration

You now have a good grasp of database application development. One of the most common tasks in constructing a database is converting data from either another program or a raw data file. The growth of the Internet has caused an explosion of text files that contain data that might be read into a database and used.

Visual Basic provides robust capabilities to read and write either text or binary files. Therefore, if you know or can figure out the format that is used by the file, you can write a converter in VB to read the data and store it in a database.

The highlights of this hour include:

- Reading a simple file
- Examining the Open method
- Using Type structures for formatted loading
- Introduction to the new File System Objects

Reading a Simple File

For these examples, you will need to create a simple text file (using Notepad or another text editor) and save it with the filename test.txt at the root of your C: drive. Enter the following text (the entries in the brackets are a single character):

```
"Apples","Fruit",1
"Oranges","Fruit",2
"Carrot","Vegetable",3
"Chips","Junk Food",4
"Taco","Junk Food",5
```

This sample file has three fields separated by comma characters. The file is similar to many data input files you will encounter. This format, known as comma-delimited format, is a common structure used for data export from most programs and spreadsheets.

After the file has been created, it will be useful to create an extremely simple example to merely read and display the data in the file. The data will be read one record at a time.

Visual Basic includes the Input # command that will read a piece of data directly into a variable. This command automatically parses the comma-delimited file and reads the data inside quotation marks, ignoring the comma and quotation marks to return only the actual data.

Create a new project and add a command button to the form. Insert this code into the Click event of the button:

```
Private Sub Command1_Click()
    Dim j As Integer, a$, b$
    Open "c:\test.txt" For Input As #1
    Do Until EOF(1)
        Input #1, a$, b$, j
        MsgBox a$ + ":" + b$ + ":" & j
    Loop
    Close #1
End Sub
```

When you execute this routine, each field of each record will be read into the proper variable and displayed. Notice that the type of variable is set in the initial Dim statement for each of the input variables. Because the type is set, the Input # routine will expect the value to match the variable type.

If you alter the third field (the number field), for example, to include text, a data type error will be generated. Although you can trap these errors, they are a good indication during your import that the file format is not homogenous.

When you begin file processing, it is a good idea to set a breakpoint during the import and use the Immediate window to examine variables. Often, the way you believe the data is being read is not accurate. Rather than wasting time on many executions, the first time through you should track each piece of data as it is read from the file. This will make errors immediately apparent.

After the file is opened in a particular format, you are limited in the type of import functions that can be used. Therefore, considering how you are going to configure the open routine is a key aspect of creating an effective import.

Open Method

The Open method is the command that governs which features will be available for use when processing the file. You can open a file as a variety of file types as well as select the mode that the file will be used in.

The Open method will open files in these modes:

- Sequential (Text) Input/Output
- Sequential (Text) Append
- Random Input/Output
- Binary Input/Output

The sequential file is used for reading simple text. The example that you already created reads a file using this open type. Visual Basic automatically processes many of the formatting characteristics (such as commas and quotes) automatically for you.

Random input treats a file much like a database. You can use a Type declaration to define a type of record. The file can then be read in a random access fashion, inputting the record number desired.

A binary file is the most effective for byte-by-byte input and processing. Any character can be read directly into a variable without any preprocessing.

The syntax of the Open method looks like this:

```
Open fname$ [for mode] [Access access] [locktype]
As [#]filenumber [Len=recordLength]
```

In Table 24.1 you can see the settings available for the Open method. These various parameters allow the locking, file type, access mode, and filename to be specified. The parameters shown in brackets are optional.

24

TABLE 24.1   PARTS OF THE Open METHOD

Parameter	Description
fname$	A valid path and filename.
mode	Dictates the type of opening, such as Input, Output, Binary, Append, and Random.
access	Specifies the modification privileges such as Read, Write, and Read Write.
locktype	Determines the locking mode and can be set to Shared, Lock Read, Lock Write, and Lock Read Write.
filenumber	Any valid file number between 1 and 511 that isn't already in use.
recordLength	Either the number of characters to be buffered (Sequential) or the record length (Random).

The Open method should be used in conjunction with the Close method. If a file remains open, it uses one of the allocated file buffers. You can use the FreeFile method to determine the next logical available file number for assignment to a file.

File Types

Different open types have different capabilities. Table 24.2 shows the difference in supported commands for various file types. You can see that Input, because of the open-ended nature of its read operation, is not included in the commands supported by the random file type.

TABLE 24.2   COMMANDS RELATED TO FILE INPUT

Type	VB Statements
Sequential	Open, Line Input #, Print #, Write #, Input #, Close
Random	Open, Put #, Len, Close, Get #
Binary	Open, Get #, Put #, Close, Seek, Input #, InputB

Determining the file type you will use has the most to do with the type of data you need to import. Is the data stored in discrete records? Is it one long string of text? Was it written to the disk with a C++ program as Byte data types? All of these options will impact your decision.

Sequential Files

Sequential files are the most commonly used for file importing. Because both `Input` and `Line Input` conduct preprocessing, the sequential file type is best to use for either general text or files stored in comma-delimited format.

In a comma-delimited file, it is very common to have text entries enclosed in a set of quotation marks. For example, a text field might appear like this:

```
1,"This is a test",36
```

Using quotation marks prevents commas, spaces, and other characters within a string from faulting the read.

Binary Files

Binary files can be used to read unprocessed data directly from the file stream. Using the `Byte` data type or an array defined in that type, you can read exactly the data you need to read.

Reading binary files can be tricky because Visual Basic is not made to do substantial byte operations. If you are going to read binary files, it is a good idea to start by using the `Byte` data type to write a sample file in the format you intend to read. Then use your read routine to read the file, to make sure you're reading what you intend.

Random Access Files

Unlike sequential or binary files, a random access file can be easily read in any order. After the fields of a record are defined, the file can seek a particular record immediately (see Figure 24.1). This extra flexibility comes at the price of having to explicitly define the length of the record definition.

All records must be stored in the same format. Variations are not allowed. Text, such as that needed in a traditional word processor, cannot be easily entered into a specific record size.

If you have a random access file that stores contacts in a standard record format, you can easily read the records in the file simply by defining a structure with the `Type...End Type` structure.

In the following example, a file is assumed to contain fewer than 50 records in a standardized format. It reads each record into an array of the defined type.

24

FIGURE 24.1

*A diagram of a general
random access file.*

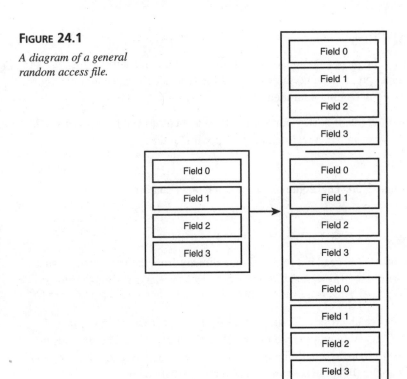

Insert the following code into the General Declarations section of the form:

```
Private Type ContactType
    ID as Long
    Name as String * 20
    Address as String * 75
    CityStateZip as String * 40
End Type
```

Place this code in the Click event of the command button:

```
Private Sub Command2_Click()
    Dim testContact() As ContactType
    ReDim testContact(50)

    Open "c:\test.txt" For Random Access Read Write Shared As #1 Len =
➥Len(testrec)
    numRecords = LOF(1) / Len(testContact(1))
    For j = 1 To numRecords
        Get #1, , testContact(j)
    Next
    Close #1

End Sub
```

You can see from the code that the Get command is used. Because the Get command allows a second parameter to specify a record number, you could modify the code to explicitly read a specific record.

> A Type structure can also be used with a sequential or binary file. It is simply most commonly used with a random access file type.

File System Objects

Visual Basic 6 includes File System Objects (FSO), which provides an object-oriented method of file access. Available in all the Visual Studio applications as well as Active Server Pages, this technology seems to be the new standard for file access.

Visual Basic programmers can easily make the choice of whether to use native commands or FSO at any time because they work in nearly identical fashion. The specific advantages of using FSO include:

- Compatibility with other development systems (Visual C++, Visual J++, Visual InterDev, and so on)
- Unicode bias
- Robust international support

If any of these factors figures heavily in your coding decisions, you should choose to use FSO in preference to standard VB file commands.

> FSO is an object model just like other libraries (such as Outlook). To use FSO, you need to add a reference to the library that is registered in the OLE Registry. The File System Object is located in the Microsoft Scripting Runtime object model in the References dialog.

A simple file-reading example can show you the similarity to standard file methods. The largest difference between the two systems is the fact that all the files are stored in textstream objects instead of stored as numeric file references.

24

The following code opens a file named test.txt and reads the first line to be displayed in a message box:

```
Dim fso, myFile

' Create a reference to the FSO
Set fso = CreateObject("Scripting.FileSystemObject")

' Open a text file in read mode (1 = Read file)
Set myFile = fso.OpenTextFile("c:\test.txt", 1, True)

' Read a single line and display it in a message box
MsgBox myFile.ReadLine()

' Close the file
myFile.Close
```

The Visual Basic manual contains all the information regarding use of FSO, but it is very straightforward. If you use the Object Browser to examine the FSO object model, you will be able to accomplish most of the tasks that your project needs.

Summary

Using the Visual Basic 6 file commands, you can load almost any type of data into Visual Basic for insertion into a database. Whether a random access file, sequential file, or binary file is used, the strength of the VB capabilities should allow you to accomplish the conversion without much difficulty.

File System Objects, new to Visual Basic 6, provides a common way to access file data among all of the Microsoft development products. The similarity between FSO and native VB file commands makes conversions between the two methods simple and quick.

Q&A

Q Can an entire file be loaded at once?

A The typical variable limit in Visual Basic is 64KB within a single variable. Arrays can be made bigger than this, but become memory and processor inefficient. If you have to process a larger file, it would probably be a good idea to process it in smaller chunks.

Q Should I process a file one byte/character at a time?

A When initially developing your conversion routine, it is often a good idea to read the data a single byte at a time. That way you can see exactly what is being input. However, this is much slower than a multi-character read. For the full conversion, you might want to revise it to read multiple characters.

Workshop

The quiz questions and exercises are provided for your further understanding. See Appendix C, "Answers," for the answers to the questions.

Quiz

1. What are the three primary file types available in VB?

2. True or False: In a random access file mode, you can instantly read a record from anywhere in the file.

3. What are the three primary data-reading commands for use with files?

Exercises

1. Create a file using one of the Excel export options. Write a Visual Basic routine to import the file in a readable format.

2. Use a `Type` declaration to write the Northwind customers table to a text file. Read the file back into VB using the type structure.

24

Appendix **A**

Error Handling

When programming a Visual Basic application, creating the code to catch possible errors can be tedious, but it is very necessary. Database applications in particular can have additional problems that should be gracefully handled.

The time spent creating effective error handling and error avoidance routines will help the application function more smoothly. In a database application, losing data is the worst possible consequence of an error. Therefore, creating code for effective error management is critical.

The highlights of this appendix include:

- General error handling routines
- Examining the Error object
- Logging errors
- Minimizing data entry errors
- Using advanced prevention technology such as referential integrity and business rules objects

Error Handling Routines

General programming presents a number of error handling obstacles. Database programming is even more challenging in the number of potential errors. Some problems specific to database programs include:

- Broken connections
- Missing drivers
- Entry of inappropriate data in a specific data type field
- Entries with invalid data such as mistyped date fields or non-existent states
- Attempted writing to a locked record

By constructing effective Visual Basic code, you can prevent many of these errors and catch the rest for effective explanation to the users rather than an inexplicable program crash.

Some routines can simply provide the error code for consultation with the tech support department of the application. Other problems can actually suggest ways to resolve the problem as is common in most Microsoft applications.

Visual Basic is particularly bad at handling errors that you do not provide handling to accommodate. Visual Basic will display an error code dialog box and will then quit the program, losing all data the user had entered.

The most effective error handling systems include recovery, reporting, suggestion entry, and access to more help. A help button that launches the appropriate section of online help can be among the best remedies to a user error.

Ideally, the user should be able to ignore the error and continue processing. For example, Microsoft Office used to require aborting an installation if any file was missing or corrupted. This would sometimes result in aborting an installation of Office on the 31st of 32 disks because of an invalid clip art file. Thankfully, Microsoft has remedied this situation, but you should try to avoid including it in your application.

When designing a database system, the longer an operation takes to complete, the more recovery options should be available. Losing data entry completed over the last half hour for a simple mistake can be extremely frustrating.

Returned Error Processing

The simplest type of error processing simply ignores the error. In Visual Basic, the `Resume Next` feature will ignore an error and attempt to process the next line of code. By simply placing the following code at the beginning of a procedure, any error will just skip to the next line:

```
On Error Resume Next
```

To catch an error and return its error code requires only slightly more advanced code. You can use a traditional message box to display the error and allow the user to continue or cancel the operation. The following simple code will present a message box that asks to continue:

```
result = MsgBox("Do you want to continue?",1,"Error")
```

If the user clicks the OK button, the `result` variable will contain the value `0`. Using a routine this simple is probably good for your own routines when an internal error is determined, but doesn't handle the more important system level errors.

> When you're writing error routines, try to include them within conditional compile statements such as #if and #else. Doing this will allow you to turn off the routines during testing.
>
> Usually you don't want any routines to catch the errors because execution will halt inside your error detection routine. When you're developing, you really want execution to stop exactly where in the code the error occurred. This way variables and surrounding operations can be immediately evaluated.

Using the standard `On Error` routine can actually trap the errors. You can use the `On Error GoTo` statement to actually jump to a particular routine for handling such as the code shown here:

```
Private Sub Form_Load()
    On Error GoTo myHandler
    MyRoutineA

    Exit Sub

myHandler:
    MsgBox "An error of type: #" & Str$(Err) & _
        " - " & Error & " occurred", 16, _
        "Error Occurred"
End Sub
```

After the error itself is trapped, the hard part begins. How is the error handled? Do you abort the operation or jump to the next statement? This decision will have to be made for each individual program construction. However, you will need more information in the routine to determine how to progress.

The Error Object

System level errors are generated by the Visual Basic system itself. Violating the bounds of an array, accessing an item that isn't in a collection, and other problems will cause Visual Basic to stop executing the program and display an error dialog box. After the dialog is dismissed, the program will end execution, close the application, and return to the operating system.

To prevent this from happening, you can create error handling routines. All the information regarding the error that occurred is stored within an Error object. Use the Object Browser included with Visual Basic to examine the two primary versions of the Error object you will use in your database development: the standard VB object and the ADO Error object.

Generating Errors

For testing purposes, one of the most useful routines is the Error() function. With the Error() function, Visual Basic can generate any error type desired anywhere in your program.

When you are getting ready to put your application through its final paces, liberally add these functions to various parts of your program. Can the program survive a simulated connection loss? How about a piece of Null data from a field in the database? By using this function, you will be able to know approximately how your program will handle a wide variety of unexpected events.

Unanticipated Errors

Visual Basic handles error routines as a chained hierarchy. If an error occurs and no error trapping code is present in the offending routine, the error is passed up the chain of calling routines until an error handler is encountered (see Figure A.1).

If no error handlers exist in the chain, the error finally is passed to the Visual Basic system itself. Therefore, make sure that you have a generalized error handler in the top level calling routine to prevent your finished application from quitting when it encounters a problem.

FIGURE A.1

The error chain for Visual Basic routines.

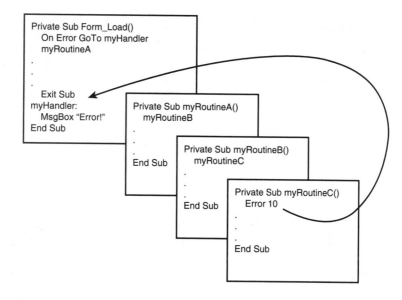

```
Private Sub Form_Load()
    On Error GoTo myHandler
    myRoutineA
    .
    .
    Exit Sub
myHandler:
    MsgBox "Error!"
End Sub
```

```
Private Sub myRoutineA()
    myRoutineB
    .
    .
End Sub
```

```
Private Sub myRoutineB()
    myRoutineC
    .
    .
End Sub
```

```
Private Sub myRoutineC()
    Error 10
    .
    .
End Sub
```

Error Events

Many different parts of the Visual Basic database system have custom event procedures that allow localized reaction to a specific error event. The Data Control and the Data Environment both allow code to be added and received and to process these events.

Placing the error code directly inside the object that generates the error has a great number of advantages when re-attempting operations (such as re-establishing a connection).

Error Logging

Logging errors to a file or database can be one of the most useful features you can add to a program. You can log the time the error occurred, what the error code was, and the condition of important variables.

The log file then becomes the basis for a statistical analysis to determine the most often encountered problems. Recording all the error information also supplies you with critical information about the problem that users often neglect to record.

For the most effective logging procedures, use standard file commands (such as Open "test.log" For Append) to write the errors into a traditional text file. Because a broken connection with a database could be the error you wish to record, attempting to write it to a database might not be a good strategy.

Database Error Problems

Database systems have a number of errors that must be handled specifically. Many of the most common problems with databases occur during the data entry stage and have more to do with error prevention than error handling.

The fewer opportunities an application presents for unusual input information, the better the system will become. The user will feel more comfortable with the solid interface of the application because fewer abstract choices are required and entry becomes routine.

By adding additional safeguards such as referential integrity and encoded business rules, the number of potential problems with a database application will be minimized.

Values Out of Range

One of the most tedious aspects of error handling is catching inappropriate values. These values are entered by users that if saved to the database will at best cause an error, and at worst will be stored as bad data.

You can use some common techniques such as using Masked Edit controls, favoring list and combo boxes, and providing notes fields to minimize these problems. Bad or inaccurate data can be one of the biggest threats to having accurate information in a database. Therefore, effort expended trying to plug some of the most common holes will result in vastly more trustworthy information.

Use the Masked Edit Text Box

The easiest method to prevent problems in this area is to use the Masked Edit text box for fields that have a limited format. Masked Edit allows you to specify exactly the format that must be entered. This prevents incorrect entries.

The control itself offers a template format (in the form of entry blanks) for the user. The user is then not confused as to what type of data is to be entered in this field.

Favor Combo and List Boxes

Rather than including text boxes for fields, consider using a list box or combo box for entry. These controls can ensure common entries are correctly selected and spelled.

Visual Basic uses this method even for numeric constants. If you look at the DrawStyle property on a form, you will see a combo box used to select from a number of constants (for example, 0 - Solid, 1 - Dash, 2 - Dot) that prevents any misunderstanding from occurring.

If you don't want to limit the user to a specific range of selections, the combo box can be set to allow general text box input. The combo box list can be used to fill in the most common selections.

Provide a Notes Fields

Often, inaccurate data entry occurs as users attempt to squeeze information into data fields that were made so they don't incorporate all the necessary information. Users frequently abbreviate full terms in an effort to add critical data to a record.

Unfortunately, these efforts might generate bad or difficult-to-query information. The solution to this problem is to provide an additional catch-all field in which extra information can be placed. When the field will not hold all the necessary information, additional data can be placed in a Notes field.

> Be sure to occasionally audit the information stored in the Notes field of the records. By examining extra information stored in this field you might be able to quickly see some aspect of the database that was overlooked in the design. Necessary fields can be added to accommodate information that users have already been recording.

Various Error Types

Because database applications require numerous technologies to work together (that is, ActiveX, ADO, ODBC, and so on), most of the technologies include some type of custom error definition routines.

For example, ODBC returns a particular type of error code, often specific to the driver. However, ODBC includes a function, `SQLError`, that provides SQL error information to explain exactly what problem has occurred.

The ADO system provides its own `Error` object type specific to database conditions. You can receive error information through the object's properties such as `NativeError`, `Description`, `Number`, `Source`, and `SQL State`.

Be sure to examine the exact technology you are using for methods and objects that map directly to that technology. Access to a data source through ADO can be handled by a combination of the native VB error-catching system and the ADO error objects.

A

Business Rules

Business rules are an increasingly dominant way of preventing data error. Rather than put the logic for checking the validity of the entry in each individual program, checks are placed in an ActiveX object, so all interfacing to the database actually occurs through the object itself (see Figure A.2).

FIGURE A.2

Diagram of the use of components for business rules.

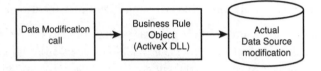

Because the ActiveX object can execute any type of code, complete checks for accuracy can be conducted, even against other tables. These objects are added to a Visual Basic project through the References dialog just like the Excel Object Library.

Visual Basic can easily be used to create such objects simply by defining a class within an ActiveX DLL project. When you select a new project, an ActiveX DLL project wizard can be used.

> The VB Data Form designer will create a class file as one of the generation options for access to a particular data source. The wizard can create this class and modify it for use in an ActiveX DLL.

Referential Integrity

Creating relations to a set of tables in a database can provide referential integrity. Unless you're using the Enterprise Edition of Visual Basic, the best method of accomplishing this task is through the Microsoft Access program.

Because both Access and Visual Basic use the same file format (MDB), any relations created in Access are valid and used from VB. Therefore, you can use the Relationships option from the Tools menu.

The first time you use the Relationships window, you are presented with a dialog box allowing you to add tables within the database to the window. After you've added the tables, relations can be created simply by dragging a field onto the field you wish to connect.

Figure A.3 shows the relation that can be created in the hr5.mdb database you used in this book. By dragging and dropping the ProjectID field from one table onto another and setting the referential integrity properties, Visual Basic will automatically make sure integrity is maintained.

FIGURE A.3

Double-clicking the relation after it is created shows the properties window.

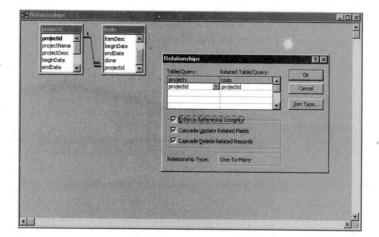

APPENDIX B

Glossary

2-Tier   See **Client/Server**.

Access   The ability to connect to a data resource for the purpose of querying, reading, writing, or deleting data within it.

ActiveX Control   A control is a self-contained miniature program that can be inserted and used within another program or development environment, such as Visual Basic. An ActiveX control is for use within any programming environment (such as VB) or browser (such as Internet Explorer) that supports the OLE protocols. Originally called OLE custom controls or OCX controls, ActiveX controls have evolved from the original Visual Basic extension (VBX) controls. ActiveX controls can be constructed using Visual Basic. See also **Control**.

Ad Hoc Facility   Allowing a free-form query that allows custom retrieval of data from a data source to be constructed by the user within an application.

Algorithm   A computer process defined by an explicit series of steps. An algorithm is generally a small, math-intensive program made to complete very specific tasks such as compression algorithms, image processing algorithms, or financial algorithms.

API An application programming interface (API) is a published standard way in which a program may interact with another program. For example, the Windows API allows custom programs (written in VB, Visual C++, and so on) to interact with the Windows system.

ASCII See **Unicode**.

Asynchronous Processing The ability to have a process, such as a query, execute in the background and activate an event when that process is complete. Asynchronous processing allows the execution of a program to continue.

Attribute A property or description of a particular object that determines what that object is or does. In database terminology, the term *attribute* is also used to indicate a data element such as a field.

Audit Trail Logged trail of operations that allows determining of every step that occurred over a time period. Audit trails are most commonly used for databases to monitor alterations to data.

Backup A copy of existing data for the purpose of preventing data loss if something happens to the primary data store.

Band An area on a data report that is repeated as necessary, such as a page header or a detail band.

Batch Process A number of independent operations that are all performed together. In database usage, the term usually refers to a number of instructions that are sequentially sent to a database for processing at the same time. See **Batch Update**.

Batch Update In the ADO model, changes to multiple records may be made, but those changes remain cached until the method is called to process all of the changes in a batch update.

Benchmarks A program or set of programs that holds certain variables constant and can execute similar processes on dissimilar systems for comparison. Many database benchmarks exist to determine how many simultaneous operations can be performed or users can be connected.

BLOB Undifferentiated data within a database is treated as a binary large object (BLOB). For example, a bitmap image cannot be searched or any other complex database operation performed on it, so it is stored as simply a chunk of data within a BLOB field.

Boolean Values that are either True or False, Yes or No, and 1 or 0. Boolean values are usually used in combination with logical operators such as AND, OR, or NOT to combine multiple comparisons.

Bound Controls   Controls that display information accessed by a Data Control. Bound controls handle all the behind the scenes work and can be easily graphically linked to the Data Control.

Breakpoint   A stopping point within the execution of a program at which variables and procedures can be examined. A breakpoint is used when debugging an application.

Bubble Chart   A graphical diagram used to explicitly show the relations (one-to-one, one-to-many, and so on) used in a database.

Business Process   The business rules and procedures used to complete a particular operation. When database systems are built, they usually mirror the business processes used in the actual work of the organization.

Child   A node or child of an object in a hierarchical relationship. In a data environment, a child may be defined for any `Command` or `Connection` object.

Client/Server   A two-tier network system in which multiple client machines (individual desktop machines) access a centralized server. Unlike the master/slave processing model used by older mainframe/terminal systems, much of the processing actually occurs on the client systems. The server exists to provide a central point of data coordination.

Collection   An array of objects that can be referenced either by an index number or the name of an object contained in the collection.

Command Object   An ADO object used to access a table, view, or stored procedure when connected through a `Connection` object.

Commit   The final method executed to write all available operations contained within a transaction to a database. See also **Transaction**.

Component   See **Control**.

Concatenate   To combine two or more elements into a single element. This term is usually used to describe the process of combining two text strings into a single string.

Condition   Processing based on circumstances, usually defined in Boolean comparisons. Statements such as `If A Then B` are conditional statements.

Connection Object   The ADO object used to define a connection to a data source.

Control   A standalone grouping of code within an object that can be installed on a computer system and re-used within multiple projects. For Visual Basic, a control represents a user interface function such as a text box, combo box, the Chart control, or a Data Control.

B

Cursor   A memory structure used to keep track of the current position within a resultant data set.

Data Control   Visual Basic includes an ActiveX control known as the Data Control. It is a visible component placed on a form to provide database access.

Data Decay   When data is loaded into an application in a multi-user setting, that data might be subject to relevance decay. If other users are actively modifying the data, the information in memory can become outdated and irrelevant.

Data Dictionary   A catalog of a data source that details the structure and data types of all elements defining the database.

Data Flow Diagram   Process diagram that indicates the path taken by information through a data processing system. Usually used to document the procedure used to handle pieces of data for a particular operation.

Data Model   Description of a database and the tables it contains including the structure, field data types, and relations.

Data Provider   In newer ADO terminology, data sources that are accessed through the data objects are known as data providers.

Data Rule Integrity   The enforcement of record consistency between records across multiple related tables. For example, when a record is deleted in one table, associated records are also deleted so no dangling references exist.

Data Source   A store of information that is typically some type of database or file. Usually referred to when describing what database technology must connect to in order to retrieve data.

Data Type   Definition of the type of value to be held by a variable or a field. For example, a variable defined to have a data type of `Integer` can only be used to store integer numbers.

Data View   The window within Visual Basic that holds global references to data sources.

Database   The central structure that holds all the data that relates to a particular purpose. A company database might hold a list of customers as well as information for sales invoices.

Database Engine   Unlike a word processor or another application with a user interface, a database typically operates behind the scenes. Any interface the user sees is most often constructed for a particular application. The functionality of the database is provided by a program called the database engine.

Database Server   A server dedicated to receiving and processing database queries, updates, and insertions. The specialized nature of a database server allows it to handle a large number of users.

DBMS   An acronym for database management system, which refers to the general field of database creation and management.

Default Value   A value used if no value is specified.

Dependency   When one resource needs another to function correctly. For example, when one table contains a relation to another table, the primary table has a dependency on the secondary data supplier.

Design-Time   The mode of the computer when the application is not executing, allowing changes to be made to the foundation of the program. See also **Runtime**.

Dialog Box   A window that presents information and is then dismissed. Typically, when a dialog box is present on the screen, clicking outside the dialog results in a beep.

Error Handling   Routines that accept an error code and in some way parse, decode, or overcome errors generated by a process.

Events   Activations that occur within a computer, based on external events (such as a mouse click or key press) or internal events (such as a disk access or timer activation).

Fields   A field is an element of a table record. The city field of a record would contain the city of a particular person. The state field would contain that person's state.

Flat File   Sequential file or data that does not have any inherent connection to other tables. The precursor to relational databases. See also **Relational Database**.

Foreign Key   A field in a database that holds ID values to relate records stored in another table.

Granularity   The precision possible when placing security settings for individual users and groups.

Groupware   Most popular in the form of Lotus Notes or Microsoft Exchange, groupware provides a central place to exchange information, files, and data. The structure of most groupware servers is a flat-file database.

Hierarchical Structure   A tree structure with some items subordinate to other items. Used in an operating system (for folders and files) and VB data environments (for `Command` and `Connection` objects).

Index   An index is a list of record pointers in a presorted order.

B

Instance   The creation of an object in memory from a class definition.

Instantiate   The process of creating an instance of an object. See also **Instance**.

Integrity Rule   See **Referential Integrity**.

ISAM   For access to some databases (such as dBASE), the Jet engine uses indexed sequential access method (ISAM) drivers. These drivers simulate a SQL language interpreter so SQL queries can be made to traditional non-SQL databases.

Join   A query that connects two or more tables by a primary/foreign key relation.

LAN   A local area network (LAN) is a short-distance network, usually limited to a single floor of a building. The most popular type of LAN uses the Ethernet technology to provide the foundation for communication. See also **WAN**.

Legacy Software   An old system or program being actively used is often referred to as a legacy system. Although useful, legacy software usually uses out-of-date formats or protocols.

Logical Database   See **View**.

Many-to-Many   In a many-to-many relation, multiple records in the first table are linked to multiple records in the second table and vice versa.

Method   A function or procedure contained within an object. A method typically makes modifications to the object itself.

Middleware   A bridge between two normally incompatible types of software interface is known as middleware. Middleware traditionally has no visible user interface but works as a translator between the two interfaces.

Node   Objects or collections within an object diagram that resemble leaves on a tree.

Normal Form   The level of normalization is divided into several normal forms that indicate the extent of normalization that has occurred in the database. Traditionally, the first to third normal forms are acknowledged.

Normalization   The process of simplifying a complex data structure by breaking it down into simple connected parts. In the case of database design, this means constructing simple related tables.

n-Tier   Multiple levels of objects that interact on a computer network. Advanced database systems use n-tier architecture to divide business processes among machines and distribute processing and security responsibilities across a network.

Null   When a field in a record is completely empty, such that it does not even contain a blank value (such as an empty string), it is known as a Null. A Null essentially identifies that no value is currently stored in the field.

Object Browser   The window within the Visual Basic environment that allows object models and individual properties and methods to be examined.

Object Model   The structure of a number of objects and their relations to each other. The Excel object model, for example, defines how the Worksheet, Workbook, and other objects can be accessed and which methods and properties are available for use.

OCX   See **ActiveX Control**.

ODBC   Open database connectivity (ODBC) is an industry standard for providing generic database access.

OLE   The object linking and embedding (OLE) technology has evolved into the ActiveX technology. Originally only containing the ability to embed or link objects between programs (for example, to embed an Excel table in a Word document), the technology has expanded to include OLE components (OCXs), OLE Automation, and OLE document storage. The OLE technologies are now unified under the ActiveX umbrella.

One-to-Many   When one record can relate to multiple records in another table, the connection is said to be a one-to-many relation.

One-to-One   In a one-to-one relation, one record in one table is linked to only one record in another table.

Optimistic Locking   A record is only locked in the exact moment an update to the record occurs.

Page Locking   Locking mechanism supported by Microsoft Access and the Jet engine that locks all records located on a 1024 byte "page" on the logical disk.

Pessimistic Locking   When a user accesses a record, none of the other users can access it in write mode.

Primary Key   A primary key is the field that uniquely identifies each record so it can be referenced from a related table.

Query   Set of instructions that dictates how data will be filtered when read from one or more tables.

Random Access   The ability to read or write data in any position without being limited by a sequential stream. Small databases can be created using Visual Basic's random access file capabilities.

B

Record   The primary unit of information contained in a table. In an address book data-base, each entry would be stored as a record containing name, address, phone, and so on.

Recordset   A recordset is a memory structure designed to load information from a data source for querying, modification, and examination. A recordset contains all the records that comply with criteria defined when the recordset is created.

Recordset Returning   A Command object can be a table, view, or SQL statement that is executed. If the object will return a recordset on execution, it is said to be recordset returning.

Recursion   A process that calls itself in a program. Recursion routines are most often used for hierarchical data to address every node within the hierarchical tree.

Referential Integrity   The technology that forces all related tables to keep consistent records for relations so the database is said to have integrity.

Relational Database   When multiple tables are contained within a single database and connected by logical relations by a combination of primary and foreign key pairs.

Replication   The process of keeping two or more copies of a single dataset that can be updated individually. When the replicated copies are once again brought together (through a network connection or other process), differences between the replicates are synchronized.

Report   Visual Basic 6 includes the capability of creating data reports for inclusion into standalone projects. The files for reports are stored in files with the .DSR extension.

Rollback   Revocation of all the previous operations contained within a transaction because some failure condition has occurred. See also **Transaction**.

Root Node   The primary node on the tree is known as the root. All other nodes descend from the root.

Runtime   The mode of the computer when an application is actually executing. Changes to fundamental aspects of a program are often limited in runtime. See also **Design-Time**.

Schema   A map or definition of the overall structure of a database. The `OpenSchema` method of a Connection object can be used to obtain information about the data source structure.

Security   Security on a database is used to restrict access to those who have permission to objects within the database. Visual Basic allows security for the entire file or down to the table level.

Self Join   A self join occurs when a primary key of a table is used to link to a foreign key field in the same table. For example, a self join can be used to indicate a superior in an employee database in which the employee record points to another employee record in the same table.

Set   The Visual Basic command that allows a reference to be created to an object.

SID   A SID or system identification code is a unique identification number stored in the security file System.MDW. A SID identifies a user or group by the user login.

SQL   SQL or Structured Query Language is a results-oriented query language used to access data sources for querying, insertion, updating, and structural modification.

Stored Procedure   A procedure of SQL code actually stored within the database that can be executed by an external or internal call. Most commonly available on complete database servers such as Microsoft SQL Server.

Table   Within a database, one or more tables actually hold the data with each table defining a particular structure. An address table might store the name, address, city, and state of a customer. The invoice table, in contrast, might store the information of quantity, description, and cost of each item in an invoice.

Transaction   A method of encapsulating several database operations into an all-or-nothing framework. Either all the operations within the transaction must occur or none of them are used. See also **Commit** and **Rollback**.

Unicode   New international standard for storing text that uses two bytes (16 bits) for every character instead of one (8 bits) as used under the current ASCII standard. Unicode expands the international aspects of computer systems by allowing languages that contain pictograms (such as Chinese) to be used on the same systems as Roman languages.

Union   Concatenation of two resultant sets from two queries that is returned as a single dataset.

User-Defined Type   A variable structure of a combination of other variable types. After the type is defined using the Type...End Type keywords, variables can be defined with the new user-defined type.

Vertical Market   Most popular applications have a broad or horizontal appeal. Specialized applications (for example, dental accounting, real estate tracking, and so on) have a selective or vertical market appeal.

View   An artificial grouping of databases or tables that makes them appear to the data consumer as if they were an actual data unit. For example, fields and data from two tables can be combined in a view that can be treated by a querying program as a single table.

B

WAN   A wide area network such as the Internet that connects computers that are usually in geographically distant places. See also **LAN**.

WYSIWYG   An acronym for What-You-See-Is-What-You-Get meant to define a particular type of user interface experience. Usually referred to in terms of the similarity between an onscreen presentation and the resulting printed output. The closer the screen resembles the printed version that will be generated, the more WYSIWYG the program is.

APPENDIX C

Answers

Here are the answers to the quiz questions located at the end of each chapter.

Hour 1

1. Can multiple tables be stored in a database?

   Yes, a single database can store up to 255 tables, although it's not recommended that you have that many.

2. What is a field? What is a record?

   A field is an element of a record, such as the lastName entry in a customer record. A record stores all the information relating to one entry in the database, such as customer information in a customer table.

3. What is the purpose of the Data Control?

   To provide a connection to a data source (such as a Microsoft Access database) that other controls such as the text box can be connected (bound) to use.

4. The database engine included with Visual Basic is compatible with what desktop application?

   The database engine uses the Microsoft Access database file as its standard file type.

5. On the navigation bar of the Data Control, what functions do the four arrows perform?

   The leftmost and rightmost arrows (with the bars) display the first and last records, respectively, in the data source. The other two arrows move through the data set either forward or backward one record.

6. Databases are sometimes described in terms of spreadsheets. What are the synonyms for fields and records?

   A field is the equivalent of a column in database terminology. A record is equivalent to a row.

7. What is a profile (used by the VB Data Form Wizard)?

   A profile saves all the selections made, so a save profile can automatically set all the same settings in the Wizard.

8. When a new record is added to the database, will it be sorted in the correct order automatically?

   No, the Refresh method must be executed before the new record will appear in the proper order.

Hour 2

1. What is a bound control?

   A bound control is a control that can be connected to a Data Control. It then displays a field from the data source accessed by the Data Control.

2. What is Hungarian notation?

   By adding a prefix to the names of objects and variables, the type of structure being accessed becomes apparent in coding. Hungarian notation is the process of adding consistent prefixes (such as frm to the form frmMyForm) to increase readability.

3. Must ConnectionString contain the complete file path to the data source?

   No. If the complete path is not supplied, the default directory is used.

4. True or False: A recordset is stored on disk.

   False. A recordset is a memory structure that holds accessed data.

5. What properties on a Data Control must be set to properly access a database file?

   ConnectionString holds the connection information, including the data source type and data path. The RecordSource property determines the table or query within the database to access.

6. True or False: Double-clicking on the DataSource property of a bound control will automatically place the name of the first Data Control in the property.

   True.

7. Which two properties are set on a bound control to reference a Data Control and a particular field?

   The DataSource property specifies the Data Control to access. The DataField property determines the field of the database to be displayed in the Bound control.

8. What functions are supplied by the Data Form Wizard through additional buttons and code?

   The Add, Delete, Edit, and Update functions are supplied through code rather than being built into the Data Control.

Hour 3

1. What is the purpose of the Data Control?

   To provide a standard connection to a data source through which controls can be bound. It also includes an instant user interface for record navigation.

2. Does the Data Form Wizard use a special form of database access?

   No, the Data Form Wizard simply creates code that uses the standard Data Control or ADO programming environment.

3. What is the Microsoft Jet engine?

   The Jet engine is another name for the Microsoft Access database engine used by both VB and Access.

4. Why set the DataSource property on a bound control before the DataField property?

   By setting the DataSource first, the control can access the data connected to the Data Control. That allows the DataField to display a popup menu of possible fields for binding.

5. Why is the Command Type setting of the RecordSource property set to adCmdTable?

   The Command Type defines the type of access. Since you don't need to write a query to selectively display records, the table setting will display all of the records in the current table.

C

6. What are the limitations of using the Data Control?

   A single Data Control can only access one table at a time. Data Controls must also be placed on a single form, so global project access is difficult. Also, a Data Control cannot be created dynamically at runtime, but must be placed on a form at design-time.

Hour 4

1. Why is planning at the beginning so important?

   Because changing the database structure when the project is half-done can be an incredibly difficult and time-consuming task. Imagine trying to make adjustments to a building foundation after 10 out of 20 stories have been constructed on top.

2. How do you decide how to separate data into tables?

   The data within each table should relate to other data in that table. For example, customer address information should not be stored in an inventory table.

3. What are the primary purposes of an index?

   An index is used to speed sorting and searching of a table.

4. What is a key question you should ask yourself when beginning design of a new database?

   What does the database need to do?

5. When is the proper time to add an index?

   After all the fields have been added so the most important and accessed fields can be indexed.

6. True or False: Adding many indexes to a table can slow down record additions or updates.

   True.

Hour 5

1. What program is used to construct a table?

   Visual Data Manager.

2. Can the Visual Data Manager open Microsoft Access database files?

   Yes. In fact, although the Data Manager can open many database types, the Access file format is the default.

3. What is a NULL value?

    A NULL value signifies that no value has ever been entered into the field and therefore the field doesn't currently occupy any space on the disk.

4. Can the value stored in a field that is set to AutoIncrement be changed?

    Yes. Only when the record is initially created and updated is it unchangeable.

5. How is a primary key set?

    By setting the Primary check box in the Field Information dialog box from within the Visual Data Manager.

Hour 6

1. What three categories are displayed in the Database window?

    Properties of the database, Tables contained in the database, and SQL language queries.

2. What is the wildcard character?

    For database queries from VB, the asterisk (*) character is used for the wildcard.

3. True or False: No problems will occur if the security for the database is set up improperly.

    False. You could be locked out of your database.

4. What function does the Like keyword serve in a query?

    It functions similarly to the equal (=) operator, but it ignores the capitalization or case when searching a string.

5. Why bother compacting a database?

    Compacting a database rids the database file of deleted records. It will therefore clean up the database and make it faster.

6. Should indexes be added to every field?

    No, because each additional index slows down insertion of new records or modification of existing ones. Each index also takes up disk space.

7. How is a query used?

    A query will filter out only the records that match the criteria specified in the query. It can also be used to organize or sort the returned data set.

C

Hour 7

1. What type of objects can be used within the Data Environment?

   Command and Connection objects.

2. In what way does the Data Environment support drag-and-drop insertion?

   Fields available in the Data Environment can be dragged onto a form and a data-aware control (such as a text box), along with an appropriate Label control, will be created. The control will automatically be bound to the proper field and the Data Environment as the data source.

3. What is a Data Link?

   A Data Link provides a global connection storage environment that may be used to maintain and examine connections to data sources.

4. Are Data Links shared by multiple projects?

   Since a Data Link is part of the Visual Basic environment, it is not attached to any particular project.

5. True or False: Each Data Environment in a project may support more than one connection.

   True.

Hour 8

1. What items are included by default when a new Data Project is created?

   The Data Project contains an empty form, all of the primary data-aware controls, a data environment, and a data report (that you won't need for this project).

2. True or False: A Data Environment can be accessed from any form, class, or code module in the project.

   True.

3. How can you change the type of bound control created by default when using the drag-and-drop interface?

   Using the Options selection in the data environment context menu.

4. What two properties must be set in the DataGrid for it to display a recordset?

   The DataSource and DataMember properties.

Hour 9

1. What two properties determine how an ActiveX control is listed on the system?

   The `Name` properties of the Project control and User control. The control will then appear in the list as `projectName.usercontrolName`.

2. How can properties be exposed from within an ActiveX control?

   The `Property Get` and `Property Let` coding must first be created. The Procedure Attributes window must then be used to set the properties as bindable.

3. What property is used to bind an ActiveX control to the Data Repeater?

   The `RepeatedControlName` property.

Hour 10

1. What is a table relation?

   A connection between two tables that enables records in one table to be linked or related to those in another.

2. How is a relation created?

   By having a primary key field in one table and providing a foreign key field in the other to store a reference to the connected record.

3. Explain the meanings of the primary and foreign keys and how they are used together.

   The primary key is the ID field in a table that uniquely identifies each record within that table. A foreign key field is used to store the primary key values from another table to create a relation between records.

4. True or False: Database normalization is the process of breaking down tables to minimize duplication of information.

   True.

5. In what way does database normalization provide extra expandability when storing information?

   In the current use of the database, multiple records can be added to a table rather than expanding the record definition of the source table to include extra information.

C

Hour 11

1. True or False: The most used features are also the most important features of a program.

   False. Important aspects of the program might be used only intermittently.

2. What common program provides flowchart symbols?

   Microsoft Word.

3. How do you choose whether to display multiple records on a form?

   Determine if two or more records need to be compared.

4. Why shouldn't operational password dialogs be used as often as possible?

   If there are too many operational password dialogs, users will probably circumvent them by creating a "cheat sheet" containing all the important passwords.

5. What question should be asked to determine how difficult deleting particular information should be?

   "How hard is it to replace this data?"

Hour 12

1. True or False: The data environment doesn't require initialization.

   False. All data environment objects require initialization. If the data environment is bound to a control, however, the control will initiate the environment automatically.

2. Is the data environment the only way to share a recordset across multiple forms?

   No, there are several ways, but the data environment is the most elegant and flexible.

3. How do you create a Command object as a child of another Command object?

   A Command object is created as a child of another Command object by selecting the Command object to which a child needs to be added and clicking the Add Command button on the toolbar.

4. What does setting a relation for parent/child objects do?

   Setting a relation for parent/child objects makes the child object display information related to the selected parent record.

5. What property is used to set ToolTip text for a control?

   The ToolTip property is used to set ToolTip text for a control.

Hour 13

1. Can an HTML report be generated by the Data Reporter?

   Yes, an entire report can be output as a series of HTML files.

2. True or False: Images can be displayed on the report from linked fields in the database.

   False, only a static image can be included in a Data Report.

3. How can multiple tables can be used in a report?

   Multiple tables can be used either directly or as related children of hierarchical Command objects.

4. What report control can be used to display a calculated field?

   The Function control.

5. Can code be executed within a report?

   Yes, like a form, code can be added to events in the report.

Hour 14

1. True or False: The Microsoft Graph control is data-aware.

   True.

2. What two properties must be set to bind the Graph to a data source?

   The Data Source and the Data Member properties are used to bind the Chart control to a data source.

3. Can the Graph be bound to a data source at runtime?

   Yes, by using the ADO recordsets, a data source can be created dynamically at runtime.

4. Is a SQL statement required to use the Chart control?

   No, the Chart control can be attached directly to a table, but much of the data that the control will attempt to graph will be useless.

5. What could be the problem if the labels for one of the chart axes don't appear?

   The Chart control on the form is probably not large enough to display the axis labels.

6. How do you make a series invisible?

   In the Custom properties window, series may be hidden, excluded, plotted on a 2nd Y axis, or shown with markers.

C

7. What is a `Data Grid` object?

This object is part of the Chart control used to store the series data being displayed.

Hour 15

1. Why is locking necessary?

To prevent data collision when multiple users are trying to access the same data at the same time.

2. What is the maximum number of users that can access an MDB file at the same time?

255.

3. True or False: The LDB file holds the current locks for an open database.

True.

4. What is a page?

A page is a block of disk space used internally by the Jet engine to quickly manage changes to a database. Locks perform their functions on page units within the database.

5. Can a record be locked even though no one explicitly requested a lock on it?

Yes, if the record is located on the same page as another record being edited.

6. True or False: An Exclusive lock can be placed on a resource that is already being shared.

False; all Shared lock users must have left the record or page before an Exclusive lock can be enacted.

7. What type of lock is used to prevent more than one machine from logging on to the same account?

User lock.

8. Is optimistic locking the default method of locking for MDB files?

Yes; optimistic locking is the default, not pessimistic locking.

Hour 16

1. True or False: Many instances of an object can be created from a class.

True.

2. What is the difference between an object and a collection?

A collection is essentially an array of objects. Unlike an array, the objects within the collection can be referenced either by name or an index.

Hour 17

1. How does using ADO differ from the Data Control?

   Because ADO is a programmable object, it can be used across an entire project rather than be placed on a single form. ADO objects can also be created dynamically at runtime rather than have to all be added at design-time.

2. What is the Command object used for?

   To execute SQL queries or execute SQL code stored on a database server.

3. What keyword is use to create the ADO objects?

   The New keyword is used with the Dim statement to create the ADO object.

4. What other programs support ADO?

   Any program that includes VBA (including all Office), the Internet Information Server Web server, and other Microsoft development environments.

5. True or False: A snapshot can be used to modify and update information.

   False—a snapshot is read-only.

6. What method is used to refresh the data contained within the recordset?

   Executing the Requery method will access the database again and update any new additions.

Hour 18

1. What does SQL stand for?

   Structured Query Language

2. Are all versions of the SQL standard compatible?

   No. Although most of the basic commands are compatible, there are often variations. Check the appropriate manuals to determine the exact diction of a particular SQL implementation.

3. Which clause is used to determine which records are or aren't included in the final data set?

   The Where clause.

4. True or False: SQL is a procedural language.

   False, it is a results language. The SQL commands instruct what should be returned, not how to execute the query.

C

Hour 19

1. True or False: A multi-field index can be defined in a table.

   True.

2. What is p-code?

   Pseudo-code (p-code) is code created by Visual Basic that is stored as a number of references that call routines in the Visual Basic runtime to execute, rather than being natively compiled.

3. Besides a specification, what is another method that can be used from database application design?

   User-selected design.

4. What is a CAB file?

   A Cabinet (CAB) file is a compressed file that can store multiple files for installation through the Setup.exe program or via the Internet.

Hour 20

1. What type of object are most pieces of information stored as?

   Most pieces of information within Outlook are stored as *item* objects.

2. Do all item types have the same properties?

   No, each item reflects the properties that are appropriate to the item type. A `TaskItem`, unlike a `ContactItem`, has no `FullName` field or property.

3. True or False: The Outlook Object Model only provides access to a limited number of fields.

   False, every property (including user properties) is available through the Object Model.

4. Which method can be used in place of `CreateObject` to acquire an application object reference?

   If an application is already open, the `GetObject` method will retrieve a reference to it.

5. How are items organized within the Outlook object model?

   All items are located in folders that group them by type.

6. Can items be referenced by an index value?

   Items are contained in a Collection of objects so they can be referenced using the `For Each` structure, by their indexes, or using the individual reference names.

7. What method is after the initial `Find` method to advance through the filtered list of items?

   The `FindNext` method will advance to the next record that meets the filter criteria.

8. Which data type is used to store the `EntryID` value?

   An `EntryID` is stored as a String data type.

9. What are the two consecutive double quotes (`""`) used for?

   Two consecutive double quotes (`""`) when defining a string adds a single double quote to the string rather than ending the string definition.

Hour 21

1. What is a transaction?

   A transaction encapsulates a number of database operations and treats the operations as a single unit. A transaction will either record all of the changes within it or record nothing.

2. If a `CommitTrans` method is used to accept a transaction, what is used to abort a transaction?

   The `Rollback` method is used to abort all of the individual operations within a transaction and restore the database to the state it had before the transaction began.

3. Do transactions make the MDB database system more durable?

   Yes. The recoverability available because of transactions to an MDB file helps make the database system durable.

4. True or False: Transactions can be nested.

   True.

Hour 22

1. What are the three primary reasons for adding security to a database?

   The three primary reasons for adding security to a database are to protect confidential information, prevent misinterpretation, and guard against accidental corruption.

2. Where can you print a list of all security levels, users, and groups for an MDB file?

   A list of all security levels, users, and groups for an MDB file can be printed from Microsoft Access through the Security Report option.

3. When is the best time to add security?

   Adding security is best immediately before the first test deployment. That way it doesn't get in the way of development, but provides enough time to resolve conflicts before the application is deployed.

C

4. True or False: The proper way of adding security is to place the permissions on groups and then add users to the appropriate group.

   True.

5. What is the System.MDW file?

   The System.MDW file holds the security identification codes, the usernames, and the group names used to provide permission levels.

6. True or False: It is possible to allow a user to add new information, but make the user unable to see any existing information in a table.

   True.

7. What folder is the System.MDW file usually located in?

   The System.MDW file is usually located in the Windows\System folder.

Hour 23

1. True or False: DAO is not included in Visual Basic 6.

   False. DAO has been included and upgraded in Visual Basic 6 to provide compatibility with older projects. However, using ADO is recommended on any new projects.

2. What is a VBX?

   A VBX is a control type that was the 16-bit precursor to 32-bit OCX and ActiveX controls. Unlike an OCX, the VBX would only function in the Visual Basic environment.

3. Does Visual Basic 6 support both 16-bit and 32-bit projects?

   No, VB 4 was the only version to simultaneously support both types.

4. Should I convert my 16-bit database to 32-bit format?

   Only if you no longer need it accessible from 16-bit systems. Otherwise, simply use the Jet engine or define an ODBC data source that points to it.

Hour 24

1. What are the three primary file types available in VB?

   The three primary file types available in VB are sequential, random access, and binary.

2. True or False: In a random access file mode, you can instantly read a record from anywhere in the file.

   True.

3. What are the three primary data reading commands for use with files?

   The three primary data reading commands for use with files are `Get`, `Input`, and `Line Input`.

INDEX

W-Z

Other Related Titles

Sams Teach Yourself Database Programming with Visual Basic 6 in 21 Days
Amundsen & Smith
0-672-31308-1
$45.00 USA /
$64.95 CAN

Sams Teach Yourself Visual Basic 6 in 21 Days
Greg Perry
0-672-31310-3
$29.99 USA /
$42.95 CAN

Sams Teach Yourself More Visual Basic 6 in 21 Days
Lowell Mauer
0-672-31307-3
$29.99 USA /
$42.95 CAN

Sams Teach Yourself Internet Programming with Visual Basic 6 in 21 Days
Peter Aitken
0-672-31459-2
$29.99 USA /
$42.95 CAN

Sams Teach Yourself Object-Oriented Programming with Visual Basic 6 in 21 Days
John Conley
0-672-31299-9
$39.99 USA /
$56.95 CAN

Visual Basic 6 Unleashed
Rob Thayer
0-672-31309-X
$39.99 USA /
$57.95 CAN

The Waite Group's Visual Basic 6 How-To
Breirly, Prince, & Rinaldi
1-57169-153-7
$39.99 USA /
$57.95 CAN

The Waite Group's Visual Basic 6 Client/Server How-To
Noel Jerke
1-57169-154-5
$49.99 USA /
$71.95 CAN

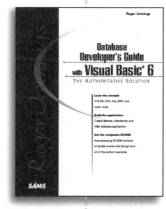

Roger Jennings' Database Developer's Guide with Visual Basic 6
Roger Jennings
0-672-31063-5
$59.99 USA /
$85.95 CAN

The Waite Group's Visual Basic 6 Database How-To
Winemiller, Roff, Heyman, & Groom
1-57169-152-9
$39.99 USA /
$56.95 CAN

SAMS

www.samspublishing.com